Praise for
How We Love Our Kids

"Milan and Kay provide us with the tools of self-awareness which can enable us to consciously examine the love styles of the past and become conscious of the stored feelings and emotions that we carry forward into parenting. This book will now be one of my primary reading recommendations."
    —MICHAEL W. SHANNON, MD

"Another home run for Milan and Kay Ye
    —SHERRIE ELDRIDGE, speaker and au
    Adoptive Parents Need to Succeed

"After reading this book, our first thoughts were, *Every parent needs to read this book—regardless of the ages of their children,* and, *Reading this book could not only protect children from the pains of growing up but also heal the parents' hearts.* This book offers insightful, practical ways of understanding children and parenting. We recommend it."
    —ROGER AND BECKY TIRABASSI, authors of *Let Love Change Your Life*

"This book is a true gift to parents who yearn to understand and communicate with their children, thus bringing about healing and restoration. Milan and Kay remind us that God is our perfect model for parenting. This book has touched my life, and I know it will touch yours too."
    —ELIZABETH JOHN, MD

"Milan and Kay provide us an entirely new way of looking at parenting. Rather than focusing solely on the how-tos of parenting, they help us explore the powerful forces of our own upbringings on how we parent and provide a path to change those forces for good in the lives of our children. As a parent educator for over twenty-five years, I see this book as the resource we've been missing!"
    —LAURA TAGGART, licensed marriage and family therapist

"Finally! A treatment of parenting that acknowledges the eight-hundred-pound gorilla in the room: parents working out their personal issues on their children. If you want to transform your child's life, then let Milan and Kay gently, firmly, and skillfully guide you on this amazing journey of personal change."

—KENNY LUCK, author of *Soar, Fight,* and *Dream*

"Imagine decreasing the drama in your home by simply learning how to comfort one another. This book unfolds five distinct love styles in parenting—their traits, strengths, and pitfalls. The real-life stories allow us to see ourselves and how we naturally express ourselves to our children. Whatever blend of love styles is under your roof, Milan and Kay will show you the direct route to building deeper love, intimacy, and connection."

—SHERI DENHAM, PhD, MFT, and co-host of *New Life Live*

"If you've ever struggled with being a good enough parent, ever been triggered by your child's behavior in ways you'd be too embarrassed to recount, or ever compensated with your child to override your guilt, then you won't want to miss *How We Love Our Kids*!"

—JILL HUBBARD, PhD, co-host of *New Life Live* and author of *The Secrets Women Keep* and *The Secrets Young Women Keep*

"Milan and Kay have given us great insights into how our own attachment issues affect our parenting styles. Every parent needs to read this book, regardless of the ages of their kids."

—DAVID STOOP, PhD, author of *Just Us* and *Forgiving the Unforgivable*

"Whether you need a parenting tune-up or a major overhaul, *How We Love Our Kids* will help."

—STEVEN ARTERBURN, founder and chairman, New Life Ministries

"*How We Love Our Kids* holds out the possibility of creating the loving, healthy family you always dreamed of."

—KAY WARREN, founder, HIV/AIDS Initiative, Saddleback Church

How
We
Love
Our Kids

The 5 Love Styles of Parenting
One Small Change in You...One Big Change in Your Kids

Milan & Kay
Yerkovich

WATERBROOK
P R E S S

How We Love Our Kids

Scripture quotations are taken from the New American Standard Bible®. © Copyright The Lockman Foundation 1960, 1962, 1963, 1968, 1971, 1972, 1973, 1975, 1977, 1995. Used by permission. (www.Lockman.org).

Details in some anecdotes and stories have been changed to protect the identities of the persons involved.

Trade Paperback ISBN 978-0-307-72924-8
eBook ISBN 978-0-307-72925-5

Copyright © 2011 by Milan and Kay Yerkovich

Cover design by Kelly L. Howard

Published in association with Stephen Arterburn: sarterburn@newlife.com.

Published in the United States by WaterBrook, an imprint of the Crown Publishing Group, a division of Penguin Random House LLC, New York.

WATERBROOK® and its deer colophon are registered trademarks of Penguin Random House LLC.

Library of Congress Cataloging-in-Publication Data
Yerkovich, Milan.
    How we love our kids / Milan and Kay Yerkovich. — 1st ed.
        p. cm.
    Includes bibliographical references (p.   ) and index.
    ISBN 978-0-307-72924-8 (alk. paper) — ISBN 978-0-307-72925-5 (electronic : alk. paper)
    1. Parenting—Religious aspects—Christianity. 2. Personality. 3. Personality in children.
4. Child psychology. I. Yerkovich, Kay. II. Title.
    BV4529.Y47 2011
    248.8'45—dc22

                                          2010043304

Printed in the United States of America
2016

10 9 8

SPECIAL SALES
Most WaterBrook books are available at special quantity discounts when purchased in bulk by corporations, organizations, and special-interest groups. Custom imprinting or excerpting can also be done to fit special needs. For information, please e-mail specialmarketscms@penguinrandom house.com or call 1-800-603-7051.

To April, who penned this poem after overcoming a chaotic attachment
and discovering what bonding feels like in a secure relationship.
Our hope for all you who read this book is that someday
your kids will say this about you as a parent.

• • •

You are gusts of gentleness
Cool, swift movements of grace
My Wind

You are drops of truth
Wet, clean pieces of trust
My Rain

You are shades of safety
Green, sheltered canopies of peace
My Tree

You are heights of radiance
Blue, calm spaces of kindness
My Sky

You are acres of freedom
Fresh, new blades of courage
My Grass

You are blankets of promise
Soft, comfortable layers of protection
My Bed

You are an ocean of love
Deep, strong currents of beauty
My Heart

Contents

Part 4: The Healing Journey for Parents and Children

Appendix: Parent Toolbox

Acknowledgments

We would like to thank our agent Steve Arterburn for his efforts in making this book a reality.

We are thankful that WaterBrook Multnomah Publishing Group believed in us enough to take a leap of faith and publish a second work.

We are grateful for our primary editor Mick Silva who helped shape the presentation and wording of the book.

Finally, we wish to thank our beloved kids—Kevin, Amy, John, and Kelly—who helped us to grow up and taught us all that we know about being a dad and mom.

The Amazing Result of One Simple Change

One fall, at the conclusion of a weekend marriage seminar, a young mother named Melissa approached us. Her eyes sparkled, and she grabbed my (Kay's) arm as she spoke. "I had the most amazing experience," she said. "Because of your teaching, my husband and I have started seeing our marriage problems in a whole new light. But I didn't expect to get parenting help as well. This morning, when we dropped our seven-year-old girl off at the baby-sitter's, I remembered what you taught yesterday about the importance of self-awareness and offering comfort for others' feelings. We've had difficulty with this in our marriage, but even more so with our kids."

Melissa continued, "Our seven-year-old, Gina, is superemotional, and honestly, it's always annoyed me. Every October she gets scared by the Halloween decorations, and she has crying fits if she gets anywhere near them. I've been telling her all week that they are just plastic—that none of it is real and she's a big girl now. This morning at the baby-sitter's house, the entire front porch was covered in Halloween decorations. Gina started to have a fit in the car. I got so irritated and was just about to launch into my 'It's all pretend' speech when I remembered the feeling question. So I asked, 'Gina, how do all those decorations make you feel?'

"She wailed, 'Scared!' I didn't know what to say. But I walked around to open her door, and before she got out, I knelt down and said, 'It's okay to be scared, Gina. How can Mommy help you right now?' Her sobs turned to whimpers, and she looked right in my eyes. I could see her little mind racing.

"'Mommy,' she said, 'you hold me and let me hide my eyes on your shoulder. I'll keep them covered while you ring the doorbell. And then you go inside and close the door, and I'll keep my eyes shut tight. After we're inside I can open my eyes and I'll be fine.' So I did. I followed her instructions, and when I put her down in the house, she looked up at me and said, 'Thanks, Mommy. That really helped me.'

"I was shocked! Not only could she tell me what she needed, it was so *easy*! Maybe I don't need to change her at all. Maybe I just needed to change my response."

By this time, Milan and I were getting excited with her. "Think about that one change, Melissa," Milan said. "One small change in you made such a big difference in your relationship with your daughter. What if you made it a goal to continue working on that—to become comfortable with all kinds of emotions in Gina? Today, you helped her manage her anxiety instead of telling her why her fears were silly. You can change her life forever, and give her a different future, by making that one change a way of life."

It has been numerous encounters like this that have made us excited to write this book. Melissa isn't alone; we've received literally thousands of stories, e-mails, letters, and comments from people who've read our book, learned about love styles, and found countless great ways to apply the ideas. It's so gratifying to hear of lives changed and relationships restored, but it's all because of the inherent strength in responding to others' natural emotions rather than ignoring, diminishing, or rejecting them.

Of course, there are so many parenting books that it can be more than a bit overwhelming. That's why we've tried hard to make this one different. The main focus isn't curbing behaviors with discipline or using techniques to get kids to behave. We've found such books can be helpful, but our parenting took a dramatic turn when Milan and I discovered specific changes we needed to make in ourselves, which automatically changed what was happening with our kids.

Taking a close look at how *we* were brought up helped us to pinpoint our defenses and difficulties we learned in our original families. We realized that often our kids were not the problem. We began to recognize *how* we loved our kids was often at the root of the struggles, and that understanding and changing our damaged love styles affected our children's behavior dramatically.

Once we changed as parents, almost *everything else* in our relationships with our kids began to change as well. There was less defensiveness, less misunderstanding, and less heartache all around. Best of all, we began to develop closer, deeper connections with them almost immediately. Maybe the greatest news for a parent is that once you know how to change yourself to be that better parent you've hoped to be, parenting can and does become far easier, as well as more rewarding!

Imagine that for a moment—simple, relational parenting. Are you tired of sabotaging your own fulfillment and happiness as a parent? Are your children tired of seeing how frustrated you can get?

As any discouraged parent can tell you, trying to change your kids is hard. The easiest thing you can do as a parent is to learn what you can do to change yourself for the better. And, ironically, this is the only thing that creates the peaceful home you've been longing for.

Here's our hope: once you discover what you've been bringing to your parenting from your family of origin and learn to overcome your personal challenges and *parenting baggage,* you'll be able to respond to your children in a way that greatly reduces the behavior problem you're currently facing.

When we first discover our own deficiencies and begin making the positive changes that improve our performance as parents, it leads to more enjoyable relationships overall. Now Milan and I didn't start our parenting careers with this profound wisdom in hand. With the exception of our youngest, our kids were much older when we first discovered our damaged love styles. It came as quite a surprise after more than a dozen years of parenting, because we had learned to hide our personal difficulties so well, even from ourselves, as dysfunctional-but-functioning adults.

If you're parenting with your spouse, you may also want to read our first book, *How We Love,* to get an idea of how your love style is playing out with your partner and how that naturally affects parenting.

Whether you're planning a family, currently a parent, or have grown children, freeing yourself to feel and deal with emotion appropriately will give your children solid, secure foundations as adults. As you use this book to foster open, healing conversations with your children, you will realize just how true it is that one small change in the parent can make a huge difference.

As I write this, I'm thinking back to just last night when a mother told me, "After seeing you and Milan demonstrate active feeling and dealing, I realized we'd never shown our kids how to really listen to others. So I apologized to my adult son and asked him to share how he felt about it. At first he didn't want to, but soon we started talking, and we've continued now for a long time. One little change—just learning to listen—has totally changed our relationship, and I can actually see his wounds healing."

Many parents who call Milan and me for help with their kids are surprised when we ask to see them—the parents—instead. Nearly every time the problems are greatly alleviated or completely solved when parents become aware of how they are contributing to the difficulties.

How you love your kids is a matter of learning to become the truly great parent you've always wanted to be. Ironically, the greatest gift you can give your child is to be the best you've ever been. And who doesn't want that? By learning how you love, initially by becoming more self-aware, you will know exactly how to love your child better. It won't always be easy or a walk in the park, but the decision to see yourself clearly and identify those places you have blind spots will give you a road map to reach your full potential as a parent.

Beyond that, learning to love well will require a bit of training and some regular practice. But if you're patient and remember that you're just like anyone training for a challenging task, with those blind spots that will hold you back, you'll gradually improve in time. With an open mind, you'll begin to see yourself as you really are for the first time, and your view of your child as the source of your problem will begin to change.

And in our experience, that's when you may realize your problem is being solved.

With the right perspective, behavioral, emotional, and relational challenges can be improved—even future generations will benefit. Who doesn't long to hear their kids say, "My parents are the best! They've taught me everything I need to know in life"? To us, that sounds like the highest compliment any parent could receive.

If you're ready now to make that one change—to see yourself honestly and learn to listen and grow—we believe you'll be hearing your child say those words to you someday.

Part

1

Helping Yourself
as a Parent

One

The Miracle and the Mess

Kay, have you seen my socks?"

I was bummed. I had just arrived home from work and wanted to go for a run, but I only had forty-five minutes before dinner. I checked the usual places: drawers, dryer, and washing machine. I even rummaged through the dirty clothes, but the lineman-strength stench knocked me on my heels and made me resume my search for a clean pair.

Then I remembered my secret stash, hidden from view on the top shelf of my closet. I dashed to look. *No!* They were gone as well. Now I was starting to get mad.

"Those kids snaked my clean socks again!" I yelled. I thought back to a bumper sticker I had seen earlier that day. "Driver carries no cash… has three teenagers." Evidently, the driver didn't realize they also take your clothes.

Who knew living with three teenagers could create such a high demand for white crew socks?

"I just bought a dozen," Kay hollered up the stairs.

She's always buying socks, I thought bitterly, *but are any left for me?*

No. There were none. Not a pair to be found. And I wasn't about to go running in business socks; it was a matter of principle now. In my frustration, I decided to take matters into my own hands. I stalked to the kids' rooms.

Amy's netted me nine, but I wasn't satisfied. I passed up little Kelly's room, took a deep breath, and plunged into the boys' room. Hunting through the thick layer of clothes, books, papers, skateboard parts, magazines, and shoes—down to the surfboard wax that had melted into the carpet—the clean freak in me rose up, bursting into a rampage for my socks. I tore through the room, every square inch of floor space, every horrible corner of the closets, every drawer. Privacy was more than invaded, and I was well past the point of caring. Any lofty idealism I'd had about ethical parenting codes was gone. I was regaining *my* property.

The sock pile in the middle of the room grew like a magical snowdrift in the middle of the wasteland. It grew and grew: white, dingy brown, gray, many in advanced stages of decay. I couldn't believe how many socks I found.

Forty minutes later—I kid you not—I loaded the massive pile into the washing machine downstairs, threw in a cup of soap, a cup of bleach, and slammed the lid. I huffed to the couch to wait, considering that I might finally have found where our discretionary spending was disappearing every month. When the wash cycle was complete, I threw the giant load into the dryer. Once the socks were dry, I sorted them into piles of like colors and relative elasticity. I then stomped back up the stairs to hide the best ones in more clever hiding places. I left the remaining carnage on the living room floor for them to rummage through.

By now my window for a stress-reducing run was long gone. So I went upstairs to the shower to decontaminate and decompress.

Kids, I thought to myself. *What a mess.*

I slid to the floor of the shower and thought back to the days each of them was born. How little had really changed. Each one was still such a fascinating miracle—wrapped in such a convoluted mess.

THE MIRACLE OF BABY

Hot water streaming over my head, my reverie stretched out for several minutes. As angry as I was, I thought how different they were, and how each unique quality first presented itself. Kevin's wide, enthusiastic smile.

Amy's sweet voice singing through the day. John's wonderful free spirit. I was just as amazed to meet Kelly and see her sweetness, her persistence, and bubbly energy. I laughed as the water soothed away my frustration. They were still the same kids. I'd see the same characteristics that night when they all came home and did what teenagers usually do…consume food and make messes.

Though each of them was different, they'd begun taking their first cues from us during their nine months of gestation. As embryos, among the first parts to develop are the brain and spinal cord—the capacity to feel and receive sensations. As babies grow, their brains begin to recognize new data about their environment—Mom's heartbeat, her breathing, the amniotic fluid, the muffled sound of voices. Everything makes imprints on the developing brain. Because they lived with Kay for nine months, she became familiar to them. Newborns recognize their mothers from the very beginning.

Ironically, the incredible mystery of the process began to calm me. Even in the first hour after birth, God wires babies for connection. You'd think they'd fall asleep following the ordeal of entering the world. Yet for a very important reason, all babies have a period of wakeful alertness for one to two hours after birth. We didn't know this when our own kids were born, but those initial few hours following baby's arrival provide the first opportunities for the miracle of bonding. When our kids were becoming parents, we had a chance to see this amazing imprinting happen right before our eyes.

At our granddaughter's birth, our son John and his wife requested that if she was healthy, Penelope stay with them immediately after she was born. In the quiet of the birthing room, John spoke to Penelope for the first time, and her head turned toward him. He sang a quiet song to her, just as he had when she was still in the dark, and her little face looked up at him and she listened intently. Just think of this brand-new life encountering humans for the first time. They let her hear their voices, smell them, and feel their hands. She even looked into their eyes. Years later as a toddler, Penelope was soothed by music and fascinated by John's guitar and singing.

THE MIRACLE OF GOD'S DESIGN: WIRED FOR CONNECTION

Think of a baby's new brain as a computer coming off the assembly line. It's waiting to download its new operational system. And unless some specific, intentional adjustments are made later on, it will carry that initial programming it receives for life. Dr. John Bowlby first wrote about imprints in the early 1940s to describe what happens as newborns acquire their emotional coding in the first two years of life.[1] Of course, it isn't based on computer technology, but as a metaphor, the idea of new computers helps us explain and understand this initializing process better.

Over the first three months of life, infants seem fairly unresponsive. Yet within the first two hours of birth, the baby is taking in the new world around him, and this imprinting is already taking place. In modern hospitals, routine procedures often overlook these precious first hours between the baby and her parents, interrupting the opportunity for connection. The baby may be whisked away to a nursery or placed in a sterile warming crib. While birthing rooms have adapted to the new understanding of the importance of mother-infant bonding, this wonderful opportunity for connection is still too often unappreciated.

After the birth of our granddaughter Holland, our son Kevin and his wife, Stephanie, took advantage of her first hour of alertness. They whispered and spoke to her, and we watched as she took everything in. A year later her responsiveness was just as strong. She listened, learned, and imitated them as her personality formed from the inside out. And as she grew, she enjoyed connection with her parents that literally shaped and wired her little brain for connection and social interaction. It was marvelous to witness, and this may be something you have seen yourself.

In his book *The Neuroscience of Human Relationships,* Dr. Louis Cozolino provides the following explanation:

> Like every living system—from single neurons to complex ecosystems—the brain depends on interactions with others for its survival. Each brain is dependent on the scaffolding of caretakers and loved ones for its survival, growth, and well-being. So we begin with what we know: *The brain is an organ of adaptation* that builds its structures through interactions with others. So maybe it is better that we forget we have brains. Because to write the story of this journey, we must begin our guidebook with the thought: *There are no single brains.*[2]

A fascinating thought. According to Cozolino, it's the interconnectedness of our minds—and in this case, the parent's developed mind to the child's developing one—that defines our existence and survival. That interaction defines who we become.

Another expert on child development said,

> The infant's inner sensations form the core of the self. They appear to remain the central, the crystallization point of the "feeling of self" around which a "sense of identity" will become established.[3]

God's miraculous design involves an inherent readiness to connect with and be shaped by our caregivers. This is why it's so important for parents to be ready and willing to connect with their children from the very beginning. God has literally designed you to form the mind that will serve your child for a lifetime. As a parent, you have the most influence in building and shaping your child's brain.

Now if you're like us, you may find this a bit daunting. As a young parent, many days I found that my shortcomings were getting in the way of this brain downloading, and I often felt woefully inadequate.

THE MESS OF NEEDINESS

Looking back to that sock tantrum, I realize I was trying to sort out many things besides socks. Why was I so irritated despite my strong affection for my kids? Linking up the past with my present feelings was a new concept to me then, and I couldn't see what became so clear twenty years later. Yes, they had robbed me of my socks and my time to have a run. But I was beyond agitated, pushing well into twisted-undies territory. Other parents might not have responded quite so strongly to the same situation.

The truth I only realized much later was that for some reason, I was *triggered* by the sock-stealing.

And the question was, why did I care so much?

The very presence of children exposes messes in parents' lives. That mom in the store yelling at her five-year-old to "Shut up!" Your child's friend in second grade with the house overflowing with toys. The neighbor kids whose mom won't let them out of her sight. Each likely indicates a mess from that parent's past. Wounds from childhood create triggers in the present that make parents overreact with their kids. Long before my kids even entered my world, I was set up for the Great Sock Sabotage.

Not only were kids messy, they were exposing *my* mess.

And I *hated* the feeling of being exposed.

The truth of that startles me even now. There's no doubt in my mind that my reactions to them at that time came directly and nearly completely from my childhood.

Pause and consider that. Do you know what I'm talking about?

As a child, my home life alternated between love, smothering, anger, overprotection, and fits of volatility. The unpredictability caused me huge anxiety; the eruptions set off horrible screaming sirens of impending danger in my head. I began to worry about everything and developed obsessive-compulsive tendencies. I created a neat, orderly world around me and carefully hid my special things from imaginary intruders—even checking them several times a day to reassure my threatened mind.

When my cousins or friends came over, I would proudly display the items but not let them hold them too long, lest they be damaged in some inexplicable way. I became Possessive Guardian, preserver and protector of order. My refuge from the outbursts of anger was to hide the few things I owned. I had forgotten how I had hidden my cap gun, my pocketknife, and my flashlight, but as I reflected back, I realized why I had hidden my "sacred" socks—they weren't really sacred to me, but I was protecting them and myself from the same feelings of intrusion.

The sudden spotlight on my past injuries left my pain exposed. What I felt in the shower that day was the same vulnerability and loss of control I'd had when my cousin ran off with my cap gun, laughing, taunting me.

The reemergence of these old feelings shocked me.

And I wasn't alone. Little did I know, but Kay was having similar challenges as well. Babies and teens are a bundle of feelings and needs. Facing this as a new parent will draw upon how feelings and needs were handled in your home growing up. A sensitive child, Kay was deeply affected by the pain she saw in the world. She moved through adolescence and adulthood battling the wide gap between idealism and the harsh realities life brought. And because her parents divorced, she was committed to being a stay-at-home mom.

As a young mother, she endured, with grace, mothering three young children all under four years old. She always maintained her cool. But when Kevin started high school football, things began to change. While Kevin's intensity and aggression were valuable assets as an offensive lineman, it wasn't working well for his mom. Suddenly, confident Kay began to freeze up, struggling to speak when Kevin would display power or noise. In those moments, she saw her dad, lashing out with reprimands and displaying impatience with her sensitivity. Against her will, her mess of neediness was exposed, and just like I experienced, a door to her past was opened.

Kay was not an adult at those moments. She reverted to the feelings of a six-year-old in front of an aggressive dad. Now Kay had a choice: face her lack of a strong adult voice, or ignore her weakness and give Kevin free reign.

THE MESS OF INADEQUACY

Of all the things about parenting I dislike, this one may be the one I dislike the most: our children's messy development reveals the mess within us as parents.

Performing competently in my personal and professional life is very important to me. Like many, I take pride in good performance. If there weren't any kids around, I would look pretty good most of the time. There would be far less opportunity for my weaknesses to be exposed. But every child increases the chances of exposure and failure exponentially in ways that confound and frustrate me to no end. Kids have a natural knack for revealing the things we like least about ourselves. Even shortcomings we're completely unaware of, things we deny, things we've successfully hidden for years. All of them suddenly begin to parade around your neat little life when you have children.

Another unfortunate fact: kids instinctively know how to mess with your weaknesses. I was twenty-five and a seasoned Southern California driver when I found myself chaperoning our first newborn son home from the hospital. Hours before, I could have effortlessly changed lanes, downshifted, popped sunflower seeds—all while singing "Layla" at the top of my lungs. Yet within moments of the five-mile drive, I fumbled with the brakes, screeched to a halt on the freeway, and almost caused a major accident as Kay wondered what in the world had gone so very wrong with me (and whether we should turn back and pick up any required medication).

I didn't realize it quite then, but being responsible for others, espe-cially our newborn, made me a nervous wreck. The simple drive home exposed an anxiety in me I had no idea was so deeply buried. Even before the little culprit in the backseat was able to say my name, he'd ferreted out one of my major issues.

When my mother came to help the week after the birth, her hovering and intrusive tendencies made Kay very uncomfortable. Raised to expect a lot of autonomy and space, Kay nonetheless tolerated it for several days and internalized heavy anxiety. After a few days, Kevin began to vomit forcefully every time he nursed. We hurried to the pediatrician.

"Your mother-in-law is making you anxious, Kay. And you, in turn, are making Kevin sick. Milan, you need to have your mom go home." We both sat in shock at the doctor's prognosis. I began to wonder if there wasn't something easier I could do—maybe swim to Catalina Island or hope my mom would get a sudden case of the flu. Surely there were better options than asking her to leave.

But somehow I got through the confrontation with my mother and she went home, and the vomiting stopped. Kay's anxiousness disap-peared. But our little exposer had struck again.

Not only do kids reveal our weaknesses, they frustrate our need for control and predictability. Of course, we know logically that there's very little we control in life, yet we still fiercely defend our illusion and desire for it. But life changes. Somebody moves the cheese. We have kids, and on the day you've just started to understand them, they grow up and change and become completely different people.

This leaves us parents with a choice. We can allow our inadequacies to help us grow, or we can choose not to. Like little coaches pointing out weaknesses and defining our training, children and teens point spotlights on places we need to grow in our lives. In the area of faith, James put it well: "Consider it all joy…when you encounter various trials, knowing that the testing of your faith produces endurance…that you may be per-fect and complete, lacking in nothing" (James 1:2–4).

If we deny the truth about ourselves, then by choice or default we choose not to grow. These are the angry parents, the ones who have no purposeful solution. For them, it's a constant battle to shield themselves from the spotlight and figure out how to manage the discomfort when they find escaping it impossible. Their children end up alienated and neglected, eventually becoming angry adolescents and bearers of hand-me-down emotional injuries.

Trials in child rearing are opportunities to become more perfect and complete, yet the change must first be embraced. And the sad reality is that most parents will never take this first step to grow and will stay stuck in the old patterns they see as inescapable.

We recently asked an audience two questions: "How many of you had parents who grew and matured during your childhood?" Few hands were raised for that one. "How many had parents who apologized for some way they hurt you?" Again, only a few people raised their hands, but to those, we asked, "How did it feel when parents admitted their shortcomings?"

And what do you think they said? "Great." "I loved them for it." "I felt validated and seen."

CHANGING HOW YOU LOVE YOUR CHILD

You may not have had parents who admitted their weaknesses or attempted to learn from them. But you can be that kind of parent. And it may be easier than you think. The focus of this book is not on getting your children to change. As Jo, the professional nanny from the hit TV show *Supernanny,* points out, despite their behaviors, kids are usually not the problem. It's about *you* as a parent.

This book will reveal some blind spots in you as a parent. How are those unseen forces shaping your parenting? Through the course of this book, we'll discuss how to respond to your children, free from the dictates of your past. If you're willing to accept your children's spotlight and set some goals for yourself to improve your responses, you *will* change your children by changing the quality of love you are giving them.

And you'll change their lives as well, even for future generations.

Imagine that. If you're like most, you didn't get this from your parents. You have probably already messed up with your kids in some big ways. The good news is that there's always time for redemption. It's always possible for parents to set things right. The great news is that brains are remoldable, especially kids' brains. And as we know from experience, all mistakes are redeemable.

No matter what water has gone under the bridge, there is hope for a better parenting future if you are willing.

And just in case you're still wondering how large that sock pile became that day: *one hundred twenty-three* socks.

Discussion Questions

- What have you learned about yourself since becoming a parent that you didn't know or hadn't faced before? *I'm selfish about needing down time*
- If you're married, what have you learned about your spouse since becoming a parent? *He is better at making fun of a sit./being silly*
- What are some things your kids do that make you feel inadequate? *ignore me when I make requests*
- How do you typically respond to those feelings? *I get mad & start giving cons &*
- Did you ever feel inadequate as a kid? If so, did anyone know this and help you? *often, rarely*
- If you did not receive help for feeling inadequate, is it possible that some feelings from your childhood could be bleeding into the present when your child makes you feel inadequate? *totally*

Two

What Determines How We Parent

While the parent-child bond can create moments that are exhilarating, it can also be exhausting, especially the first year of the child's life. Every new parent will experience times of being overwhelmed, yet for many, the negative emotions can be overpowering. Depression, anxiety, fear, helplessness, uncertainty, panic, or a constant state of stress can be some of the extreme effects of being around a baby or young child. And for most of these parents, it is because they're being reacquainted with the children they once were.

"When one becomes a parent, the buried, unresolved pain is shaken loose."[1] When parents feel these strong emotions, they react without understanding what's driving their behavior. They may withdraw from their children (physically or emotionally) or fearfully hover; or they may get angry, or look for something to distract themselves. In the worst case, if there is a lot of unresolved pain in their past, they may abuse, neglect, or abdicate their parent role by turning their children over to someone else. There are plenty of grandparents functioning as primary caregivers whose adult children have not fully grown up yet.

So where did this messiness come from? Our families of origin, of course, or what we call the "FOO factor." As well-meaning as our respective parents might have been, they were broken people raising broken children in a broken world.

We all are.

The FOO factor and what our individual experiences were like will determine how we each parent. The parenting (or lack thereof) your parents provided was your training ground for all your adult relationships, including those with your children. Your love lessons growing up impact how you love your kids now.

One therapist says, "When the parent establishes an atmosphere of respect and tolerance for the child's feelings and emotions, the child is able to let go of the parent and more easily become their own individual and healthfully separate from the parent." She goes on to say that if the parents are to furnish the environment for this to successfully occur, the parents themselves ought to have grown up in such an environment.[2]

A similar thing was said two thousand years ago: "A pupil is not above his teacher; but...after he has been fully trained, will be like his teacher" (Luke 6:40). If we want to have great kids, we need to first be great parents. Our kids cannot rise above our level, so seeing where we need to grow is essential. We know from experience it's possible to overcome the past, and it's our hope that this book will help you to do just that.

By discovering the unseen forces that determine how we parent, we can learn to respond to children free from wounds of the past.

As we examine what successful parenting really looks like, let me begin by telling you a real-life story from the family archives.

A few years ago, my daughter Amy told her then-four-year-old son, Reece, that they were coming to Nana and Poppy's for dinner.

He was quiet for a moment. "I don't like going to Poppy's. He kisses me too much."

Now let's first jump back a few decades to my family of origin for a moment.

My (Milan's) father was the son of an immigrant whose practice was to hug and kiss family and friends on the cheek as a greeting or to say farewell. Until the day he died, I still kissed my dad on the cheek every time we met or departed. My mother was a midwestern small-town girl whose family called kisses "sugars," and when my aunts saw me coming, they would suck at least ten or fifteen sugars from each cheek. "Train up a child in the way he should go" (Proverbs 22:6). This kid was trained to be a kisser.

Kissing in the Yerkovich family is as second nature as breathing, eating, and sleeping. I turned kissing into play while wrestling with my four children. They'd ride around on my back, and eventually I would stop and say, "Kisses make the horsie go." They would laugh and lean over to plunk a few kiss tokens into the ride, and I'd start up all over again.

So what should I have done with Reece's request?

I could have chosen to reject *his* individuality and insisted he conformed to my preferences, "the Yerkovich way." After all, I'm the poppy and he's four.

Sadly, many families routinely make this kind of demand, which amounts to a total dismissal of a child's real feelings. In fact, few family systems (and marriages) allow for, much less celebrate, others being different.

Whether with opinions, preferences, tastes, ideals, decisions, ideas, politics, specific knowledge, or simple suggestions, we all have a tendency to insist that others think, do, feel, and say the same things we do.

We're looking to validate *ourselves* at others' expense.

And what is the effect when children are overlooked? Gifts are not developed, adult voices never mature, talents are not cultivated, and dreams are never realized. What does occur? When kids' feelings are dismissed repeatedly, they become resentful, angry, disconnected, depressed, anxious, and hopeless.

At first when Amy told me, I was a bit hurt. Yet I took a moment and said, "Okay, Reece is different from me. I'll adapt to *his* desires." We had a great time playing, and when he left that day, his dad, Steve, carried him, and Reece and I had a high-five on his way out.

In a marriage when one person constantly dominates, the other is eclipsed. In parenting, if a mother or father continually insists on his or her way, the child is eclipsed. The child loses his voice and, in some ways, ceases to exist. Many adults have learned as children not to risk or show their real selves because it's pointless to do so.

In those with dominator personalities, insecurity causes them to make others' opinions and actions go away. This constant anxiety over others possibly gaining any control over them makes them unable to tolerate differences in others. Assertions of independence and uniqueness threaten their fragile inner world and cause a familiar internal distress. Because they can't listen to others, they tend to dismiss everyone who doesn't agree with them.

Know anyone like that? We're betting you probably do.

Many people have been victims of such tyranny and had their personhoods eclipsed. They commonly struggle with internal fears to speak up and be heard and often fight feelings of being invisible. They're usually extremely afraid of others' disapproval.

We're betting you may know some people who tend toward this extreme as well. Why is this so common?

LULLABIES THAT LAST

Your parents gave you your first lessons in love. They were lullabies that lasted. They are with you to this very day.

What was modeled in your home? What were the written and unwritten rules in your family of origin? My grandson Reece is in his formative years, and he's received some good love lessons from his mom and dad. How about you?

We all know no parent is perfect, yet in a healthy home with good parenting, children develop three essential abilities from good love lessons: (1) the capacity to see oneself clearly, (2) the expertise to deal effectively with a wide range of emotions, and (3) the capability to repair relationships by dealing with conflict and reaching resolution.

Did you learn these lullabies?

Self-Awareness

The ability to know oneself is *the* essential lesson parents teach.

When we make this claim, some parents will say, "I love my child just fine, and my parents loved me. Isn't that what counts?" Of course, love is what good parenting is all about. But what we're talking about here is *how* love is given and received. *How* we love our kids determines whether they will learn to discern the true qualities of love. And *how* we model love for our children teaches them either to know themselves or to struggle with the same emotional challenges most people do. As researcher Robert Karen says, "If there is one thing, then, that the anxious parent in each of us is truly guilty of—and that our culture colludes in—it is not necessarily a lack of love, but a failure to look at and to know ourselves."[3]

At four years old, Reece was able to know his internal state and was fortunate enough to have a mom and dad who were sensitive enough to listen and take him seriously. So many of us would have simply made him deal with it. Amy had to confront her dad with unpleasant news that might have made her uncomfortable.

But instead, Reece's parents drew him out by listening to him and asking questions. They showed him that his feelings were safe with them and they would be his *advocates*. And finally, they assured him I would do the same and be okay with his feelings. We decided to ask Amy and Steve about what they did. "It was amazing what he could tell us about his feelings and needs when we took the time to inquire and listen," said Amy. "Reece is so much like me," Steve added. "He's an introvert, and he warms up slowly. It's great we could affirm his preferences and support his needs and desires."

Self-awareness is a learned skill that develops when parents *stop, listen,* and actively *love* the heart of their child. A child requires guidance to learn the words to describe his confusing and overwhelming internal world of thoughts and feelings. And children who learn to describe their feelings, motives, and behaviors will be better parents and spouses.

Ultimately, knowing our internal selves allows us to define what we need, which allows others to see it and respond. This is part of our makeup as humans—we were designed to connect with others in relationship, to define ourselves through bonding with others.

By four years old, Reece demonstrated self-awareness and the ability to describe his feelings. These imprints are created early, when the brain is actively receiving such lessons. Over time Reece will have a reservoir of comfort to draw from. He will also learn to manage his emotions and feel safe to express his feelings in relationships. Of course, reinforcement will happen throughout grade school and into high school. He'll develop deeper abilities to evaluate his emotions, which will increase his ability to understand his responses and choose behaviors. He will mature in his capacity to know what makes him tick and what makes others tick. He'll be known as a person who cares for others, is open and flexible to others' input, and is self-controlled and understanding.

When most people become parents, they will struggle mightily to rise above the experience of their own parents. As attachment researcher Dr. Robert Karen says, "Only the parents who had the capacity to reflect on inner states could provide this function for their children.... What happens when a parent lacks this capacity?... He will continue to be a slave to his own early patterns, persisting in strategies and maneuvers with his own child that he first learned when dealing with a rejecting or erratic parent."[4]

If we don't work to change our parenting, we will unconsciously train our kids to do what we learned in our families of origin. And children *only* learn these lullabies by example and direct instruction.

So how can a mom or dad teach this stuff? With a baby you might begin saying things like, "Your crying tells Mommy you're not a happy boy. How can I help?" With a toddler, "I know you're mad because you can't have ice cream. Let's think of something else you want that you can have." To a preschooler: "I understand you're mad because you can't have ice cream, and that's okay, but you may not hit or throw a tantrum.

If you're tired, we might need to take a rest, or sometimes a hug helps us to calm down when we're upset. Would you like a hug? Yes or no is okay."

Teaching emotional awareness and helping children learn to assess what's inside them is more caught than taught, but when coupled with direction, they're given a gift that will keep on giving.

When Amy responded to Reece's statement, she said something like, "I could see how Poppy's kissing makes you feel uncomfortable. He loves you and that is one of the ways he shows it. He's been kissing me since I was a little girl. Just watch, he'll hug your daddy and kiss me when we come through the door. But I will talk to him, and he will be okay with your decision. You can walk into his house by my side so you can be comfortable."

Amy and Steve did a great job that day! And come to think of it, so did I.

Feeling and Dealing

Were you taught to feel emotion and deal with it appropriately? Most adults who come into my office for therapy frustrate very easily and have poor coping skills. Usually, their adult relationships are suffering immensely as they lack patience and the capacity to deal with the strong emotions that overtake them or respond effectively to passionate emotions in others. Let's face it: life is a real pressure cooker at times. If we weren't taught good love lessons in the "feeling and dealing" department as children, as adults we will lack the ability to self-regulate; that is, manage strong emotions effectively. We may look twenty-, thirty-, forty-, or fiftysomething on the outside, but we can still react to challenging situations by withdrawing, pouting, having tantrums, being defensive, and generally being children in an adult world.

One special memory stands out in my mind. One day when our second son, John, was about ten, he came home from school and I could tell something was wrong. As he slowly shuffled past my home-office door, I asked, "How was your day?"

"Okay," he mumbled.

"You sure there's not something wrong?"

"No, and I don't want to talk about it!"

During this time Kay and I had just begun to learn to identify our feelings and express and discuss them in the family. We had our Soul Words list taped to the refrigerator door, so I said, "John, I can tell something inside of you isn't doing well. Go look at the soul words on the refrigerator and pick two that you're feeling, and come back and tell me before you go out and play."

You can imagine the reaction I got: whiny, mournful sounds; some moaning, and even a little wailing. "Aw, come on, Dad. Everybody else is outside already." I remained silent and eventually he trudged off to the kitchen to pick some words off the fridge. "Stupid list," I heard him mutter.

Of course, it took him fifteen minutes to get back to my office, but once he'd had two bowls of cereal and delayed sufficiently, he came back to my door. "Sad and embarrassed."

"John, what happened?" I asked.

He suddenly broke into tears. "I forgot my homework again, and the teacher yelled at me. Then the whole class turned around and laughed at me."

I pulled him onto my lap, and he cried. I held him and rocked, thinking back to many of my school days where I'd done poorly because of my intense anxiety. I remembered being put on the spot by many a teacher and not having any answers. "Yes, that must have been really embarrassing," I said, validating his emotion. "I can see why you're sad."

After a few minutes, he sat up and started playing with stuff on my desk. I let him play for a while, and then he looked at me, gave me a big hug, and said, "I love you, Dad."

"I love you too. More than you could ever know."

Then he jumped down and went out to play. His entire demeanor was different, and it wasn't long before I heard him outside with the other kids, cutting loose.

How about you? Do you have memories of being comforted? Those who do will be natural comforters of their own children. John is now thirty-two, and I watch him naturally wrap his arms around his daughter, Penelope, when she's distressed—and she's comforted too.

Children need to be allowed to experience some levels of stress in order to learn to manage it. Yet too much stress becomes traumatic, setting up defense patterns that can hang with them a long time. Since we can't shield our children from all stress and pain, we have to be prepared to help them learn to *feel and deal* by being attentive caregivers, ready for hidden reefs of pain lurking below the surface. As we gently coax them out, helping our children overcome their natural bent toward shame, hiding, and fear, they learn to get through life's troubles successfully—because what's *shareable* is *bearable.*

What are some good ways to talk to your school-age children? "You have been grumpy since you got home from school. I wonder what is stressing you inside. It's hard to have fun when you're upset. Let's figure out what's bothering you by picking a few soul words off the list." For adolescents who might be a tad bit resistant: "We both know you're upset. I see frustration, but there are probably several things behind it. Let's talk later this evening and try to sort some of that out. Think about it and let me know when you've identified some other feelings."

Experts have clearly concluded that parents who train their children to have higher EQs (emotional quotients) will be way ahead of their peers socially and academically and, as they grow up, will be more secure and capable spouses and parents. Putting feelings into words allows kids to look at them and *change* them. Additionally, learning to be a feeler-dealer parent will allow you to be more affectionate and nurturing. People who pay attention to feelings use touch more to show affection. When people are confused about their feelings or unsure they tend to avoid touch and have negative reactions to touching.[5]

Think about it: were you touched as a child? It's never too late to start learning and teaching your children.

Resolving Conflict

Couples who come into my office with conflicts often come from two extremes. Bill was fearful of his wife and struggled with being honest due to his discomfort with conflict. He tended to lie and minimize. I asked him about this. "Oh, my parents *never* argued or had fights in front of us kids. I don't think they even did in private. I had a great home."

His wife viewed him as weak, disrespected him, and was convinced she'd married a pathologic liar. She didn't like it when I disagreed with her and suggested he was simply afraid of her.

In another case, Leslie grew up used to battles and an angry, terrorizing dad who slapped children who stood up to his tantrums. In her marriage, Leslie was a controller who demanded conformity to her opinions and rules. Over time her dominance squeezed the life out of her passive husband.

Bill and Leslie had learned no love lessons. Neither knew anything about self-awareness or how to feel and deal. They had no models for managing anger, resolving conflict, or expressing feelings and negotiating compromise. And that lack of healthy role models stifled love from one generation to the next.

Chances are, if you learned self-awareness and how to feel and deal, you most likely learned how to resolve conflict. You were listened to and learned how to listen to others. There was mutual respect in differences. They were either tolerated or managed, or ideally, celebrated. Individuals were allowed to think and feel differently about many things. These are the simple tools to successful parenting, and if you know them, you will experience the various stages of your child's development with enjoyment and little distress.

If you didn't learn these love lessons, your first job as a parent is to discover them. Over two decades ago, we were two such parents. In many homes today, there are adult children raising children, and none of them will enjoy much or go very far until these lessons are learned.

Now is the time for you to choose. You can strive to appreciate and celebrate differences, or you can stay stuck trying to change everyone to your way of living. As Kay often says, pick your pain. Either is painful, but growth is productive. And the promise of reward to everyone involved is great. Growth, and the subsequent freedom that ensues, occurs when we "live with the reality of our past and give up the most flagrant of our illusions."[6]

To not grow is to remain trapped in distorted views of oneself, filled with illusions, facades, and denial—all of which emanate from our own pain in childhood. To lose your feelings is to lose yourself. And what is the result? "Depression...experienced as emptiness, futility, fear of impoverishment, and loneliness [all come from] the tragedy of the loss of the self, or alienation from the self, from which many suffer in our generation and society."[7]

You and your child may be struggling, but take heart. Have faith! Muster up your courage. Your God-given brain *can* repair and rebuild around new love lessons.[8] The exciting fact is that your parenting is about to improve dramatically as you become more observant and expressive with your kids. Relief is in sight.

The next few chapters will pass quickly, so hold on. We'll start by identifying your love style and the effects of each. Then we'll discuss what changes you can make to impact your family forever. So get ready to pass on these essential lessons to your children, and learn how you truly *transform* how you love your kids.

DISCUSSION QUESTIONS

- Think about your love lessons growing up. Do you have memories of being emotionally upset and having a parent draw you out, validate your feelings, and offer comfort?
- Did your parents build self-reflection skills by asking about feelings?
- How were emotions handled in your family growing up? What were the unspoken rules about feelings?
- How did each parent tolerate or encourage differences? Was your uniqueness seen and celebrated? If so, how? If not, what did your parents miss?
- What were your love lessons about resolving conflict? What did you learn about being angry?

Three

The Avoider Parent

(Kay) was playing Peter Pan with my four-year-old granddaughter Penelope at the park. She was Tinker Bell, as usual, and I was playing several parts—Peter, mostly, but occasionally Captain Hook or one of the mermaids. Another little boy around the same age joined in, announcing, "I'm Sam, and I want to play."

"Okay," said Penelope, "but I have to sprinkle you with pixie dust first." She bent down and picked up a pinch of sand and sprinkled it into his hair. I wasn't sure Sam's mom was going to appreciate this, but I wasn't sure which one she was among the other moms chatting. Sam brushed the sand out of his eyelashes, and we continued to explore Neverland. Just as we had spied the Lost Boys, our play came to a screeching halt when Sam let out a painful cry. I watched as he brushed a bee off his hand, and I realized he had been stung.

"Let me get the stinger out," I said gently, but Sam turned his back and squeezed his eyes shut tight, trying to stifle his tears.

"Where's your mom, honey?" I asked, scanning the nearby moms.

"She's at work," Sam said.

"Who brought you to the park?"

"My dad. He's over there." Sam pointed to a man reading at the far end of the park. I hadn't even noticed him. "The baby-sitter's late, so my dad brought me here until she comes."

"Come on, sweetie. I'll walk you over to your dad."

Sam rather reluctantly followed me.

"Now what, Sam?" said the father impatiently when we reached him.

"He got stung by a bee," I explained. "I think the stinger is still in his finger," I added sympathetically.

"Come here, Sam, and let me see," his father said. Sam stepped forward but held his finger protectively in the other hand.

"Give me your finger, Sam," his father said without the least bit of compassion. As his dad pried his hands apart, Sam began to cry again.

"Big boys don't cry; it's just a bee sting." He pulled out the stinger. "There, it's gone. Now stop your crying." After picking up his book, he dismissed Sam with a downward glance.

My heart broke for this little guy. What was his dad teaching him? *Don't show me your feelings. Don't expect comfort from me. Your needs are an interruption.*

And Sam was getting the message, loud and clear.

As we were walking away, I said in a voice loud enough to be heard, "Those bee stings really hurt, Sam. I think you just need some comfort." And I gave him a hug as we walked back to play, leaving Captain Book to guard his precious bench.

Now, to be fair, Sam's dad may not have a single memory of comfort from his childhood. Perhaps, like me, he didn't know what he missed. A bit later, I looked over and he was gone; the nanny had taken his place. "Is that your baby-sitter?" I asked Sam. He looked over at the bench. "Yeah, that's her," he said with disinterest. Apparently, a hug and kiss good-bye were not on this dad's agenda either. But Sam was already learning to get along without him.

I parented my kids for thirteen years as a full-fledged avoider.[1] I had no idea then, but looking back, I can see how the bonding injuries from my childhood shaped how I parented in countless ways.

One particular day comes to mind, when my oldest, Kevin, was about two and a half and Amy was seven months. Once again, I was looking for Kevin's "night-night" blanket, which he wanted frequently and left everywhere. Although I tried not to show it, I resented that stupid blanket. We had to find it to take along wherever we went, and it had to be in his bed before he could sleep.

While searching under piles of laundry, we heard the trash truck roaring slowly in our direction and the clanging of trash cans. This was one of Kevin's favorite weekly events, and he ran to the screen door, and begged me to "go see twash towuck!" I stopped my search for the blanket, checked Amy in the swing, and scooped him up to walk to the curb for our weekly ritual. He waved his whole body at the trashman and watched with wide eyes as the big metal arms scooped up the cans. And suddenly a plan formed in my brain.

We waved good-bye, went back in the house, and after a few more minutes of searching, I found his blanket under his daddy's desk. "I have a great idea," I announced. "You are such a big boy now. You don't really need this blanket anymore. Let's do something very special with it and give it to the big trash truck." He looked at me and felt the satin on the edge of the blanket, his thumb in his mouth. No response. So I naturally took that as assent and proceeded to talk it up all week.

The fateful day arrived. I opened the front door so we were sure to hear the truck. Out we marched, blanket in hand. Kevin acted very brave. He believed what I had told him: he *was* a big boy. The magic moment arrived, and I explained to the trashman about our plan, fully ignoring his dubious look. All three of us watched the blankie get scooped up with the trash. "Yeah!" I clapped. "Kevin is a big boy!" I felt victorious. One more thing I didn't have to think about, hunt for incessantly, and try to get clean. But before that driver hopped back in the seat of his truck, Kevin began to cry. "I want my blue blan—(gasp)—*kie!*"

"Don't cry," I backpedaled. "You are a big boy, remember?" It did not help. Still, I knew he would get over it. Meanwhile, he consoled himself by hunting for a replacement. He strode out of his room still sniffing, "I have a yeyow piwow now," he declared. And from then on, he made sure his yellow pillow never got near the trash truck.

I've told this story publicly several times. I've been known to tear up recounting it. Some laugh and Kevin always gets a few sympathetic "ohs." In reality, it's a very sad story about *my* injuries getting in the way of loving my child.

So why did I do this? What forces inside me were driving my need to force my child into growing up faster? I didn't have the self-awareness to understand what was really happening then, but that blanket represented his great need, specifically, his need for comfort *from me*—this same neediness I had learned from my family to live without. His blanket and what it symbolized made me more than a little uncomfortable. I had no idea about age-appropriate behavior or that neediness is not something to be dismissed or grow out of. Rather, neediness is a part of being human that we never outgrow.

But any avoider—male, female, young, or old—will understand this story. We all share similar traits. Since avoiders come from homes where they received little comfort, nurturing, physical affection, or concern for their emotions, they enter adulthood placing little value on these things. Emotions are something avoiders learned to ignore. Avoiders value mastery, performance, tasks, and a job well done.

Most often, avoiders grew up in homes where mastery and performance were valued with a consistent underlying message of hurry up and grow up. Independence is prized and dependence is discouraged. Remember, these love styles exist on a continuum, so a mild avoider will identify with these traits to a lesser degree than an extreme avoider. See if you relate to the statements listed below.

AVOIDER ASSESSMENT

- It seems my spouse has more emotional needs than I do.
- What is upsetting to my spouse or kids seems like no big deal to me.

- My childhood was fine, but I don't have many memories from my upbringing, let alone positive ones of receiving comfort.
- I'm independent and self-reliant, and those are values I've worked to pass on to my kids.
- I would rather work on a project alone than sit and have a long conversation with someone.
- I've been told I don't show enough affection.
- When something bad happens, I get over it and move on.
- If a kid is upset, I reassure her with, "You're fine."
- I tend to guard my space and feel annoyed when I'm required to spend a lot of time and attention on family matters.
- I like to make decisions on my own.
- When someone is very emotional, I find a way to escape, especially if they think I'm supposed to help. I don't like tears and lots of emotion. It makes me uncomfortable I don't know what to say
- In my family growing up, everyone pretty much did his own thing and kept to himself.
- I have siblings with whom I have little or no contact today.
- I have rarely never felt particularly close to my parents.
- Nothing gets me too bothered or upset.

If you identified with this assessment, congratulations. You're that much closer to being a better parent. And you might want to thank your kids for helping you to grow and recognize yourself better. But let me assure you, avoiders have positive traits too. They raise responsible kids who are often extremely accomplished and uncommonly resourceful. You can learn to balance your focus on achievement as you expand your ability to connect emotionally. Your kids will benefit and so will you. So let's look at some of the tendencies avoiders have in parenting to learn what you can do better.

WITH INFANTS AND TODDLERS

How do avoider moms and dads deal with these early stages of parenting?

Sandy is a good example. She walked into my office toting a six-week-old in a carrier. No sooner was she seated than she got right down to business.

"I'm not cut out to be a stay-at-home mother," she explained. "My husband hated day care when he was a kid, so he doesn't want that. But I feel trapped, and I'm missing the office. Being with two kids all day is driving me crazy. I didn't think it would be this hard."

"What do you find most difficult about being home?" I asked.

"The crying, the whining, the laundry, the messes, snotty noses, tripping on toys. I can get it all done, but the crying makes me nuts. What's the point of staying home if I don't like it?" she asked.

"Well, in order to weigh all your options, it might be important to understand more fully why you find it so difficult. Tell me about your experiences growing up."

Sandy spat out the facts. "Good family. I'm the first of five. Dad was gone a lot. Moved ten times. I mostly remember Mom packing and un-packing boxes. My parents loved us, and we all turned out great." She punctuated this last part with a quick nod.

From there, Sandy continued to confirm my speculation that she was an avoider. She was competent, devoid of emotion, and task oriented. Women who are avoiders often have some ambivalence about becoming a parent. They don't feel a maternal instinct, and it's difficult for them to adequately prepare for parenting, as they tend to dismiss their fears.

By our sixth session, Sandy began to understand why mothering was so difficult. "I never realized how self-sufficient I was as a kid," she said. "Mom popped out the babies and was perpetually tired and basically a single parent. Actually, I was the other parent. She depended on me."

"So you functioned as the helper parent from six until you left home at eighteen. Did anyone enjoy you, play with you, help you?"

"Not really."

"No one recognized your loneliness after every time you moved?" I continued gently. "Or when you struggled to make new friends?"

She shook her head.

"So you had to get rid of feelings and needs and do the best you could to be the good little soldier. And now you're a mom again—giving, giving, giving. It must remind you of those lonely years. You had so little time to be the receiver."

Sandy looked out the window, and her eyes welled with tears. "No wonder I put off having kids so long." She was finally quiet and reflective. "I don't want to resent my kids. I remember taking care of my brother when I was seven years old. It was always so hard to get my brother to stop crying. Every night he would cry, and Mom would beg me to hold him. I hated it. I realize when my baby cries, it's like…I'm seven again and completely powerless and overwhelmed."

When avoider moms or dads become new parents, they are thrown into a world they could not have imagined. Babies are tightly wrapped packages of constant needs and emotional demands. Fathers are usually able to distance themselves from a mom's territory, but an avoider mom usually has to face everything she's learned to minimize, dismiss, and ignore in herself, twenty-four hours a day. Her unbearable job becomes to cuddle, feed, change, wash, nurture, and otherwise tolerate intense feelings and nonstop demands day and night.

To make matters worse, avoiders learned long ago not to depend on anyone for help, and they're extremely resistant to asking for any kind of assistance. This compounds the problem, as an avoider mom believes she must manage motherhood on her own, while not being needy herself. Skilled at dismissing her distressing feelings, she may tend to detach from her baby, never enjoying the experience. To manage the stress, avoiders gravitate toward parenting styles that are structured, predictable, sched-uled, and won't "spoil" the baby.[2]

That day I told Sandy her tears were a good sign—she was beginning to have sympathy for herself and what her children were feeling. Going back to work would lessen her discomfort. But could she use the oppor-tunity to learn to acknowledge, understand, and accept her feelings? Could her children help her regain what she'd had to give up as a child? It may seem the more difficult route, but healing usually requires the harder choice; however, in the long run it pays off.

We recently went to dinner with a young couple who attended a church we were visiting. They had just taken part in our workshop on love styles. "I had a big 'ah ha' moment today during the workshop," Sara shared between spoonfuls of ice cream. She rubbed her belly, due any day. "When I told Frank we were pregnant, I was crushed by his reaction. I thought he would hug me and twirl me around, but he just sort of nod-ded and grinned. I called my mom and told her, and you could hear her down the block."

Frank squirmed in his seat. "I'm excited," he said rather flatly.

"I realized today that Frank is an avoider. He doesn't show much emotion about anything. And I'm a bundle of emotions with hormones blasting through my body!" She laughed. "I know he's not trying to hurt me when he tells me to stop crying and get it together." She looked at him. "It's what his dad taught him. When we told Frank's dad about the baby, he said, 'Well, I hope you get a raise, because kids cost an arm and a leg.'"

Frank's face relaxed slightly. "My dad has never shown much emo-tion about anything. To be honest, having a kid scares me. I don't really know what to do."

Milan and I shared a quick glance to say, *Yeah, this might cause some unwanted tension in the house.*

Avoiders retreat under stress. And becoming a parent is stressful even when the baby is planned and wanted. Faced with new emotional changes, avoiders feel inadequate and, of course, uncomfortable.

Most couples can remember getting the news about being pregnant and their reaction. How do you think most avoiders react? Not with the exuberance one might expect. Avoiders rarely have emotional responses to anything. A public display of feelings is uncomfortable. Like Sandy, Frank needs to discover how his love style is affecting his closest relationships.

If you're a new parent (or have been one), can you identify with any of the statements below?

- I don't like the baby stage.
- I can't stand not being able to figure out what my baby wants.
- If I pick her up every time she cries, I'll spoil her. It's better just to let her cry it out.
- I'm not sure what I'm supposed to feel, but I don't feel close to my baby.
- I get excited when my baby masters some new skill or toy.
- I'm very annoyed by crying and fussing.
- I wish babies were more like me; I don't need much touch.
- I'm annoyed by pacifiers, blankets, and so on.
- I'm grateful for pacifiers, blankets, and so on because they make my child need me less.
- I don't like neediness, nurturing, or lots of affection.
- My baby needs to learn to need me less when I'm gone.
- I prefer bottles to nursing. Propping up a bottle gives me some freedom, and the baby can learn to feed himself.

WITH PRESCHOOLERS

One of the most difficult challenges preschoolers bring is knowing what is age appropriate. As a preschooler, Kevin fussed and cried when I left him. At the time, I assumed his behavior pointed out some failure in me as a mother. I believed happy, secure children didn't cry. However, just the opposite is true.

Kids who are well adjusted and bonded may protest when separation occurs, because preschoolers are supposed to prefer their moms and dads. A baby's temperament can play a part—some children are more bothered by separating than others. But my own imprint from childhood told me to see crying at separation as bad instead of appropriate and normal. I didn't soothe Kevin much because I felt it would encourage his fussing. If I could go back, I would make more effort, saying things like, "It's okay to cry when we say good-bye. You're sad because you will miss me, and I'll miss you too. Here's a big good-bye hug, and I'll have another big hug for you when I come get you in just a little while."

In general, avoiders expect too much too soon from their preschoolers. Milan and I met David and Susie during a weekend marriage seminar. David introduced himself as a classic avoider. "We see how these love styles apply to our marriage, but we've spent a lot of free time talking about our three boys who are two, five, and seven. Susie is always telling me I'm too hard on them, but until this weekend, I didn't believe it. It actually makes me mad if they cry over anything. Until hearing you both speak, I never realized I didn't get comfort as a kid, and it never occurred to me their emotions were valuable. If I give in to their crying, won't it make them crybabies?"

"Great question," Milan said. "Your phrase 'give in' is interesting, as though it's a power struggle, where you lose and your child wins. Was it like that for you growing up? Did you have power struggles with one of your parents?"

"No struggle," David said. "Dad was the boss, and it was his way or the highway."

"So he related to you in a controlling way rather than a relational way?" Milan asked.

"I never thought of it like that, but yes. He didn't allow feelings at all. You think maybe that's why I get mad when my boys whine or cry?"

"Maybe. But look at it this way," Milan continued. "Responding to your children's feelings in a tender way validates their emotions. It's not 'giving in,' but merely recognizing they feel distress and helping them *understand* their feelings. Once they understand them, they can learn to manage them instead of ignoring them. This is one of the greatest lessons you can teach your kids."

Below are some common problems avoider parents have raised regarding their preschoolers:

- "My three-year-old should be more mature by now."
- "My child won't do enough things on her own, and it frustrates me."
- "I distract my child with something else when he wants something from me, especially comfort."
- "I ignore negative emotions and only respond to positive ones."
- "When I leave my child, I generally try to do so quickly and avoid the fuss."
- "I get exasperated when my child cries on my return. I'm back, so what's the problem?"
- "I don't usually enjoy playing with my child unless she's learning something."
- "I wish my kid would learn to play on his own."

Avoider moms and dads say things like: "Go to your room if you are going to cry," "There's nothing to be scared of; don't be silly," "Don't make a scene," and, "You're just trying to make a bigger deal out of things."

Maybe your kids are past this stage and you're worried you made mistakes. Don't worry. Kids of any age are amazingly resilient and more capable of change than adults. It's never too late to begin to pay attention to emotions. We'll discuss some growth goals at the end of the chapter.

WITH SCHOOL-AGE KIDS AND TEENS

Adolescents describe avoider parents as busy and hard to get close to. While avoider parents may show some affection to very young children, older kids are too big for hugs and kisses. Many teens say they seldom, if ever, hear, "I love you" from their avoider parent.

Accomplishment is how avoider parents express love, so raising responsible, productive kids becomes paramount. While certainly a worthy goal, avoiders don't make soul connections with their children. The advantage for teens over younger children is that they're able to identify this weakness and respond to it (which can put avoider parents at an emotional disadvantage).

I was traveling in the car with some friends when one mother of a teenage daughter lamented, "Teenagers are tough. I caught my daughter in bed with her boyfriend several weeks ago, and I can't get the picture out of my mind. It's been very tense between us."

"What did you say to her about it?" I asked.

"Nothing! I didn't know what to say. How do you talk about something like that? She's so moody anyway, I don't want to get into it and risk setting her off."

I felt so sad for this mom and daughter. Tension and no talking—a sure recipe for disconnection and detachment. I decided to take a risk and asked if she would answer some questions, and she readily agreed. As we rode along I inquired about her childhood, quickly learning that her family ignored her emotions and needs and left her to fend for herself in her turbulent teen years.

After hearing some sad stories of disconnection and loneliness, I asked, "So you can understand why it's difficult to knock on the door of your daughter's heart if your parents didn't do that for you? Your parents didn't know you deeply and gave you no experience to draw from."

"Yes," she said. "It makes so much sense. In my house growing up, questions meant I was in trouble. I did want my parents to pursue me and know me." Then she looked at me, a new realization dawning on her. "My daughter must feel the same way."

"You can help her if you're willing to be a little uncomfortable. Say I'm your daughter. What would you say to me?"

"Now?" she fumbled.

"Yes." I nodded in encouragement. "You have to practice being uncomfortable. I'll give you words if you get stuck. Start by recounting our conversation and what you learned today. Let her know you feel afraid and lost, but that you care deeply about her and you want to try to share more deeply."

After thirty miles she had it down. "Think you can do it?" I asked.

"Yes," she said. "I feel ready to try."

Several weeks later I received a beautiful gift and a thank-you note from this wonderful mom. She described having the best conversation with her daughter she'd ever had. And I know that today they're enjoying the kind of relationship both of them always hoped for.

When teens move toward self-sufficiency and independence, we have heard avoider parents typically express these feelings (note that these aren't necessarily bad feelings):

- "I'm uncomfortable giving affection or tender words to my older kids."
- "I tend to avoid personal discussions or anything too emotional."
- "Teens need to learn to solve their own problems and experience life to learn to get along."
- "My teen should be out of the house by eighteen, get a job, and take care of herself."
- "When something bad happens, it's probably my teen's fault."

- "I'm eager for my teen to grow out of his problems."
- "I have high standards for my teen that are in his best interests, even if he doesn't understand that now."

PARENTING WITH AN AVOIDER

Being the spouse of an avoider parent can be a lonely experience. As competent as avoiders are in many areas, parenting is messy, unpredictable, and ever changing. Avoiders often defer to their spouses, not because they're uninterested or don't care, but because it's overwhelming and they feel inadequate. And, of course, they won't admit this. Avoiders often describe their childhoods as being wonderful, without recognizing that an emotional connection was missing. Their conceived wisdom is that they can parent as they were parented and everything will turn out fine. Below are some suggestions on how to encourage avoider coparents:

- Remember the wound under their parenting inadequacies. They don't know how to give or receive emotional connection and comfort. Ask about their childhood experiences and show them compassion.
- Avoiders show love by doing tasks. They need to grow and expand beyond this, but appreciate and compliment them for the tasks they do.
- Gently coax them to give comfort or ask about feelings when you see an opportunity. For example, "I know your mom and dad would have never asked you how you feel or what you need, but Sammy just got cut from the basketball team and he is hurting. Could you ask how he feels and try to offer him some comfort?"
- Use the Soul Words list on page 269 as a part of conversations. If this is an accepted tool in your home, everyone will benefit, but it's a necessity for avoiders.

- Look for opportunities to comfort them so they begin to learn that comfort has value and does offer relief.
- Praise and appreciate any small changes. Every step counts.

GROWTH GOALS

One of the strengths avoiders have is their work ethic. They often raise high-performing, responsible kids. But this strength needs to be balanced with emotional connection. As an avoider myself, I had to change my perspective to be a better parent and love my kids more fully. Otherwise I'd simply offer them what I had experienced. Our book *How We Love* includes a workbook that outlines important growth goals for the avoider and a plan for changing your responses and developing your natural empathy. But when it comes to parenting, one of the most important areas for growth is to *learn along with your kids.*

Kelly was a baby and our older three kids were in late elementary and junior high school when I finally identified my bonding injuries. We explained to the older kids our inabilities as parents to know and express our feelings, and our desire for all of us to grow in self-awareness and expression. Using the list of soul words during a conversation made it less awkward and easier to get going. As you begin to link feelings with daily events during conversations at mealtime, bedtime, or while driving in the car, you'll grow more comfortable with messy emotions. Even though we started late, now that three of our children are parents, we see they have this skill to pass on to their children.

Reece, our grandson, was five when he saw his mom and dad crying. "Mom and Dad are sad because Grandma is so sick," his parents explained. "Mommies and daddies cry too when they're sad." Reece accepted this and later announced it to his neighborhood playmates, "Mommies and daddies cry too." One child argued and kept insisting, "No, they don't. My mom and dad never cry." Reece knows that emotions are normal and acceptable and that comfort is offered when family members are sad—no matter how old they are. We hope his neighborhood friend catches something of this truth.

Avoider, remember, if you're uncomfortable, it means you're growing. Not one of these ideas will be easy. But that's why they're important.

- Encourage everyone in the family to be aware of and express feelings. Name feelings for toddlers who don't have words yet. Identify and talk about your feelings.

- Learn to notice what behaviors, attitudes, and reactions your kids display when they are stressed out. Every family member will be different. Are they moody, angry, quiet, or funny? Do they withdraw, overeat, lash out, sulk, or complain? Watch for red flags that indicate your children need to talk and process. Find out what feelings are driving the outward behavior. What triggers those feelings? Pursue conversations about them. While you do this for your kids, ask yourself these same questions too.

- Look for opportunities for comfort. Notice when *you* need comfort, and be on the alert for occasions to comfort your kids. Say what you see. "You look sad and upset. I'm wondering what you're feeling inside and how I can help you."

- Learn to give and receive more physical affection and touch. The more you do it, the easier it gets. It's hard to believe, but eventually you will enjoy it!

- Express tender words of love, acceptance, and affirmation. Notice and praise positive personality and character traits in your child, not just successful performance.

- Look for guidance on what is age appropriate when you have expectations of your kids. If you are not sure, it's okay to ask for help. You don't have to figure everything out on your own anymore.

- If you have older kids, let them know how you came to be an avoider. Tell them about your difficulty with emotions and neediness, and express your desire to grow and change. Kids, and especially teens, hugely appreciate this kind of honesty.

Four

The Pleaser Parent

Most pleaser parents would make great patrol leaders in the Boy Scouts. The Scout Law says, "A Scout is trustworthy, loyal, helpful, friendly, courteous, kind, obedient, cheerful, thrifty, brave, clean, and reverent."[1] Does that sound like many men and women you've known? They're room mothers, team moms, coaches, after-school supervisors, crossing guards, and the first to put up neighborhood safety signs in their front yards.

Pleasers[2] can be wonderful parents with many great characteristics. Their main problem is that they cannot tolerate discomfort. Pleasers intensely dislike discomfort, in any relationship or for anyone else. They tend toward overprotection of their children, existing as *fear-based* parents. They avoid conflict and are afraid of criticism, confrontation, and disapproval. Most pleasers are so accustomed to anxiety that they don't even realize it's a part of their daily life.

Peace and approval are their highest values, and they'll do most anything to preserve them. They are highly protective by nature and often volunteer as caretakers and helpers to keep an eye on their children. For some, it's an unconscious reaction to keep anxiety at bay.

As a recovering pleaser myself, I (Milan) am here to tell you that pleasers can make really fun parents. Pillow fights, water fights, wrestling matches, whatever. And they'll make scrumptious delights, usually way more food than is needed, just in case somebody else shows up. But as a recovering pleaser, I have empathy for my pleaser brethren. First, I feel for your past, the fear and anxiety you experienced as a child. Maybe you worked to win approval or avoid criticism. Maybe you were surrounded by conflict or you worked to compensate for a wild sibling. You could have soothed a distressed parent or tried to appease an angry parent.

Yet I also have empathy for your present. I know how hard it is to be you. As Bill Cosby once said, "I don't know the key to success, but the key to failure is trying to please everybody."

I used to believe otherwise. As a church planter in the late 1970s, I tried to be the pastor (a glorified parental role) who was everybody's friend. Ten years later, exhausted and cynical, I resigned knowing something was wrong. See if you identify.

Pleaser Assessment

- I'm usually the giver in relationships.
- I'm a peacemaker and peacekeeper.
- I anticipate my spouse's needs and meet them.
- Sometimes I'm dishonest to avoid conflict.
- I fear making my spouse or kids upset or angry.
- I tend to give in to get conflict over with.
- I don't like to be alone.
- It really upsets me if someone is mad at me.
- When someone requests help, I usually say yes and get overcommitted.
- I tried hard to win a critical or angry parent's approval.
- Sometimes I get mad, but I don't show it, and I smile a lot.
- I had a parent who never stood up for himself, but passively accepted poor treatment.
- When I sense others distancing, I try harder.
- I'm on the cautious side; I definitely wouldn't call myself a risk-taker.

- I had an overprotective parent who worried a lot.
- I crave reassurance and affirmation from others.

With Infants and Toddlers

As Kay and I sat looking out at the ocean one day, we saw a young mom struggling to get everything down to the beach in one load. She had an infant in a harness on front, a stroller piled high, and in the stack was a pop-up tent for the baby, an umbrella, a beach chair, three or four towels, a cooler, and a large tote bag. And perched like a cherry on top was the diaper bag, and let me tell you, *whoa*. What a diaper bag.

I struggled with my desire to offer help and looked for the entourage that had to be following. When I realized no one else was with her, I decided she was a colonizer. About an hour later, her friend showed up with her baby and a small backpack, just about the time camp had been fully set up. When it comes to planning and provisions, the pleaser parents (especially pleaser moms) are the unchallenged winners. If there's ever a national disaster, find a new pleaser mom with a diaper bag.

A pleaser may be handy to have along in case you run out of anything, but their amazing abilities come with a price. Pleasers are very nurturing and enjoy caring for their babies, but the closeness is often spoiled by worry about what might eventually go wrong. Overattentive, they become distressed easily. They often need a lot of reassurance that the baby is okay and are nervous about doing everything right. If any of the attachment styles is going to end up knowing their pediatrician on a first-name basis, it will likely be pleaser parents.

Some may have never thought of themselves as anxious, but most pleasers become extremely frustrated if they can't make situations peaceful. Catastrophic thinking takes a toll on them. Often, the entire family can be held hostage by a pleaser's protectiveness.

Pleasers are attentive and tend to touch more often than other types.

As close-proximity seekers, they enjoy holding, nurturing, and playing with their babies. And just in case you wondered, they're usually the ones rubbing the necks and playing with the hair of their partners in church, the theater, or the car.

They've had lots of training in their families of origin as hypervigilant mood readers. When it comes to babies, they are good at reading babies' cues and have high levels of attunement. Pleasers are skilled at reading the emotional weather patterns to brace themselves for storms or to attempt to change the climate at home. This comes in handy when parenting an infant, as pleasers are good at anticipating a baby's needs. Particularly fussy babies can make pleasers doubt their ability and feel overwhelmed with anxiety.

WITH PRESCHOOLERS

When Kay and I were waiting to be interviewed about our marriage book on a local cable television channel, we watched another episode being filmed where the therapist was describing a "helicopter parent." There was footage of an anxious pleaser parent who followed her four-year-old around the entire playground. There was no danger present, yet her child was equipped with a helmet, elbow pads, wrist braces, and knee guards! Her overprotection probably seemed like the loving thing to do, but some trauma in her past was making her act out of that pain unconsciously.

Overprotecters
Where avoider and controller parents err on the side of underprotection, pleasers and vacillators overprotect, and neither extreme is good. Too much stress is harmful to a child, but too little stress and the child becomes weak and defenseless. When toddlers and preschoolers go off and explore while their moms are nearby, they learn valuable lessons about tolerating frustration. Too much help and they never have to build a tolerance for stressful situations.

Child development expert Dr. Bruce Perry says some children who grow up insecure and frightened have not experienced a trauma per se during childhood. Instead of exploring and returning when they need to refuel, these children are prevented from exploring by their fearful parents. Without learned stress-response mechanisms and coping skills, they never learn to be okay by themselves. And when it comes time for kindergarten, these children freak out because they have never had to go it alone.[3]

Fearful Parent, Fearful Child

Fear-based parents are more tuned into their children's fear than other emotions. Fearful mothers (or fathers) have difficulty separating from their toddlers and foster anxiety in their children, discouraging independence. The parents' fear is absorbed by the children. More is caught than taught.

Pleaser parents can try to hide their fear, but in several ways they still give the message that the world is scary and that their children can only be safe with them. I'll often ask pleasers to pay attention and rate their anxiety throughout a week, to get them to realize just how anxious they really are. An anxious state is normal for many pleasers, but children can sense fear even when the parent isn't aware of it or tries to hide it.

While controller parents frighten children with outbursts of anger without providing resolution, research shows that the frightened parent causes harm as well.[4]

A wonderful but anxious single mother came up to me after one of our parenting workshops. She'd just been told by the preschool that her almost three-year-old daughter was always checking up on the teacher, asking, "Are you okay?" For some reason the school felt it wasn't typical behavior for a three-year-old.

I asked the mom how much she asked her child, "Are you okay?" She blushed slightly and said, "Oh, all the time. I thought that's what a good parent does." I asked her to tell me why, and she explained that in her home growing up, changing moods meant trouble, so they were monitored. I explained that mood shifts were normal in three-year-olds and that by constantly questioning normalcy, she was teaching her child not to be okay.

By this age the diaper bag has expanded to include Cheerios, applesauce, Goldfish crackers, veggie sticks, fruit snacks, cheese, and juice boxes. You never go hungry with pleaser friends.

Pushovers

Pleasers are among the least respected parents of all the love styles. Why? Because they do not say no, set limits, or get mad appropriately. Pleasers tolerate disrespect from their kids, appease, give in, and placate. Preschoolers learn to assert themselves and say, "No!" It's at this stage that many kids gain the upper hand over the pleaser parent.

When pleasers do make a decision, they frequently cave in under pressure or protest because they fear rejection by the child. A protesting child saying, "I hate you," will usually ruin the day of the pleaser parent. A strong-willed preschooler can run the pleaser ragged. We heard a wife say to her pleaser husband, "You are negotiating with a two-year-old. Just say no and make it stick."

Minimizers

Pleasers rationalize and excuse bad behavior of their children and always give them the benefit of the doubt. They tend to minimize pain and discomfort by seeing problems as originating from other people, children, or situations. They often believe that their children were just misunderstood, and so they will just love them through the storms of life. For the pleaser, love equals protection, not confrontation. They are like the three monkeys all rolled into one, with eyes, ears, and mouth all covered. The pleaser parent will praise to no end, but lacks the counterbalance of constructive criticism, which acknowledges the child's weaknesses and holds her accountable for bad behavior.

Pleasers minimize because they cannot tolerate discomfort between family members or the anxiety a child suffers from the inevitable relational distress that life brings. As fear-based parents, they minimize problems and avoid conflict due to fear of criticism, confrontation, and disapproval.

Neglectful

Pleasers are helpers, but because they are greatly fulfilled by parenting, they often are too tired and out of energy to take care of themselves. A pleaser will also struggle to find the time and attention needed in a marriage. Remember, the most important gift you can give your kids is a great marriage. And someday your kids will grow up and leave, so make sure you save time to remind your spouse how much he or she means to you.

WITH SCHOOL-AGE KIDS AND TEENS

I must have been nine or ten when the Little League game came to a halt and the coach asked me to move from first base to catcher. The first-string catcher had just been nicked by a fastball and was crying. (I think he was eight.) I told the coach he'd have to ask my parents, and he turned to the bleachers and asked my dad. My dad said he'd have to ask my mom, who was in the car because it was cold. I'll never forget the craning necks and stares as my coach and my dad stood at the window of our car trying to convince my mom to let me put on the catcher gear.

Finally, I saw her arms fly up in the air, and they both turned around and told me to suit up. It was one of the most embarrassing times of my life. To the anxious parent who sees catastrophe around every corner, her child is the one who will die by pop fly.

My mom was a wonderful Christian mom and the best cook in Los Angeles, and her care for my sister and me was impeccable. Yet, as a small child born seventh of ten, my mom was teased a lot, suffered from a bout of polio, and was devastated when my older sister was born breech with a brain injury resulting in cerebral palsy. I can't blame her for being frightened about her only healthy boy. But no matter our history, all of us must finally face our fears and decide to take risks and grow.

Because of their fear, protective pleaser parents tend to hover, protect, interfere, rescue, defend, smother, and overprotect even into teen years. Additionally, they find themselves triggered and agitated when a child passes through a developmental stage or phase of life where they themselves experienced some sort of pain or trauma as a child or adolescent.

A pleaser dad was in one of my classes when I explained this principle, and his wife gasped out loud, which made us all jump. She was embarrassed but went on to say to her husband, "So that's why you freaked out when our son was sixteen and you wouldn't let him drive. You were paranoid when he turned sixteen because of your car accident at the same age." He stared at her for a minute and said, "You're right. I've never connected the two events." Fear is common to us all, but to pleasers, it is the dominant animating force in their parenting, whether conscious or subconscious.

The teenage years are often a time of turbulence and conflict as children begin to further individuate and have their own thoughts and opinions. As they grow, toddlers and teens go through natural levels of separation from their parents, and these developmental periods make the pleaser parent anxious. Often, teens raised by pleaser parents can be spoiled and overindulged, and grow up with an expectation of always being bailed out by their moms or dads. As a result, they tend to be less responsible with material things and various responsibilities. If a child has grown up knowing that if he leaves his baseball mitt out all night in the rain, Mom or Dad will buy a new one before the next game, he learns to not be responsible for his possessions. It's hard for a pleaser parent to let the child face the consequences of poor choices. When a kid suffers, the pleaser parent suffers, and therefore offers a way out rather than allowing the consequence to be the teacher.

Failure to Launch

The teen years mean launching your child into adulthood is just around the corner. Failure to launch is a dual problem. One half of the problem is the weak, needy child who is undeveloped, afraid, and does not know how to flap his or her wings. The other is the weak, needy parent who is afraid to let the child go, for fear that the child will be hurt. The parent is internally fighting the question, "What will I do when I am alone?" What will the pleaser parent do with no kid to need him? A pleaser mom raised her hand in class one night and asked, "How can I get my grown twenty-nine-year-old son out of the house?" I asked back, "Do you still make his breakfast?" The sheepish look on her face said it all. I went on to ask, "How dependent are *you* upon him?" At first she didn't get my point, so I restated the question. "What would you do with yourself, and how would you fulfill your mothering needs if he were to leave?" Her deer-in-the-headlights look continued, and I then said, "Perhaps he is not leaving because you've inadvertently trained him to stay. That is, maybe *you need him at home* as much as he wants to stay home?" After a long pause she looked at us both and said, "Good point."

See if the descriptions below of the pleaser parent sound a lot like you. Let's remember most of these traits are born out of anxiety.

- enjoys taking care of kids but worries a lot and wants to keep a close watch
- tends toward overprotection, trying to shield child from any stress or pain
- likes to be needed, so does for kids what they should be doing for themselves; for example, doesn't require kids to build skills toward self-sufficiency like cooking, cleaning, laundry, homework
- doesn't recognize how a child's confidence is sabotaged by giving the message, "You can't do that on your own; you need my help"

- rescues kids from consequences and mistakes, because it pains the pleaser parent to see her kids distressed—takes lunches, types papers, defends, solves problems
- praises strengths but doesn't give constructive criticism; not honest and direct about weaknesses that may be exhibited by the child; tends to give kids the message, "You are all good"
- believes his child is most often right and others are to blame when there is a problem
- asks kids a lot of questions to get information to soothe his own anxiety
- allows and gives in to a kid's persistent nagging—a push-over parent
- may undermine other parent by minimizing problems, not implementing consequences, secretly giving money, gifts, or favors

Remember, knowing what is not working gives you a road map for change. We'll discuss some growth goals at the end of the chapter.

PARENTING WITH THE PLEASER

Amid the many pleasures, there are real challenges for the spouse of an insecure parent. I want to discuss the three most common struggles Kay and I see in our offices and from callers to *New Life Live,* a radio program I cohost.

First, pleasers can be the softies for children to exploit. The other parent might not be rigid, but that parent ends up as the "bad cop" or persecutor, the child becomes the victim, and the pleaser parent becomes the rescuer (and trust me, this little triangle does not lead to wonderful marital intimacy). The more the pleaser rescues, the harder line the other parent must take. This polarizes parents, and the kids know how to work this to their advantage.

Second, a spouse might complain, "I have to make all the hard decisions." While looking like adults on the outside, when triggered, pleasers are still emotionally little internally, and their spouses sometimes feel like they have another child on their hands. With this comes a natural loss of respect and admiration.

Third, pleasers fix or distract versus really facing a problem and wading into it. There is a consequence of "conflict aversion"; it completely loses sight of the long-range goal—a child who can handle stress. To not allow the child to become stressed or uncomfortable is to take a short-sighted parenting track, which ultimately weakens the child. The spouse with the "long view" often feels undermined.

Below are some ways that Kay helped me as a recovering pleaser parent:

- encouraged me by recognizing how much fun I brought to our home, which was a good counterbalance to any areas she pointed out that needed growth
- recognized when I felt provoked, asked how tired or anxious I was, and got me to talk about my feelings
- asked me to slow down when I'd want to rescue a kid from consequences, and to also consider the long view, allowing the child to experience temporary discomfort
- asked about my most distressing childhood moments, so we could both understand the root of my anxiety and need to please
- supported me in developing my ability to make independent decisions to draw boundaries with the kids and in developing my "no" muscle
- coached me on the side, instead of interceding and correcting me when she felt I was overly protective or too accommodating in my responses to the kids; I could then correct myself with the child.

Of course, it should never be a one-sided deal. Give your spouse the opportunity to help you in your journey and discover ways to help your spouse as well. Together you can help *re-parent* each other.

GROWTH GOALS

Remember, fears only go away when you face them. Only when you can say, "I am a fearful person!" can you begin to overcome your fear rather than avoid it. Don't contaminate your children. Help them to experience an anxiety-free adulthood!

Growth involves deciding to grow up in the areas where you are still emotionally a child. Pleaser parents are competent adults in many ways, yet, as mentioned, they are emotionally young inside. I was thirty-seven when I began to face my fears, feeling like I was thirty-seven going on seventeen. Fearful childhoods will continue to sabotage us as long as we can't tolerate saying no and deal with any resulting rejection, conflict, or alienation. You will survive, and maybe even thrive.

"When I was a child, I used to speak like a child, think like a child, reason like a child; when I became a man, I did away with childish things" (1 Corinthians 13:11). Healthiness involves taking risks and moving forward after failure or success. Like the kid at the ice rink holding on to the side, you have to let go to experience what skating really is.

Growth involves discomfort. My growth journey toward adulthood involved examining my childhood fears, with therapists, friends, and Kay. I learned to get mad at the people who inflicted the pain and to learn to cry and receive comfort instead of compulsively caregiving. As I grieved my past, I learned to acknowledge that scared little kid was still inside me. Instead of dismissing him, I helped him grow up, but not until I saw him with compassion.

With a developed adult voice, you can find the adult you. Don't wait. Start that journey and finally feel on the inside the age you resemble on the outside.

- Determine to grow up and face your fears daily.
- Share your journey with others and solicit their support.
- Grieve the pain in your past that created your emotional dependence.
- Face reality daily and acknowledge any tendency to minimize and avoid reality.
- Learn to speak truth, and reveal your true state and need for help.
- Learn to tolerate disapproval and criticism.
- Purpose to launch your children, not keep them close for safety.

If you've set up patterns of permissiveness, you should expect some resistance when you choose to grow. Whiners may emerge from every bedroom. "Why do I have to do my own laundry?" "I'm too old for a bedtime." "You're kidding...right?" But over time, as with all change, new habits will develop and protests will subside when they see your resolve. So, pick your pain.

Also realize that your new assertiveness will sometimes lack good judgment and be extreme or inappropriate. Reactions will not always match the infractions. Give yourself grace when you overcorrect. It's okay not to be perfect. As new attitudes and behaviors begin to replace the old, you will improve in your parenting day by day. You might work with your spouse by role-playing and accepting coaching. And remember, every small change in you will make for big changes in your kids.

Do the work. You won't regret it.

Five

The Vacillator Parent

Dutifully, Marie gets up to referee another fight between her three-year-old son, Nicholas, and his neighborhood playmate, who are both yelling and grabbing for the same truck. The crying kids are irritating and interrupting her preoccupation with the women's group she just left. Assumptions begin to take on the hue of facts as Marie reviews the morning interactions in her head.

Darcy and Jenny were unusually quiet. I bet they've been talking behind my back. Darcy must have told her about my marriage problems... I did see that judging look in Jenny's eye. And to think I trusted Darcy...

A particularly shrill wail snaps Marie's mind back to the boys. For the third time this morning, the kids are interrupting.

"That's it," Marie yells. "I'm done!" She strides into the room. "Jason, it's time to go home. Now! Nicholas, you can stay here in your room alone, and I don't want to hear another word."

Marie has only responded as any normal parent might in such a situation. But what she isn't aware of is that her anger with the kids is more about her vacillator love style[1] and the uncertainty she's feeling about her friends and their opinions of her. Highly sensitive to signs of rejection, Marie constantly reads nonverbal signs that she's being left out and overlooked. Add fighting kids to this internal turmoil and she's frequently boiling over with anger.

In the sudden quiet, Marie considers putting the final touches on her advertising project although it's not due until next week. Working at home with a toddler is more difficult than she imagined, and her round belly reminds her she will soon have even more responsibility to juggle. She always encourages Nicholas to be more independent and play by himself, especially with the baby coming, but he's seemed clingier recently, demanding more attention. *Maybe I shouldn't have sent Jason home*, Marie thinks. *Now Nicholas will probably want me to play...*

Marie sits again at her computer, but her mind drifts back to Darcy and Jenny. *How much did Darcy tell her? And who will Jenny tell? Who won't Jenny tell?* Her anxiety rises as her imagination builds on the possibilities. Again, Marie is lost in thought about the women in her group and where she stands with them. As she tries in vain to ignore the endless possibilities, suddenly the worry becomes too much. She needs total distraction.

"Hey, Nicholas! How about a walk to the ice cream shop?"

The vacillator love style often forms when a child is raised in a home where there is some connection and bonding but it's sporadic and unpredictable, governed by the mood of the parent rather than the need of the child. The mood of the parent is governed by the level of preoccupation she is experiencing. It may be the vacillator is ruminating about work, or a spouse or friendship. Uncertainty and disappointment about relationships or the idealization of something new is usually the inward focus. At times the vacillator parent feels more settled and is present and available. When this kind of connection happens, it's often fun, spontaneous, and exciting for the child. But that connection can often evaporate in a burst of parental exasperation that's confusing to the child. Where'd Mom go?

Marie is preoccupied by her thoughts more than she realizes. While she might be physically present, she is mentally and emotionally unavailable. When this happens, Marie doesn't realize she's mentally leaving Nicholas and how he'll wait and watch for her to return to be truly present with him. Like all children, he's learning to be an astute judge of whether he's really being seen and heard, or being left out and overlooked.

Just like Marie.

When a parent is frequently preoccupied, children often misbehave and increase their attempts to be seen and heard. As Nicholas shows more needy, clingy behavior, Marie feels pressure to abandon her internal world of conflicting thoughts and feelings, and pushes him away, which only intensifies Nicholas's neediness. The vicious circle intensifies until eventually Nicholas learns not to expect attention or comfort when he needs it most.

And nobody wins.

Marie is a vacillator. She isn't intentionally hurting Nicholas. She wants to be a great parent, but she's unaware how her childhood injuries are affecting her as a parent. Like most vacillators, she experienced some level of emotional and/or physical abandonment as a kid. This childhood abandonment causes adult vacillators to be very sensitive to closeness and distance in relationships. Fearing a repeat of this abandonment causes anxiety about relationships as well as a distrust of closeness. Marie desires to feel special and connected, but at the same time, she doesn't trust loving attention to last or fill her up. This dilemma causes vacillators to unintentionally create a push-pull, come-here-go-away dynamic. For the vacillator, relationships are either great ("I feel loved, included, special, and valued") or completely bad ("I feel invisible, unimportant, and rejected"). There is little middle ground.

Can you relate to any of the vacillator traits listed below?

VACILLATOR ASSESSMENT

- No one has ever really understood what I need.
- I fall in love instantly, and my relationships are initially intense and passionate, but they never last.
- I always hope for great relationships, but everyone disappoints me.
- Some people try to make amends, but it's always too little, too late.

- I'm a very passionate person, and I feel things more deeply than others.
- I know far more about being a good parent than my spouse does.
- I could describe many examples of how I've been hurt and disappointed, and I often feel unappreciated by my spouse and kids. I can always sense when others pull away from me.
- I want far more connection than I have currently.
- I love the feeling of making up after a fight.
- When people hurt me long enough, I write them off.
- If my spouse would pursue me more, things would be better.
- I don't like to be alone, but sometimes having people around makes me worse.
- My parent(s) still drives me crazy.
- Sometimes I pick fights, and I'm really not sure why.
- I make it obvious when I'm hurt, and it's only worse when no one asks what's wrong.
- I'm always waiting for people to be available, and I wonder if they've forgotten me.
- I'm convinced I have the ability to read people really well and quickly judge their motives and intentions before they even speak.

WITH INFANTS AND TODDLERS

Marie came to me (Kay) for help because she was increasingly angry with Nicholas and her husband, Tom, who was an avoider.

"Tom is distant and doesn't want much sex since Nicholas was born. And Nicholas was such an easy baby, but now I get really angry when he doesn't listen. I always try and make it up to him, but he's so clingy and it drives me crazy. What's wrong with him?"

Before I could consider, Marie went on. "I'm kind of overwhelmed with the idea of another baby even though I love holding a baby close. I so like the attention of being pregnant, but I *hate* feeling fat. Being a mother is harder than I thought. It's like sometimes I love it and sometimes I feel so trapped. I miss work where it was easy. And I don't fit in at moms' groups. I had one friend, Darcy—our boys are the same age—but I've been replaced since Jenny came around."

I grabbed my chance to get a word in. "Let me ask you a few questions that may seem somewhat unrelated. Your answers will help me understand you better. Has something like what you described with Darcy happened before?"

Marie reflected. "Yeah. But that's the way it is. I get hurt and after a while I can't take it anymore. I just reach a point where I'm done."

"How about with Tom? Have you ever threatened divorce?" I asked.

Marie chuckled. "Sure, but I don't really mean it. Like I said, I get angry and it used to rattle him, but I'm passionate and if it's been a rough day..." She trailed off.

"One more question, Marie. The last time you lost your temper with Nicholas, what'd you say to him?"

"What I say every time, 'Get over here and listen to me!' He's started running away when I call him. And then when I'm *busy*, he won't leave me alone! It ticks me off!"

"Okay. Good. Now think of your parents saying those words, 'Get over here and listen to me.' Would you have wanted to say that to one or both of them when you were a kid?"

Marie looked up at me and blinked. Her face slowly drained of color, and her eyes began to look past me into her inner world. "Oh my gosh. Oh my gosh, yes. Both parents, but especially my mom. My dad was always busy at work, like all dads. We called my mom the crusader. She was on every committee and project the church ever started. Everyone else was more important than my sisters and me. Sometimes I'd have her all to myself and then not at all. She ran off with the music director when I was fifteen, and I ended up driving my sisters everywhere."

I nodded. "Let me suggest a few things. First, I'd like to invite your husband for next time. Having his help will be very important. Second, I want you to realize that your mom abandoned you frequently, and then once and for all. Other things were more important than her time with you, and she left you with her responsibilities. That's a lot of fuel for anger right there. I'd expect you to resent that and feel some grief from the loss of your childhood. That's the source of a lot of your anger and pain. But you can get free of that now. It doesn't have to make you resentful as a parent."

Over the next few weeks, Marie and I explored her negative feelings. We discussed how children trigger old wounds and how her mom didn't respond to her pleas for attention. Disappointment and anger were familiar to her then, so when Nicholas began ignoring her, those childhood feelings would flood into the present, causing stronger anger than was appropriate to the situation. As her husband began to understand these hurts and comfort her, Marie's wounds began to heal and Nicholas's behavior became less upsetting. Marie became more aware of her tendency to be preoccupied and made sure she found daily time to connect to Nicholas, making an effort to be fully present.

Marie's feelings were what any mom or dad might experience. But for vacillator parents they're more intense, more frequent, and debilitating. And they make *no* sense until you look to the past.

Like all the love styles, vacillators are on autopilot, driven by their childhood attachment injuries. They want to be good parents and are often devoted to their kids. But they don't realize they're being controlled by feelings that started early in their lives. Vacillators tend not to realize how preoccupied they are with their unmet attachment needs. Marie was surprised to realize how often her thoughts were in another place than with Nicholas, and she began to realize that she'd often play out relationship scenarios in her thoughts that centered around themes of rejection or feeling misunderstood. Marie discovered that her anger often covered feelings of insecurity, and deep down she questioned how loveable she was.

Vacillators don't mean to be moody. They're simply unaware how often their current relationships are reminders of the feelings they had as kids. These unexamined injuries contribute to the vacillator's preoccupation and reactivity and the mood swings between feeling *good* and *bad*. Vacillators feel good when they get attention, connection, and validation, and therefore feel wanted, seen, and special. They feel angry and miserable when they feel unwanted, unseen, unimportant, lonely, or abandoned. When these feelings are triggered in current circumstances, vacillators devalue the person or relationship, get angry, and retreat.

Vacillators don't recognize these are familiar feelings that had their origins in childhood, so they overreact in the present. This causes vacillators to be unpredictable as parents, alternating between being happy and then preoccupied with negative feelings that are intense and overwhelming because they are both current and historic. When vacillators are preoccupied with relationship difficulties, they ruminate on possible scenarios, assuming they *know* the motivations and intentions of others. These assumptions turn into *facts* of reality in the vacillator's perception, intensifying the pain.

Vacillators have an exaggerated need to feel special, important to others. They want the consistent connection they missed as kids, and they want connection that feels passionate and intense. Sometimes the vacillator love style is created by a parent who makes her child the very special one. This kind of overindulgence and constant attention by a parent makes the vacillator expect such special treatment in adult relationships.

When it comes to babies, vacillators enjoy being needed. Young children provide a dependent relationship where the vacillator feels safe. This connection fulfills vacillators' needs for bonding for a time, and can serve to distract them when they're hurt or distressed in other relationships.

Once the child begins to assert independence, things might not go so smoothly.

Toddlers or preschoolers who assert their independence by saying, "No," "Mine," "Leave me alone," can make vacillator moms or dads feel rejected and unwanted.

Vacillators send kids mixed messages:

- Affection/Aversion: "Come here, sweetie, I need a hug." / "Not now, I'm busy. Go play."
- Approval/Extreme disapproval: "You're the best kid in the whole world!" / "I'm so disappointed in you. What on earth is wrong with you?"
- Needy/Resentful: "How could I possibly live without you?" / "Why can't you learn to be alone? You're driving me crazy."

Mad Not Sad

When hurt, vacillators tend to express anger rather than sadness. Sadness only creates vulnerability and more feelings of powerlessness. If they do cry, it's most often mad, frustrated tears rather than brokenhearted weeping. Anger prevents the connection the vacillator longs for. Vacillators feel their anger is justified, and they don't see the depth of its negative impact on the entire family. Pouting and withdrawal are indirect ways of expressing hurt or sadness, but these reactions don't promote the connection they hope for.

Vacillator Dads

A vacillator dad may be a workaholic, preoccupied with success, and tends to brood on disappointments with his spouse or friends. My dad was a vacillator. He could be lots of fun, and we did genuinely connect sometimes. But only when he was in the mood; that bonding could end unexpectedly as his mood changed. Like most vacillators, my dad was very sensitive, but I saw more anger, impatience, and exasperation than anything else. He left me longing for more fun and spontaneity, but often when he came home, he was off somewhere else, preoccupied with work or other relationships.

A vacillator dad rarely realizes how the baby is triggering old feelings of abandonment as his wife adjusts to motherhood. He may be irritated and blame or carry resentment toward his wife for forgetting about him after the baby arrives.

This rejection sensitivity may make a vacillator dad very uncomfortable as he feels pushed away, unseen, and unimportant compared to the attention the baby receives. When a dad feels robbed by the baby and expresses anger, a new mother may be in a difficult situation, feeling there are two needy people competing for her time. Because babies demand time and attention, a vacillator dad may be triggered by having to wait and will protest his lost attention.

Vacillator fathers may also struggle with the interruption in the sexual relationships that is universal for new moms. Recovery from childbirth and the demands of a new baby dampen a mother's sexual appetite. Vacillator dads take this very personally and feel rejected and unwanted and get mad rather than sad. This is a cause of many marital arguments, and too much pressure for sex to "be like it used to be" causes vacillator dads to devalue the marriage, and in worst-case scenarios seek a "passionate" partner elsewhere.

Moms and dads in these situations should try to determine the childhood triggers and feelings of abandonment parenthood brings up for the vacillator dad and focus on the root of the problem, not the symptom (complaining). The deepest need of the vacillator is comfort—for the childhood pain and how the present situation is a reminder of old losses.

WITH PRESCHOOLERS

Sadly, the vacillator's ideal hopes are always spoiled sooner or later. And things tend to head downhill when a baby learns to explore, assert opinions, resist, and say no. If you've been unnerved by a noncompliant pre-schooler, congratulations! We have all felt that way as parents. But if you've ever felt enraged, uncontrollable, or unreasonably frustrated over such normal kid issues, you may be a vacillator (or a controller, which we will discuss further on).

For obvious reasons, vacillators may feel intensely distressed when leaving their crying, protesting child. Rebecca came for help when her preschooler, Steven, cried to the point of vomiting when being left at his preschool classroom. Any separation was tremendously agonizing for both mom and son. I asked Rebecca to pretend she was Steven and tell me what it felt like.

"Please don't leave me! I'll miss you too much! I can't handle being without you! If you loved me, you wouldn't leave me. I can't stand it when you leave me. I'm going to throw up again!"

"So, Rebecca, is any of this similar to when you were growing up?" I asked.

"I don't remember ever throwing up," she replied.

"Did you ever miss your parent like that and feel left alone?"

"When my parents divorced, I felt like that all the time. I was ten and my dad's visits were sporadic. My mom had to go back to work to make it financially."

"Perhaps you don't want Steven to feel these same things, and that's why you're so tormented by this. He feels how distressing separating is for you, and that fuels his fears. When he sees you disturbed, it heightens his alarm. You always return, and you told me you always pick him up on time. It's okay for him to worry or be upset. That's normal for a four-year-old. But he's *not* feeling all you felt at ten years old."

Things for Rebecca and Steven improved once she understood how she was projecting her feelings onto her son and making assumptions about how Steven felt that were not true. As she grieved her losses and was able to leave Steven confidently, Steven's protests decreased.

The great news for vacillator parents is that change is not only possible but inevitable with a commitment to understanding the past. Read on for the growth goals at the end of the chapter.

WITH SCHOOL-AGE KIDS AND TEENS

As kids grow, they naturally become their own person. A child's circle of relationships widens to associations outside the family and becomes more prominent with time—relatives, friends, teachers, coaches, neighbors. In divorced families, kids may also have a relationship with a parent's new spouse. Since vacillators are triggered by feelings of exclusion, they can feel threatened when their kids enjoy other relationships.

John, a vacillator dad I know, is a good example. He definitely parented when he was in the mood. Yet other times, he was preoccupied and unavailable to his thirteen-year-old daughter, Leslie. Once, John described a father-daughter dance he'd recently attended.

"We were all dressed up, and Leslie looked so beautiful and grown up. I was so excited. We had one dance, and then she was off with her friends, and I spent the evening alone. She ignored me most of the evening. After a while I just went and talked to another dad I recognized from soccer. By the time we drove home, I was so mad at her I didn't even want to talk."

I knew he couldn't see the connection, so I said, "I'm going to tell you something that might be hard to hear. I think it would be helpful for your relationship if you could realize Leslie treated you exactly as you have treated her many times. She was physically present, but busy with other things, and this left you feeling unimportant. This is exactly how Leslie feels when you're around but preoccupied with work. You may be present, but you aren't connecting *with* her. It hurts, doesn't it?"

With vacillator moms something different can happen. Tammy came to my office with her husband, Brad, and explained their situation. I soon surmised that she was a vacillator and Brad was an avoider.

Brad complained, "Tammy only has time for the kids. I have taken a backseat ever since we had kids."

"Well, at least the kids appreciate me," Tammy shot back. "I'd rather be with them than you any day. You're like living with a ghost."

No surprise, Tammy was using her kids to feel valued. She especially leaned on her firstborn and was finding it extremely difficult to let him grow up and become his own person. When he wasn't attentive or wanted to be with his friends, Tammy would pout (hoping someone would pursue) and enforce restrictive punishments for minor infractions. Expecting kids to make up for an inadequate marriage is unfair and makes letting go difficult. Some good marriage therapy was essential to solving this parenting problem.

Teens of vacillator parents say their moms or dads have embarrassed them with displays of anger in public or in front of friends. I always ask such teens if they think their moms or dads are aware of the impact their anger has on them and other family members. Nearly every time, the familiar answer is no, they have no idea. Because when Mom or Dad is over it, everybody else is supposed to be over it too. The vacillator's moods often govern the family's interactions. Then when the switch flips, "all good" turns into "all bad" again, and the family is suddenly walking on eggshells.

Examples of how a vacillator parent often behaves with a teenager are shown below. Do any of these sound familiar?

- A vacillator may seek connection with his child to punish his spouse.
- A vacillator can be insensitive to the impact her anger or withdrawal has on her child. Also, as soon as *she* gets over an explosion, she expects her child to simultaneously appear unaffected too.
- Sometimes a vacillator will compete with his same-sex child as the child hits adolescence. For example, he wants to be

friends with his child's friends and be the cool dad to keep from losing connection.

- A teen's growing independence makes a vacillator parent feel unappreciated, rejected, and unloved.
- As her child gets recognition outside the family, a vacillator parent may feel resentful and excluded.
- Since separation feels like rejection, a vacillator parent may push for more connection by texting and Facebooking with his teen like a peer, or by being intrusive.
- The vacillator parent sometimes swings between harsh discipline when angry and being too permissive when afraid of losing the teen. Fearing rejection by the teen, she may have trouble drawing boundaries and be permissive to feel liked.

If you are a vacillator, don't feel "all bad" or overwhelmed. Your desire for connection is a wonderful, God-given desire. You need to see the childhood wounds and grieve the losses under all that anger. You can make several changes to improve your parenting very quickly. But start by having some compassion for yourself.

PARENTING WITH A VACILLATOR

Vacillators can bring spontaneity and adventure into parenting. But they need help to acknowledge their inclination toward preoccupation and mood swings. They tend to see the pleaser or avoider spouse as inferior, untrustworthy, and at times even unworthy of parenting *their* children. Vacillators often devalue their spouse at some point, not just as a mate but as a parent too.

So what can you do if you are coparenting with a vacillator? First, look for times when the vacillator is engaged and fun. Notice and appreciate your spouse's strengths. Verbalize your appreciation in specific observations. "I love the way you enjoyed the kids just now, and the way your eyes light up when you interact with them."

Second, be aware of the hurts in your spouse's past. Listen to the pain and validate and comfort feelings of abandonment and fear. This will be a healing experience for your spouse and create more trust in your relationship. Even better, it will reduce anger.

Third, anger must be dealt with constructively and assertively. When angry, vacillators need to hear, "I will support what you need to say to the kids when you are not so angry. I know you don't want to hurt the kids and your anger is upsetting." If they won't stop, lead the kids away and say, "Mom has some important things to say. We will listen when she is not so angry." This models boundaries to your kids.

Fourth, deal with your fear of negative emotions and conflict. Vacillators often coparent with avoiders or pleasers who are both adverse to conflict. Vacillators need spouses who can learn to wade into the difficulty with them and face it.

Finally, help your vacillator spouse grieve the end of the parenting phase of life and accept the empty nest. Many vacillators may be drawn toward adoption, idealizing the concept while underestimating the emotional cost to the marriage and family.

GROWTH GOALS

Be Present with Your Children and Notice Their Needs
Make it a point to spend some time each day fully present and engaged with your child. If you become lost in thoughts, tell your child, "I'm sorry, I wasn't listening/watching. I got distracted. I'm all yours now. Tell/show me again." Try your best to respond when he needs you rather than when you're in the mood.

Get Sad Not Mad
Let anger signal that more vulnerable feelings aren't being expressed. Express hurt, not anger. This will help you slow down and discover the buried feelings underneath. More time to reflect will increase your self-awareness

and help you become more responsive and less reactive. *Reactivity is your worst enemy.* Be aware of extreme statements you may say when you're angry or frustrated. The most common are, "I'm done," or, "That's it." After this, the resulting withdrawal, pouting, or leaving for a time is what causes your children to feel abandoned.

You'll say these kinds of statements when you're overwhelmed or disappointed. But you need to realize how unsettling it is to your family. It's far better to say, "I need a few moments to compose myself and/or respond properly." Use the Soul Words list at the end of the book to identify feelings under the anger and express them in a soft, low voice. Stay focused on the present problem, and use as few words as possible instead of going on and on to make your point. This will greatly increase your chances of being heard and understood.

Integrate Good and Bad

You tend to view moments or situations as either *really good* or *really bad*. When you're in a bad place, you won't be able to remember the good that just happened ten minutes ago. You need to become aware that you are going to that "all bad" place. When you're devaluing, getting angry, pouting, or withdrawing, you are sliding down the slope of "all bad." When you experience these feelings, jot down who and what has made you so upset. Then use the Soul Words list to identify specific feelings *under* the anger. As you look over the list, ask, "Is this a familiar childhood feeling?" If so, you need comfort for those childhood hurts.

The last and most important step to follow when you are in the "all bad" place is to go on a hunt for the *good*. Write a minimum of three good things about the person who has upset you. This will be hard, and you will feel a lot of resistance, believing you are too mad to think of anything good. You'll know you're making progress when you can find the good. You are really on the road when you answer the question, "How was your week?" with an honest, "Good and bad." Every day, every person, every situation contains both good and bad. Recognizing both in any given situation is an extremely important growth goal.

In the same way, recognize when you are idealizing new people or situations and ignoring the bad. Seeing new situations or people through rose-colored glasses is a setup for disappointment in the long run.

Make Communication Direct, Not Indirect

You tend to *show* your feelings (behaviorally) and hope others get the message and respond according to your desires. This is indirect communication, and it often leaves you feeling misunderstood and disappointed. Instead, practice using direct, clear, verbal communication. If you were in my office, I'd ask you to use the format, "I feel [emotion] and I need [action]." At first you'll have difficulty filling in the blanks. But learning to make a simple, one-sentence statement will require you to become more self-reflective. Ask yourself, "What do I feel? What do I need right now?" Becoming more direct about your feelings will make disappointment and anger a lot less likely with your spouse and your kids.

Don't Assume

Don't assume you know the intentions and motivations of others or what they meant by certain words, looks, or gestures. Ask.

Repair Ruptures in Relationships

You have difficulty apologizing and even trying to see your child's perspective after you've messed up. To admit a mistake makes you feel "all bad." Yet no one is "all good," so apologies should be made at times by everyone in the family, parents included. Resolution after a conflict means understanding is reached and feelings are listened to and validated, even if there is still disagreement. To reach resolution, you must admit your hurtful words and behavior, apologize for them, and leave feeling better about the relationship.

Where should you start? Start anywhere! Choose a common situation and commit to it. You'll start to see results soon enough. Wherever you start, the relationship between you and your child will benefit. Give yourself grace and keep going. We recommend taking one of the goals above and making that your only focus of change for at least three months. *If you try and take it all on at once, you're likely to get overwhelmed and stop.* When you feel more successful at implementing that growth goal, move on to the next one. We guarantee the positive change in your relationship will soon become its own motivation!

Six

The Controller Parent

Apastor and his wife brought their sixteen-year-old into my (Milan's) office, and I gave the reluctant teen his choice of seats in my office. He looked at my chair and glanced over to me, and I nodded for him to go ahead and make himself comfy. The parents, Doug and Barbara, sat on the couch, and I took the desk chair.

"I learned from your mom on the phone that you three are having difficulties in your home, and that there is a lot of conflict. What seems to be going on?"

With startling intensity the dad immediately started speaking. "Our son is not adopting our values; he's always protesting our questions and instructions. He's got a really bad attitude. He ignores me, won't speak, and is always angry with his younger sister. He misbehaves in school and is getting horrible grades. He's not 'honoring his father and mother.'" As he was talking, I watched the son, Paul, sink into his chair and stare at the ground, his face grimacing. At the same time, Barbara was completely still as she nervously stared at her husband. Occasionally she'd look at her son with a distressed look that seemed to say, "Hang in there, son. Don't do anything to make it worse."

A classic controller dad.[1]

I explained that before I could address the biblical "honoring" command, I needed to ask another question based on a different biblical mandate. "What have your parents done that has made you angry?" I asked Paul.

Doug shot me a look, and I explained, "The verse following 'honor your father and mother' says, 'fathers, do not provoke your children to anger'" (Ephesians 6:2, 4). Doug could have killed me with his eyes. "I need to understand your son's perspective," I said, then looked back to Paul. Doug and Barbara glanced at each other.

Paul's eyes rarely left the floor. "It's fine," he mumbled. I asked him to explain that, and he grunted. I tried to guide him in expanding his answer, and he returned a couple more deflective sounds. His failure to make any eye contact with me and his minimal handshake at the end convinced me he'd learned to distrust all authority and not to expect help from anyone. Over the next few weeks, I met with Paul twice and several times just with his parents.

I doubt I was the most popular person the first few weeks. Doug questioned my competency when I didn't support him, but I kept pushing to get him to share about his childhood. After a while the picture of a lonely boy, an alcoholic dad, and a mom seeking companionship at bars began to emerge. There were also several older brothers who tormented and beat him up.

As I listened to Barbara's perspective, stories of frustration and pain began to unfold. "When we were first married, Doug was so great. He swept me off my feet, and we were engaged within three months, married in six. He's always been a take-charge guy, which everybody appreciates. Everything was fine until we had our first child, and then the anger came out of nowhere."

By the third week, there was no doubt. Pastor Doug was an angry controller, and Barbara was a pleaser or victim who froze up when Doug would begin to boil. Although Paul was a typical teen with all the common issues that accompany adolescence, he wasn't the problem. Mom and Dad's marital dynamic and resulting parenting dysfunction was the major source of their problems. In our fourth session without Paul, I felt great tenderness for Doug as I was beginning to see his deep childhood wounds.

I said, "Doug, I wish I could have been your dad." A single tear, just one, trickled down his cheek. But he quickly laughed it off. It was hard for Doug to know what to do with compassion. It was foreign to him.

After four years of marital therapy, up and down on the roller coaster, he gradually saw and owned his controller love style and accepted that his reactivity was fueled by his tragic childhood experiences. Doug and Barbara heard and comforted each other's painful histories, developed empathy for each other, and by the end of our time together, they'd both grown immensely. They began re-parenting with what they'd learned, and for the first time, the playing field leveled out for Paul, and his family life was calmer. And guess what? So was Paul.

If you identify with this or know a controller parent, you need answers and a way off this runaway train. You may be wondering why controllers are so much more severe as parents than the other love styles. Avoiders, pleasers, and vacillators may have trouble bonding, but they can still protect their children. The controller *is* the source of danger who brings "fright without solution."[2] Simply, fight or flight is normal for them. This is the world as they know it.

Depending on personality and severity of the environment, the child of a controller parent is highly likely to become a controller or a victim. For the child, a constant question is, *Who is Dad/Mom right now?* Is she the scary one, the tired one, the slurring one, the sad one, or the apologetic one? And so the child is forced to ask, *Who am I at this moment?* The bad one, the hated one, the invisible one, the good one, or the parent to the parent?

As rapid shifts occur in the moods of the parent, the child must repress anger and grief, the natural responses in abusive situations, to prevent more chaos, upheaval, and more threats. And these kids grow up, get married, and enter parenthood with the same unresolved, unprocessed trauma their parents acted out of.

Chaotic children (controllers and victims) are held tightly by the dysfunctional gravitational field of their families. Having learned to tolerate the intolerable, they grow into adults on the outside only. Developmentally frozen in time, their trauma prevents them from preparing for the challenges of adulthood.

The autopilot setting of controllers is keeping everything and everyone in line, while they get out of line over and over again. Compliance, respect for disrespect, and obedience to irrational demands—this is the law, *or else*. Having been cut off from the pain, they possess underdeveloped vulnerability and sensitivity, but usually these will leak out when regret occasionally breaks through.

Those who are dominated will eventually dominate others, control or be controlled. Unconsciously, they control to keep the inescapable horrors of their forgotten terror at bay. Their goal is to never feel again what they felt as children. But of course that never works. It's only when we feel the truth and deal with it properly by sharing it, holding it out, and having it accepted, validated, and comforted by another that we get past the past.

Overwhelmed by anxiety and humiliation, childhood was a prison for these poor kids. Any breakthrough of vulnerable feelings as adults causes controllers to quickly stuff them back down with anger. Order and structure are used to prevent others from saying and doing things that could make the controller experience that familiar *one down* position ever again.

Remember, love styles all exist on a continuum, so mild controllers may identify with these traits to a lesser degree than extreme controllers. The bottom line? The greater the need for control, the greater the childhood pain. There is usually a direct proportion between the amount of childhood trauma and the amount of adult anger and need to control.

CONTROLLER ASSESSMENT

- Growing up, a parent or sibling threatened me, intimidated me, or was violent with me.

- No one protected me when I was growing up; I was on my own for the most part.
- My spouse and kids do things behind my back and that infuriates me.
- I dislike authority and feel angry when others tell me what to do or ignore what I tell them to do.
- I tend to use alcohol, drugs, pornography, gambling, or overspending to feel good.
- My life has had its share of problems, so I'm under more stress than most people.
- I try to control my temper, but it's hard not to let it out.
- My spouse does things to make me jealous.
- I know my family doesn't like me losing my temper, but they shouldn't make me so angry.
- I have hit, slapped, or pushed my spouse or kids, or I have come close to it.
- I've changed jobs frequently.
- By the time I was a teenager, people knew not to mess with me.
- I left home early, and some family members were afraid of me.
- My spouse and kids don't listen when I ask them to do things.

Controllers enter adulthood believing childhood is behind them, but therapists call these "unresolved issues" for good reason. Most chaotic adults don't want to touch their childhood memories with a ten-foot pole. And who can blame them? How do you begin to resolve the enormous amount of unresolved, unprocessed hurt and pain when there's little to no feeling left? It's all been stuffed down—all the powerlessness, fear, grief, and shame—and they're completely out of touch with what's now happening to their own children.

And so the nightmare continues.

If there is to be growth, hope, and real change, the controller needs someone with a lot of compassion, persistence, and courage. The kind they've never known, likely never even seen in real life. This is often the only way to get at the heart of the issue. If it takes the help of a spouse, a therapist, or a psychiatrist, the controller with the best chance is the one convinced he needs to compassionately face his past.

WITH INFANTS AND TODDLERS

I was watching the news one evening, and the reporter was standing next to a Dumpster in inner-city Los Angeles. The camera zoomed in on the Dumpster to reveal a sticker with a red circle and a line through it. And in the circle was an adult hand holding a baby by its heel over a trash can. No, babies aren't supposed to be dumped into the trash. Now think: why on earth would this Dumpster need such a sticker? And why on earth would it be necessary to publicize a policy in L.A. County that an infant can be dropped off at any fire station or hospital anytime, no questions asked?

Hard to believe. But anyone who's been a new parent knows the enormous demands a baby makes, often competing with the demands and immaturity of its parents. And who usually wins this control game in the first few months? Not the parent. To some degree, a child is a cyclone of chaos smashing into already damaged areas daily. The messiness of a baby's neediness is colliding with the messy pain inside the controller.

For many controllers, a crying infant can serve as a deep reminder (often unconscious) of their own childhood hurts, and as a result, controllers can be irrationally intolerant of crying babies. Is it any wonder why some such abused parents might overreact and throw their screaming bundle of needs in the trash? The intolerance is magnified if the baby wasn't wanted in the first place or if it is a reminder of a terrible mistake. Other factors can come into play too: being abandoned, financial difficulties, and on and on. And yes, poverty and ignorance take a tremendous toll, especially on kids.

Shame at being incompetent or inadequate can be suppressed under anger and rage. Without any healthy parental modeling, controllers live tilting toward extremes, either without structure or consistency to their parenting or moving to the opposite side and being overly rigid. Inflexible controllers depend on formulas for security. Christians can easily be swept up in an emotionless, "immediate obedience"–type system. Schedules and tools for controlling babies become more important than nurturing. Ultimately, they lack the patience and awareness to understand their baby's cues and simply keep pushing the system until it "works." Patience is difficult for the reactive controller, and some babies require a lot of patience.

When overwhelmed, controllers may "check out" for a while since they know no way of dealing with their unresolved pain. Addictions are the most common method of finding relief. The constant torment they once endured on the outside has traveled inside to become their closest "friend": a familiar place of pain with no apparent escape. I had a client whose father handed him a bottle of wine at fourteen years of age and said, "Here, this will make the pain go away." Addictions of all kinds put babies and young children at risk as parents act out to subdue the pain and stress.

No one has ever helped controllers. Think about that. No training in understanding, let alone regulating their emotions. With no modeling of self-awareness or self-care, they tend to draw wrong assumptions about people and their kids, often expecting them to behave as adults. They say things like, "She's such a monster; she's just looking for attention," "He's manipulating you; show him who's boss," or, "She just wanted to ruin our one night off together."

Babies are helpless. Controllers were once helpless and afraid in their childhood homes. A baby's helpless crying triggers their old pain, so they must shut down to keep it out of their awareness. And as they detach, they can't be responsive and attentive to the baby.

A controller often:

- frustrates easily and has poor coping skills.
- exhibits rage, outbursts of anger, and violent behavior toward the child.
- is understructured or overly rigid.
- is addiction prone and preoccupied with things "more important" than the baby.
- draws wrong conclusions about or attributes negative traits to their baby or children from people in the past and says things like, "The baby hates me," or, "She's a little manipulator."
- has a trancelike response or frightening reaction triggered by the baby's crying or helplessness.
- makes poor choices and neglects the baby when over-whelmed or preoccupied.

If you recognize these signs of a controller in yourself or someone you know, the best thing to do is to show compassion and realize trauma is at the root of the problem. Help is necessary, but parents can overcome these defeating patterns when they can reconnect to their emotions and come to grips with the pain, fear, anger, and helplessness.

WITH PRESCHOOLERS

Recently, I was attempting to relax and read a book when I was assaulted by a controller mother taking pictures of her eighteen-month-old girl. I was nearby, but everyone down the beach heard her. "Jordan, look here! Jordan, smile at Mom! Jordan, don't stand up, just sit. Jordan, turn this way!" After ten full minutes of this, her name being shouted dozens of times, Jordan began to wear out. Pleading, noisy Mom was now being ignored. In raging disgust, the woman shouted to the sky, "Ugh! She doesn't even know her own name!"

I wanted to say, "Lady, I'm pretty sure people in the next county know her name now."

Even if you aren't a controller, you can sympathize. And we know we've got some controllers in and around our lives. Look through the list below and see if you have witnessed any of these tendencies recently.

- has no concern for the child's needs; lacks awareness of age-appropriate expectations
- is intrusive; imposes unreasonable demands on the child to conform
- yells, disrespects, and mocks the child, or threatens violence
- is moody and unpredictable; nonchalant about things that matter
- teases or bullies the child and then says, "I'm just kidding"

Controllers may insist children conform to their timetable with little sensitivity to the developmental capacities of the child. Each child has a different personality, physiology, and style that affects everything about parenting, but for controllers, none of this matters. If it's time to eat, the kid must be hungry. If it's time to leave, the kid was done playing. If Mommy needs rest and quiet, then little Susie must feel like staying in her room and whispering to her dollies to be quiet for Mommy. The adult gets to say what the kid wants and gets to do.

And when babies and toddlers don't comply, expect sparks.

Many controllers have kept their anger somewhat in check until they marry and/or become parents. And once a family unit is created, they realize they're suddenly being triggered. I talked with a man after a seminar who said, "I was an angry child but seemed to get it under control during college and our first year of marriage. But when we had our first child, my anger exploded like a volcano." With tears in his eyes and a shaky voice, he described being so triggered that he'd shake the crying four-year-old and push him into his room to cry alone.

How many parents have taken a vow never to be like their own parents? When controllers find themselves in such enormous internal conflict, the struggle to uphold such a vow is often a losing battle. Abuse breeds abuse, and preschoolers just learning to have a mind of their own and say,

"No," "Mine," and, "Me do it," can make controller parents explode. It is an important part of a child's development to learn to separate and establish his individuality. But in any group of young moms, we find scared women who are surprised by their anger and how easily it overtakes them. When we talk about controllers and abuse breeding abuse, several will typically come up afterward and say we were speaking directly to them.

Whether outright rage or outbursts of frustration at the beach, preschoolers push controller parents' buttons.

WITH SCHOOL-AGE KIDS AND TEENS

I heard a sad story about two brothers, eight and nine, forced to put on boxing gloves and fight until one gave up. Their dad would praise the winner and ridicule the loser: "Be a man. Go to your room if you're going to cry." When fighting is key to survival, it must be learned at an early age. This father was only protecting his sons from what he must have suffered.

I've heard many a controller in my office say, "I don't have empathy or compassion for weakness." No wonder children of controllers are neglected and their feelings minimized when they're in physical or emotional distress. I once observed a dad laugh at his eight-year-old son who had just lost a Little League game. He had said, "Be a man and stop crying like a sissy." After some time in my office discussing the pain of his childhood, one controller reluctantly admitted, "I guess I don't have any compassion for myself either." This is exactly the problem, and wonderfully, the key to recovery. As he began to grieve the wounded child he once was, this hard man began to have more compassion for the distress of his children and stopped minimizing their emotional worlds.

Because controllers struggle with self-regulation and lack impulse control, discipline of children and teens is often either too severe or nonexistent. Some controlling parents are frequently unable to determine if their children are in danger. Disconnected controller parents often allow their small children to wander the streets or walk to places that expose them to dangers of all kinds, whether bodies of water, campgrounds, public bathrooms, or liquor stores. They never think, *Could my child get hurt in some way?* Remember, controllers grow up in homes that are dangerous, so as children, their alarm buttons were pushed way too many times. Now as parents, their ability to assess danger is compromised. They can be underprotective; they can be overprotective and intolerant of mistakes; or they can swing between the two.

At adolescence a natural pulling away begins, and the controller parent's world is rocked again. Even the most secure parents struggle during the teenage years, so you can imagine how controllers might feel. They'll often try to control their children all the way into adulthood.

Kids with stronger personalities will often "have it out" with the controller parents during adolescence, while quieter kids will stay under the radar and out of the way. Challenges may erupt into verbal abuse and violence, and if a teen gets kicked out, he may find a gang or some other new "family." Worst of all, he is set up to continue the next family chapter as chaotic spouse and parent.

Sex is often a problem in such homes as well, as controllers tend to have an addictive and abusive relationship with sexuality. Parents may watch explicit movies with no consideration of the kids. Sexual activity is often frequent in the controller's house, and wives and daughters learn quickly that dressing seductively gets them approval or some level of power. Yet again, rigid controllers may go to the opposite extreme, demonizing the body and distorting kids' views of God's design for sex.

Substance abuse or addictions of some kind will likely be present in controller homes, and kids and teens may be exposed to drugs, alcohol, and wild parties. As a result, resisting and disrespecting authority, getting away with something, and eventually, finding a way to ease all that emotional anxiety and pain can become strong attractors to such kids.

Religiously controlling parents often make *any* party evil, and unwittingly send their kids off to college to embrace drugs and alcohol with reckless abandon. The more compliant adolescents may simply follow the conservative path for a lifetime, never asking why they've taken the road they're on.

The controller parent of kids and teens tends to exhibit

- a lack of empathy for children and often forces them to take on the harsh world prematurely.
- disrespect through mocking or shaming kids while demanding respect.
- poor assessment of danger.
- a lack of integrating good and bad; living in extremes with no middle ground.
- a forceful imposition of their will on others at all times, unless passed out or checked out.
- annihilation of others; merciless inability to accept difference.
- competition with teens and severe reactions to noncompliance.
- little sense of home, having left home early, and/or has a child who left home early.
- sexualized behavior, objectification of girls, and disregard for purity.
- exposed substance abuse, sometimes encouraged with the teen.
- excessive boundaries, rigidity, and structure (especially religious), or lack of boundaries.

PARENTING WITH A CONTROLLER

Maybe you could relate to the pastor's wife at the beginning of the chapter. Kay and I see many Christian controller men and women, leaders and laity, whose spouses and children are faced with daily power struggles characterized by cycles of dominance, resistance, intimidation, intense conflict, and fearful submission. While some controllers are difficult to live with, others are only mildly controlling and can still be pleasant, even caring parents. Yet it can be a frustrating, lonely, and frightening experience to be a less important or invisible partner, forced to act like a child, possibly be sexually dominated, intimidated, and looking for someone to understand.

Spouses of controllers may lose their personhood, appear childlike, be forced to perform sexually, experience unwanted pregnancies and STDs, and be terrorized and battered. Sometimes they might initiate sex to "tame the beast." Yet eventually the constant pressure and grief seeks relief in addiction. And unfortunately, the downward spiral then only gets worse for the entire family, and mostly for the children.

One of the most frequent types of calls we get on *New Life Live* radio is from a wife of a man who doesn't want to change. And controllers top the list. They tend to dig in their heels and balk at any help or possible change to their lives. We always tell the caller to make a decision and grow anyway, because that's what God wants. Just one person's growth will change the dynamic of the home. Here are some of the things we recommend if you are parenting with a controller:

- Attend couples' counseling with a therapist who can become your advocate and be another set of eyes to help you see what's going on more clearly. A good therapist can offer an accurate view of what abuse and domination are, why they should be intolerable, and how to find safety and resolution. Go alone if your spouse refuses.
- Get help learning to assess true threats and making wiser judgments. Believe in your heart that you are loved, cherished, and chosen by God to protect your children and yourself now, once and for all. Be encouraged and stand up for yourself. Be the adult and let your children see how to take control back from anyone who wrongs them. You can learn to do this, or continue being complicit with the abuse.

- Call the authorities and file a report of domestic violence to establish a precedent should you ever need a restraining order. Many times, Child Protective Services needs to be called to help the family.
- Be sure to read the growth goals for the victim parent in the next chapter, which include ways to protect you and your children from retribution.

Growth Goals

Our hearts go out to anyone whose childhood was ransacked by parental dysfunction. As an innocent child, you faced neglect, abuse, terrible fear, and you did it *alone.* Your heart and your needs were ignored. It's time you had compassion for yourself, because it was you who lived through it and you *did* live through it. You need comfort for all those uncomforted wounds you have held inside.

If you are a controller, you need support. A group recovery program can help you process unresolved grief, and regular meetings with a reputable, well-trained Christian therapist is essential (1-800-New-Life can help you find one in your area). A good counselor will become a trusted friend, a mentor, and a guide. Under a counselor's care, you can begin to give up control. With your therapist or sponsor, you need to:

- address painful events in the past and develop greater compassion for the child you were.
- learn how to receive and take in comfort and care.
- develop self-control to keep your temper at bay.
- gain a deeper awareness of vulnerable feelings that you felt as a child.
- learn to develop healthy relationships and secure connections.
- find the freedom to be your own person and allow others to be as well.

- become secure in the belief that you and your family members are entitled to live up to their unique potential as individuals.
- develop a new appreciation for degrees of good and bad, and to recognize both at once, in yourself and others.

A good therapist will also help controllers learn to delay gratification and slow down impulsive behavior to help them cope better with the adult world and be more successful parents.

A grace-centered local church can be a place to find helpful community as well. Sharing burdens, confessing sin, and getting free of old patterns can be just a few benefits as we learn from others. Recovery groups can help us face addictions that developed in response to legitimate needs that went unmet by others. By learning to bring emotional needs into relationship, we become less dependent on other things to get over negative feelings. In some cases, a doctor may be best to prescribe an antidepressant or mood stabilizer as a temporary aid in the transition to your new life. I recall many kids and spouses saying, "What happened to Dad?" "What happened to Mom?" "They're not angry anymore."

Over time, as *you* heal, your children can begin the journey as well. Remember, with every change you make, your children become more secure as you become safer and more approachable.

Seven

The Victim Parent

can't believe this is even happening. He was so nice to us when we were dating, and now he's so different. I can't believe what I've gotten myself into."

Sheryl took a deep breath, chuckled nervously, and apologized for trembling. She asked if I (Milan) had a tissue.

"Are you kidding?" I joked. "A counselor's office without tissues is like a taco stand without tortillas." She laughed and pulled a handful from the box. "Sheryl, I've been overwhelmed too. There are more tissues where those came from. So take your time and tell me all about it."

She was a well-meaning single mom who fell in love with a man who swept her off her feet. As a divorcée, she often worried if she would ever have security or a loving male role model for her teenage son. "He was so engaging and seemed to be so strong and decisive. He did everything for my son and me when we were dating. He arranged everything ahead of time, and I was so impressed with his initiative and the way he'd follow through. He'd hardly let me do anything. He seemed so caring. Just the kind of leader I was looking for."

She knew he had a history of drug and alcohol dependence, and that he'd been sober for two years. But when she said, "I do," she never imagined the dream would soon turn into a nightmare.

With no premarital counseling and a relatively short dating period, she didn't know her new husband's addictions were his outlet for a violent childhood. So to cope with the danger in his home, her husband learned at an early age to self-medicate with beer and wine. He also became very controlling among his peers and got into many fights throughout high school. Though her new husband was sober, he was what you'd call a "dry drunk" with poor coping mechanisms and anger when others didn't comply.

She quickly learned he was nice when things went his way. But when things didn't go according to his plan, he'd turn on others. Intimidation was his tool to achieve compliance. When her teenage son started to oppose him, he'd become irate and scream in his face. Over the next couple of years, the teenager grew bigger and stronger, and the intensity of the arguments escalated. Finally, the stepdad challenged him to take a swing at him, and the son walked away amid a volley of verbal taunts, deciding to live with his biological dad.

He didn't actually hit the boy or his wife, so was this abuse? Certainly! He was a powder keg waiting to explode. Someone was likely to get hurt; it was only a matter of time. I supported her decision to obtain a legal separation until her husband sought help. Over the years I've seen similar scenarios, some with the female as controller.

Victim parents[1] are so dominated that they have trouble knowing who they are or what to think. They don't have well-developed critical-thinking skills, having never had a parent to demonstrate. Such skills can't be developed while dodging the assaults of others. Survival precedes development, and, as adults, they can't protect themselves, let alone their children, from the dominating parent. Stuck as children, they're often more like an ineffective big sister or brother, dodging the angry parent.

Like the other love styles, victims exist on a continuum of mild to severe, religious and nonreligious.

VICTIM ASSESSMENT

- People in my family struggled with outbursts of anger, violence, addictions, and abuse.

- I try to keep my mate from knowing certain things, to prevent him from becoming angry.
- I have been in and stayed in destructive relationships.
- I get depressed and anxious, which makes it hard for me to cope as a parent.
- I'm loyal even when others are probably exploiting me.
- For most of my life, I've felt unworthy and unlovable.
- Sometimes I'm far off, and I feel detached and disengaged. Sometimes I find myself not paying attention to my children.
- My parents had drug and alcohol problems.
- One of my parents was abusive, the other passive.
- Growing up, I functioned as the parent.
- My spouse mistreats me, but I stay because it would be horrible to be alone.
- I was physically, emotionally, or sexually abused during my childhood—or saw these things happen to other people.
- I get nervous when things are calm, and I anxiously wait for the anger to come.
- When my spouse is unkind to our children, I feel powerless to do anything about it.
- Sometimes I feel life isn't worth living.
- I don't let myself cry, because if I started, I'd never stop.

If you see yourself or someone you know in this assessment, be encouraged. There's hope for recovery! Some of the nicest, most wonderful people in the world are victims, and we have met and known many such people. Incredibly sweet and compliant, there are few who try harder than the victim to do things right.

WITH INFANTS AND TODDLERS

Years ago as a young pastor, I was visited by a woman asking for money, saying her family was in severe distress. I gave her some money, prayed with her, and didn't see her again until years later at another church, this time with a missing tooth and an infant clad in only a diaper.

"Wow. I've met you before," I said. "Things haven't changed, huh? You've been doing this a long time. What's the real story?"

I learned she and the man she was living with were homeless, camping nearby. She was sent out daily to seek benevolence from churches, hopelessly stuck in the trap of emotional sickness and dependence. The baby was obviously tired, wet, and hungry, but all he got was a few bounces followed by a harsh "hush." Her desperation won out over the child, who was protesting being dragged around crying and screaming, which soon tired him out and forced him into restless sleep.

Victims can check out or dissociate when stressed and overwhelmed. They're literally unavailable to their infant at these times and "not all there." Babies' cries can remind victims of unresolved distress in their own childhood, and their energy must be directed at keeping this out. When their best efforts fail to console the baby, they go a bit wild with panic. In this state, they can easily switch into the angry-abuser mode, shaking or hurting the child, or abandoning him either temporarily or permanently.

Victims tend to have these characteristics:

- are overwhelmed by a chaotic lifestyle; may not protect the baby from an angry or abusive spouse
- suffer with depression; may make moms less responsive to their babies
- are tolerant of intolerable living conditions and used to extreme behavior
- have little ability to read babies' cues, or respond to crying by checking out
- minimize problems and often feel overwhelmed and helpless
- may seem frightened by the baby, suddenly retreating or backing away
- are prone to addictions—alcohol, marijuana, and so on—to subdue internal childhood pain

- have role confusion, such as seeking comfort from the baby rather than providing comfort
- are easily coerced and intimidated into complying with dominating spouse's demands
- may become negative or intrusive; may mock or tease the baby
- act childlike as a parent

WITH PRESCHOOLERS

The wife of a dominating pastor came to see me. She cried and complained that she was constantly on the go—morning, noon, and night. Coming to me as "defender of the weak," she lamented that she absolutely couldn't slow her husband down. He felt called to serve and had a single-track mind. "He's like a runaway train with no brakes," she said.

I asked how old her children were.

"Three children. Daniel is three, Esther is eighteen months, and Isaac is one month. My husband believes he's Moses, that God talks to him, and he's to lead His people. Our church has three meetings a week, and he expects everyone to be at all of them. He actually told someone to get a doctor's note explaining why she missed church for a week."

I ventured a guess. "I'm deducing this means you and the kids have to set an example for the church and be there all the time. That must put a lot of pressure on you as a young mom."

She started sobbing and said, "I have to teach a Sunday school class, head up women's ministries, and go to the midweek service he teaches. If the kids are tired or cranky, he tells me to bring them anyway. He drives separately and doesn't tolerate any questions from me or the kids. He's so distant and harsh to them. I don't know what to do. Please help me."

I told her that I had no superhero outfit under my shirt, but if he'd come in on her next visit maybe I could understand a bit better. "He doesn't trust counselors. He refused to come in. He said I was the one with the problems."

I told her how sorry I was, and that with time, I'd try to help her learn to set boundaries with him.

I then asked, "Of all the things you've told me, what bothers you most?" I wasn't surprised at her answer.

"Oh, myself. I'm so over the edge, impatient with the kids, and I yell and scream at them." Her voice trailed off as she whispered, "Something I vowed I would never do…"

I pressed further, "So why did you make that vow?"

"Because it's what I grew up with. Dad was ignorant, angry, and just plain mean."

"Your mom?"

"Passive and mostly nonexistent. Her familiar line to my dad was, 'For gosh sakes, Bob, stop it!' And her favorite line to me was, 'He really does love you.' Humph, like heck he did."

While passivity helps the victim survive as a child, it makes parenting difficult. Victims feel unable to protect their children and themselves from threats and danger. Helplessness increases stress, which decreases their ability to respond to the child's needs. Parents may temporarily abandon being the parent, and the child is left afraid, alone, and unprotected. Toddlers who defy a controller may be harmed when the victim freezes.

While no physical harm occurred in this case, the young pastor bullied his wife and children, expecting complete compliance. She was suffering and the children were miserable as drag-alongs whose needs were not regarded.

And just like with infants, a victim may lash out at an uncooperative toddler, especially if there's danger of agitating a controller spouse. Inadequacy and fear of losing control are common emotions, and unexpressed anger may leak out on young children who appear weak or when victims are agitated and don't know what to do.

While stories like this are unpleasant, these scenarios are common, even among Christian families. Below are some traits typical in victim parents:

- have no concept of what's age appropriate
- are powerless: respond helplessly to an angry, feisty preschooler
- are exhausted, with no self-care
- are isolated and dishonest about the reality of life
- are helpless in providing reassurance and protection when a child needs it
- require too much when children are tired and/or sick
- sleep a lot, seeking distance from kids; leave them for extended periods
- are depressed, anxious, overwhelmed, or despondent
- have phobias, such as fear of dark and being alone
- are dependent on alcohol or drugs

WITH SCHOOL-AGE KIDS AND TEENS

Putting aside the stereotypical abusive males for a moment, some of the worst controllers are women. In one case I recall, the victim husband was dominated with threats and beatings. If he called the police, she said she'd tell them he molested one of their children and give them incriminating evidence. Paralyzed by her threats, he allowed the abuse to continue.

I asked him, "So what happens to the kids when these episodes occur?" He told me most of the time it happened when the kids weren't home and he'd fabricate stories or go to a friend's house and tell the kids he was on a business trip. Of course, that left them to the whims of the mentally unstable spouse.

Unfortunately, this scenario is much more common than we'd like to imagine. The number of battered men is astonishing. Statistics show that "25 percent of people who call police for help as domestic violence victims are men."[2] But male or female, an easily intimidated victim ceases to be a parent.

As children grow and see the helplessness or tears of their victim parent, roles may reverse. Sensitive, insecure children may take on the task of parenting the parent. Victim parents, unaware how unhealthy this is, may welcome the caretaking without realizing the burden it places on the children.

"My seven-year-old daughter is the strong one," a victim mom once told me. "She always tells me it'll be all right. I get my strength from her."

Victims often make excuses for the abusive spouse or accept blame for their outbursts of anger. When the controller is contained, victims may turn on the kids, blaming them and making them feel responsible for setting off the out-of-control parent. Angry kids may also begin to imitate the pattern of abuse toward the victim parent.

If their parents are children, how can children develop? "A blind man cannot guide a blind man, can he? Will they not both fall into a pit? A pupil is not above his teacher; but everyone, after he has been fully trained, will be like his teacher" (Luke 6:39–40). If a teenager is somehow more competent than the victim parent, the teen may become a surrogate parent or spouse. In other cases, the victim parent rescues the teen from consequences and responsibility. A victim mom may lie, steal, and overlook all sorts of things to protect the child or teen who's protecting her.

What are victims like with school-age kids and teens? Remember the severity range from mild, moderate, to severe.

- are easily intimidated by spouse and strong-willed children or teens
- are dependent on compliant children to take over responsibilities
- behave childishly

- are likely pushovers
- can have explosive and unpredictable moods
- may be alcohol and/or drug dependent
- are anxious and depressed
- have no real ability to protect the kids from the dominant parent
- are likely isolated

PARENTING WITH THE VICTIM

Victims may not always marry controllers, but they have been raised by one, so they're familiar with hiding from abuse. Those married to victims often feel as though they bear the load of the responsibility and that their partner is not engaged in the parenting process, and they're right. If the spouse is a controller, this lack of responsibility can exasperate controllers all the more. Having learned early to detach, parenting can feel overwhelming for victims. As a result, when children come along, victim parents may check out. Passive parents often struggle to provide opinions, because they lack confidence, feel indecisive, and don't want to take risks. The "yield sign" is always up, and spouses often feel alone in the parenting journey.

Victims most often struggle with telling the truth to their spouses because they fear reprisal. With a lifetime of training, they're frequently manipulative, hiding the truth from those they fear. They even hide truth from themselves, living in deep denial.

Trained by trial and error over many years, they're in a conflicting, confusing dance with the spouse who's usually dominating. Colluding with their partner, they support or withdraw, seduce or hide, smile or cry, engage or withdraw, depending on what the lead step may be. They play their learned role with the dominating spouse, tolerating, excusing, or denying the emotional unhealthiness of their partner.

Children bring depression and mounting anxiety to already overwhelmed victims. If there's a history of abuse or neglect, victims may dissociate and go to a "private place" where they are safe and no one is allowed to enter. In another world, they are unavailable and both the spouse and child are on their own.

Because they lack self-awareness and an adult voice, when it comes to sex, victims can be all over the map. Over the years they've typically been abused, mistreated, even raped. As adults, many females have had multiple abortions and/or children. They can be sensually oriented, sexualizing all intimacy with provocative dress. Or they can be sexually avoidant, minimizing sexuality and hiding. Of course, in this environment, the children will develop distorted views of sex as well.

Growth Goals

If you're a victim, passivity helped you survive as a child, but now it harms you. You must learn to set boundaries and say no to what's wrong. Don't mistake heroism for allowing abuse to occur. Yes, Jesus said to turn the other cheek, not to resist those who would do evil to us, and even took on our sins as part of God's redemptive purpose. But tolerating abuse in your home allows sin to continue without restraint. You can best love the one who's persecuting you by removing yourself. Your continued victimization is *not* part of God's plan.

Join a recovery group and get a sponsor. It's free. You can find a sponsor at many recovery groups in churches or at any Alcoholics Anonymous group. A sponsor and/or therapist will help re-parent you as you experience support, honesty, accountability, a listening ear, and genuine care. Self-awareness, revisiting your abuse, and talking about your early trauma aloud in a group of safe people will help you begin your healing journey. Grieving past abuse and neglect and getting angry at it will eventually help you learn to set boundaries as you realize the anger of others is not your fault. As an adult, you can help the little child you once were by learning to value and protect yourself.

Asserting yourself is vital to developing as the secure adult God intends for you to become. All of us must learn how to command the respect of others and establish boundaries. Respect is earned, not given. Softies and pushovers are never respected. We've had several victim women study at our kung fu studio who, with time and training, have become formidable opponents who know how to stop attackers.

True growth usually involves some discomfort. God allows you to choose for yourself to stop letting others hurt you, and to seek the help you need. You can learn to speak truth and accept distressing outcomes. God will not magically give you your adult voice without you working for it. Grow up in all aspects, He says. You are personally responsible for your maturity process. It takes time, patience, and perseverance, but eventually you will see it's a *slow* miracle.

Interventions are sometimes necessary to break addictions to alcohol, drug, and sexual mistreatment. It's important to seek out your community mental-health services and get in touch with a therapist, as well as a social worker and a lawyer. You need people who can protect you and know what to do based on the severity of your situation. Over the years many of our clients have been controller/victim couples. We provide containment, accountability, and guidance as couples begin to step out of the strong gravitational field of hurt and violence.

If you're a victim of abuse from a spouse, you need a plan. Get out of the house and negotiate from a safe distance through a third party. Seek out friends to support your decision and provide resources to help you transition to a safe environment. Safety for you and your children is the first goal. This may involve seeking refuge in a shelter if you or your children are in danger.

This also might involve taking refuge in a secret location where the angry controller can't find you and intimidate you into returning home. Fear of punishment and retaliation and financial uncertainties are the most common reasons people stay in abusive situations. Some can be trapped for years, and sadly, many of these situations have tragic endings. A legal separation with a restraining order allows you to negotiate from afar, until you can determine if your partner will face his or her past and choose to grow.

Those in chaotic homes *always* require help from others. It's also important to document behavior so a legal paper trail is established. How can you defend yourself best? By calling 911 *every* time physical violence occurs. File a police report and have a deputy escort you to safety as you get out of the house. If you or your children have been hit or abused, go to the hospital and have your wounds attended to, with pictures taken. The hospital will bring in social workers and call Child Protective Services to protect you and the children.

Go to weekly therapy and/or a recovery group, whether or not your spouse chooses to go with you. Give a full report weekly detailing any abuse in the home and ask for advice. If necessary, their records will provide evidence to the court regarding this history of violence, and they can be used to establish a pattern. If threats are used, generally, the truth will find its way to the surface. Psychologists are trained to interview children and adolescents and find the truth in their testimonies.

Some attorneys specialize in representing spouses of mentally ill men and women.

The Bible tells a story about friends of the apostle Paul letting him down over the wall of Damascus in a basket to escape those who wanted to kill him (see Acts 9:22–25 and 2 Corinthians 11:32–33). My question for you is, Who are your friends, and where is your basket?

The key growth goals for the victim parent:

- Get help in community, through church and counseling, to gain perspective and accurately assess true threats.
- Learn assertiveness training, both verbally and physically.
- Plan for discomfort and a challenge, but plan to be a changed person too.

- If necessary, devise an escape plan to seek refuge.
- Overcome guilt, misinterpretation of Scripture, and religious defenses. Tolerating marital abuse is not biblical or spiritual.
- Learn to set boundaries by grieving past abuse, as you realize the anger of others is not your fault. As an adult you can help the little child you once were by learning to value and protect yourself.

Take courage. As you begin to change and stand up for yourself, your children will become more secure. They will see what it is like to see a person liberated from danger, and you will eventually become a model of courage and bravery. You have the opportunity to become a transitional generation. Be bold.

I remember one day I was expecting a new client, a young victim woman who was coming to my office for the first time. She was apprehensive and cautious, and it had taken much for her just to come in and meet with me. She was brilliant and well educated, but she'd had a chaotic childhood and adolescence, which automatically meant her adulthood would be chaotic as well.

As I sat down at my desk just prior to her arrival, I felt inspired by her courage, and in a rare burst of creative energy, I wrote the following piece, which I quickly hung on my door where she would see it when she walked in.

I share it with you here, in hopes that it may inspire you to be that brave dreamer you were meant to be.

TO ALL WHO ENTER…WELCOME!

Welcome to the children who have children themselves and yet still feel so little. To those who still have small parts within that need to grow up. Welcome those who are frightened of the "big" people of life, who can seem so tall and beyond their reach.

REMEMBER...

*That the one who temporarily occupies this office is a fellow
sojourner feeling afraid of this confusing thing called life, where
happiness can at times be elusive, where growth is painful,
and where joy must be clung to when found!*

Part

2

Helping
Your Child

Eight

Helping Any Child

As we described the love styles in the previous chapters, we hope you discovered your love style and are motivated to make some changes. Perhaps you feel upset because you see some of these traits in your kids. Frustrating, isn't it?

Perfect parents we are not. But if we can face ourselves truthfully and realize where we've missed the mark, we can overcome our deficiencies as parents. We'd all love to live without ever hurting our children, but a better goal is to use our mistakes to admit where we've failed and to model personal growth. The great news is, kids don't really need perfect parents. They need parents who say, "I messed up. I have weaknesses in me that cause hurt in our relationship. But I'm committed to growing and changing."

Before we describe more specifically how each style shows up in kids, we want to give you some suggestions and tools that can help every family. First, learn to use the Comfort Circle for Parenting, which we detail below and which is included in the Parent Toolbox at the end of this book. Second, learn to lower your reactivity by recognizing your triggers as a parent. Last, be aware of any difficult circumstances or trauma that may have affected your child's ability to connect. Let's see how each of these can help you as a parent.

In our case, our parenting was strongly influenced by my (Kay's) avoiding and Milan's pleasing. To help our kids, we first had to help ourselves, yet we realized we could all learn new skills together. We gathered our kids (who were in elementary school and junior high) and we explained that we were learning about how our first families shaped us. We told them we didn't blame our parents, but we were taking responsibility for change.

We took some time to point out the mistakes we'd made in how we typically responded. We also talked about things we'd done that were wrong and gave simple examples of how our love styles had affected them. Finally, we mapped out some of the changes and the benefits they could have on our family.

The kids were a bit bewildered. As far as they were concerned, things were fine just the way they were. As a starting point, we focused on awareness of feelings. We admitted how we weren't very good at knowing and expressing our feelings. We explained that God had lots of feelings and that He created us in His image, so feelings were important to God. *If we don't know what we feel, we won't know what we need.*

"Feelings are like lights on the dashboard of the car," Milan said. "They tell us what's going on in the engine under the hood. If the light flashes and you don't pay attention, the car won't work well." We put the Soul Words list on the refrigerator for future reference.

The boys thought these new ideas were fine until we asked them to go get the list of words during a conversation. "Aw, Dad! We don't need that stupid list." As parents we were committed to the changes, so we gently insisted. And often they were surprised at all the feelings churning under their irritation, frustration, or bad moods. Over time they began to see the benefit as they felt a great deal of relief after talking and feeling heard.

LEARN TO GO AROUND THE COMFORT CIRCLE

The comfort circle is one of the most powerful tools a family can use. The comfort circle is used to see into the heart and soul of your child. It promotes meaningful conversations and provides a map to help you mend your child's heart when you (or someone else) cause a wound. Problems come up. Your child will face stress and difficulty living in this world. *The comfort circle makes difficulties bearable and repairable because it's shareable.* The comfort circle teaches your child that people cause stress, but they can also provide relief. We talked extensively about the comfort circle in our first book, *How We Love,* in regard to marriage. As you read this section, turn to the Parent Toolbox at the end of this book to visualize the steps at each point in the journey.

There are four points on the comfort circle:
- Seek awareness.
- Engage (speak the truth in love).
- Explore and find out more.
- Resolution brings relief and comfort.

Step 1: Seek Awareness

Behold, You desire truth in the innermost being. (Psalm 51:6)

Self-awareness is a learned skill and it doesn't happen automatically. As parents we must listen to our child's behaviors as a language, and teach them to have words to describe their internal feelings and thoughts. When you see them acting up or looking distressed, help them to identify their feelings. For a toddler, start with four feeling basic words: *happy, mad, sad,* and *scared.* As the child grows and vocabulary increases, you can introduce her to the Soul Words list in the Parent Toolbox. Helping your child learn to be aware of what is stirring around inside her heart and soul and being able to put words to those inside experiences is developing the important skill of self-awareness.

As your kids grow, point out their behavior when they are stressed or upset and help them express feelings under the behavior. "You are usually quiet when something is bothering you. Let's get out the Soul Words list and see if we can figure out what's going on and how I can help."

Step 2: Engage and Speak the Truth in Love

> A plan in the heart of a man [or child] is like deep water, but a
> man of understanding draws it out. (Proverbs 20:5)

As the parent, it is your job to be the initiator and engage with your children. The goal is to create a safe environment for feelings and upsets to be discussed and explored. Over time, your children will come to you when they need to talk. You will need to initiate almost all the time with introverted kids, as they are more reserved and less likely to open up.

Safety means your kids have permission to speak truthfully and can trust you to tolerate negative feelings even if those upset feelings are about you as a parent or something that is going on in the family. The goal of engaging is to invite dialogue.

Over time, teach your children to deal with anger by speaking the truth in love. Respect must be modeled, not just required. Ephesians 4:15, 25–26 instructs us to lovingly speak truth, dealing with anger quickly before it festers inside and turns to bitterness. Kids are not going to automatically do this perfectly. It takes time, self-control, and maturity.

To engage means you will be a good conversation starter and a good listener to keep the conversations moving in a helpful direction. Instead of reacting ("I'm sick of your attitude and you better shape up"), try inviting ("You seem extra irritable and grumpy. I often feel that way too when something is on my mind or I can't solve a problem. I wonder what's on your mind"). See the Parent Toolbox at the end of this book for good questions and conversation starters.

Step 3: Explore and Find Out More; Listen and Validate

> Be quick to hear, slow to speak and slow to anger. (James 1:19)

In step one and two you are teaching your children how to be aware of what is inside them and initiate conversation to process feelings and the reasons for their behaviors. In step three you are giving the gift of listening. A fortunate, blessed child leaves home having been deeply listened to at each age and stage. The Listener and Speaker Guides in the Parent Toolbox at the end of this book are your guide. As a parent, you are the listener and your child is the speaker. Ask open-ended questions, not accusatory or entrapment questions. You can find some sample questions in the Listener Guide on page 274.

Remember, as you ask questions, always ask about feelings.

Being a great listener means expecting the unexpected and not being reactive or defensive. Reactivity is the enemy of listening. Ask hard questions and dive into the mess. Don't be naive; don't settle for simple, superficial answers. Be a good detective and a fair judge. In so doing, you will be giving your children one of life's best gifts: to know how to share and to know how to listen.

As your children enter elementary school, they can learn to be listeners too. Solving conflicts with siblings or friends is a good opportunity to teach your children how to be in the listener role and find out about someone else's feelings and thoughts about a conflict.

Step 4: Resolution Brings Relief and Comfort

A soothing [or healing] tongue is a tree of life. (Proverbs 15:4)

Once they have shared their feelings and you have thoroughly listened and they've gotten everything off their chest, always ask them what they need from Mommy or Daddy. This teaches them to link feelings to needs. There is a list of possible ways to create resolution and comfort on the bottom of the Listener Guide on pages 274–75 of the Parent Toolbox. The goal is for both people to leave the interchange feeling better.

While this is not always possible, it is wonderful when it can be achieved. Often after a trip around the circle, the mood will be lighter and the tension dissolved.

Make Time For Meaningful Conversations

The comfort circle can be used for positive, upbeat conversations too. Sometimes we get so busy with activities, schedules, and chores that our interactions with our kids are mostly about problems:

- "Did you empty the trash?"
- "I told you to clean up this room."
- "Hurry up, we are going to be late."
- "Is your homework done?"

When is the last time you had a meaningful conversation with your kids? Good connection requires significant conversations, so parents need to learn to ask about good feelings too. Mealtime and bedtime are great opportunities to get to know what your children are thinking and feeling. You can start by asking, "What was the best part of your day, and what was the most challenging part of your day?" This helps kids self-reflect and teaches them that every day is good and bad. It's a part of life.

Control Your Reactivity by Understanding Your Triggers

Effective parents know where their sensitivities lie and what makes them prone to overreacting. A trigger is an emotional memory where feelings from the past flood into the present. The resulting response, expressed or not, will be overreaction or withdrawal out of proportion to the situation. The way to figure out your triggers with each child is to ask yourself what bugs you most about him. Is it some behavior? Is it certain words? Is it an attitude? A temperament trait?

Try to determine what triggers you have with your children. For each child, write down what bugs you most about this kid. These will likely be different depending on the kid. What causes big reactions inside you? Use the Soul Words list to write three words describing what you feel when your reactions seem exaggerated. Then write what you'd like to say to her or about her—the uncensored, raw response.

Next, link it up to when you felt those feelings before, when you were a kid. Did someone say the same words, have the same attitude or exhibit the same behavior? Is there someone in your past you'd like to say those words to now? Maybe you've been longing to say it to whoever it was.

All triggers are unresolved emotion from the past. And when dealt with they loose their intensity.

I asked Kelsey, who had an eight-year-old daughter, Tara, what bugged her the most. "I can tell you exactly what it is," she said. "Tara is so ungrateful. I do so much for her, but it's never enough. Sometimes she doesn't even say thank you."

I handed her the Soul Words list. "How does Tara's behavior make you feel?"

"Unappreciated."

"What else?"

"Annoyed, beaten down, mystified," she added slowly. "Annoyed, because I put so much effort into parenting. Beaten down, because she never seems satisfied. Mystified; well, I'm not sure why I picked that. I think I'm confused as to what to do."

"What raw, uncensored words do you want to say to Tara when she's ungrateful?"

"I'm sick of doing stuff for you, you little ingrate. You don't even appreciate me."

"Now, who in your past did you want to say those words to? Who did you try hard to please who didn't appreciate all your efforts? Who made you feel annoyed, beaten down, and confused?"

Kelsey stared at me. "My mom," she said in a whisper. "To this day, I do a lot for her, and she can never say thank you. It's never enough for her, and I'm sick of doing stuff for her, but I feel trapped."

"So Tara's ungratefulness is a trigger. You need her to be extra grateful because your mom never has been. Can you see how you are prone to overreact to Tara?"

"Absolutely," she said.

How do you get rid of a trigger? First, acknowledge the wound and feel the feelings, including any grief that attends them. Next, accept comfort for the wound from your spouse or friends. As these wounds heal in you, they have less power over you. You'll still struggle, but less and less over time, so apologize when you do overreact and learn to keep engaged if you tend to withdraw.

Sometimes triggers don't surface until kids become a certain age. My oldest, Kevin, was always a happy, extroverted kid. Yet when he turned fourteen, suddenly he was as tall as I was with a deep voice much more like my dad's, and when hormones began to produce frustration and anger in him, I began to feel intimidated. I felt exactly like a child again when his temper would flare. Eventually, I realized he was reminding me of my dad, and his flareups made me feel afraid and intimidated, so I'd back down.

Realizing this, I invested in some therapy and learned to acknowledge the wound my dad had given me and to face him with my adult self. It was a two-year process learning to draw boundaries with my dad, speak my opinions, and hold my ground. But eventually, I was able to do the same with Kevin. As Kevin learned to manage his frustration, I learned to manage my fear. Today, I remember it as an incredible time of growth for both of us.

REPAIRING CONNECTION AFTER DIFFICULT CIRCUMSTANCES

Sometimes a child's damaged love style can arise from difficult circumstances. Ryan was five when I met him and was often angry and bel-

ligerent and argued with his mom about any request. Yet I'd occasionally see sensitivity under his bad behavior. I asked his mom if he'd
suffered any trauma, medical, relational, or physical. She replied, "Like a
hospitalization?"

"Yes, tell me about that."

"He had to be hospitalized for severe asthma when he was eighteen
months old. He had pneumonia on top of that and was having a lot of
trouble breathing. Twice the emergency room doctors had to puncture
his lungs to inflate them and neither time involved anesthesia. I hardly
left his side and slept at the hospital every night. And if I had to leave, his
dad was there."

"Did you notice a change in his behavior after he came home?" I
asked.

"Yes. He was clingy. Preschool was a nightmare. He'd scream when
I left and then stay in a corner of the room and kick and yell if anyone
came near him."

"Well, see it from his perspective," I suggested. "His mom, who has
always helped and protected him, is standing right there when these
strangers come and hurt him. Do you think he understood the doctors
were saving his life and not killing him? At eighteen months old, he
couldn't tell you what he was feeling. Maybe he thought preschool was
another place like the hospital and he would get hurt."

Linda put a hand to her mouth. "Oh my gosh. I never put that
together."

"Here's what I'd suggest: you could tell him the story of his experience and help him understand."

"Oh, it was so awful. I'm not sure I can talk about it."

"Tell him it was hard for you too. He can understand. But he has
feelings that confuse him now, so he's acting out with anger and resistance as his shield. Kids can change relatively quickly if they can talk
about what's wrong with someone who helps them understand their experience. You could say something like, 'One time, a little boy named

Ryan couldn't breathe and his parents took him to the hospital where doctors could help. He wasn't old enough to talk, but when he couldn't get his breath, his eyes looked very scared.'

"Then tell him how you felt. 'Mommy yelled for the doctors to come help. They said they could help but it would hurt Ryan a lot. Mommy was very sad, but she knew Ryan needed help to breathe. So she let the doctors stick a big needle right here in his chest. Ryan cried really hard because it hurt so much. He was too little to understand why Mommy would let the doctor hurt him. And Mommy cried too. But that big ouchy needle saved Ryan's life, and soon he got better and came back home.

"'But you know what? Ryan was still afraid sometimes when new people came near him. He was so smart that he remembered how a man hurt him once and he wouldn't let that happen again. So at school, the little boy would sit in the corner and kick and scream if anyone came near. After a while, he realized school was much more fun than the hospital and he could play there. Sometimes Ryan would still get mad, but no one is going to hurt him again. And now, Ryan's mommy just wants to hold him and kiss and hug him, and especially whenever he feels scared.'"

Linda agreed, and she did tell the story to Ryan. And he wanted to hear it again and again. He remained willful but became less angry and more affectionate.

Just like adults, kids need help to make sense of their feelings and reactions. And with help, they can heal from even the most traumatic memories much more quickly and completely than adults.

Over the next few chapters, we'll look at some specific ways to help kids with harmful love styles. You can begin to build a more secure attachment with your child, even if you have older or adult children. Change is a whole lot easier if you know exactly what needs to change. But first we have to get an accurate diagnosis.

Nine

The Avoider Child

(Kay) went with my friend to pick up her dog from the vet's. The place was like a pediatrician's office during flu season. Two dogs, a cat, a bird, and various other animals were waiting with their owners for medical attention. A sad-faced girl sat cradling her hamster, who looked the worst off of the bunch, limp and panting heavily under a watchful eye. I wondered how much it was going to cost to save this ten-dollar pet.

We sat down to wait and another pet emergency entered. A young boy around ten stoically carried his golden retriever puppy with a badly mangled front paw. Mom followed behind rolling her eyes as she stood waiting for the receptionist to acknowledge her. The puppy was obviously in pain, whining pitifully, and the blond boy and his puppy sat down next to me.

The receptionist returned to the front office and asked, "May I help you?"

"Come here, Phillip, and tell the lady what happened," she said disdainfully.

Phillip rose slowly from the chair and dragged himself to the receptionist window. "My puppy got hurt," he said quietly.

"Tell her why, Phillip," his mom insisted.

"I left the door open, and he got out and jumped up while I was on my bike," he confessed quietly.

I leaned over and said to my friend, "I guess mistakes aren't allowed in that family."

"Do you know how many chores you are going to have to do to pay for this?" Phillip's mom said while Phillip used every bit of energy to keep from crying. "Crying isn't going to help," she continued. "This is what happens when you don't pay attention."

Phillip stood up and walked to the other side of the room and sat with his back to his mom.

I hope this mom was simply having a bad day. But I have to wonder if Phillip's mistakes were a common focus, and his mom was often too angry to see his need for comfort. Phillip had already learned tears were unacceptable, even over hurt puppies. His mom showed not a hint of compassion. Where could the boy go for comfort?

Phillip has already learned to bear his pain in isolation.

Avoiders become very good at distancing themselves from their feelings. Expressing emotion may begin to feel like one of the many mistakes that's not allowed. So where do avoiders go for help?

If your child is showing signs of being an avoider,[1] look at the list of traits below and then read the suggestions for help at the end of the chapter.

People do not need to go through life deadening themselves to pain, fear, and ultimately love. And since we know most kids respond to changes more easily than adults, it's never too late to help your child grow.

IN INFANTS AND TODDLERS

- avoids eye contact
- exhibits little to no protest or crying (normal six- to twenty-four-month-olds cry at separation and hug parents in new situations); quickly distracts self with toys after departure; distress is experienced but concealed
- plays with toys upon reunion; appears not to care if parents are present or gone

- is not very affectionate and avoids physical contact at a young age, even when upset

In School-Age Children and Teens

- avoids eye contact during stressful times or in personal conversations
- does not seek the parent out for comfort, nurture, or help with relational problems
- has a narrow range of emotions; seems like he is usually "fine"
- avoids talking about feelings or emotions; walks away when others are emotional
- lacks self-awareness or ability to put words to internal experiences
- smiles and/or laughs when talking about something distressing
- isolates or distracts from painful emotions when upset with activities, projects, and hobbies
- avoids in-depth conversations that put parents in a negative light and minimizes or ignores any painful realities of family life
- more interested in goals and achievements than interpersonal relationships
- may get angry and push others away when confronted with emotions and neediness in others
- has difficulty with dating and is uncomfortable with emotional intimacy

Lack of eye contact can be noticed very early in avoiders. Babies only have one method of self-protection: avoiding eye contact. A baby who's developing in a healthy way will make attentive eye contact between eight to sixteen weeks or so. When the stimulation becomes too intense, the baby looks away, settles down, and then reengages with more eye contact, coos, and vocalizations. This looking away is normal and helps the baby manage the level of stimulation.

My friend, who works in a neonatal unit for babies, reports that babies hospitalized for abuse or domestic violence do not make eye contact. No matter how gently one tries to engage them, they act as though no one is there. A baby who won't make eye contact is definitely stressed in some way. Lack of eye contact can also be a signal of a hypersensitive baby who can't take much stimulation and becomes easily overwhelmed (see "The Sensitive Child" in chapter 16). Birth trauma, early medical interventions, and premature birth can make bonding more difficult. In rarer cases, lack of eye contact can signal developmental problems such as autism or Asperger's syndrome.

As a toddler, the avoider may not protest separation from her parent and at an early age seem like a good baby who doesn't need much. While temperament certainly contributes, toddlers and preschoolers who don't cry, refuse comfort, and don't ask to be held (especially when distressed) may be exhibiting avoider traits. While some level of self-sufficiency and independence is positive, we all need help, comfort, and touch during stressful times.

Avoiders restrict and avoid feelings, having learned others were annoyed, dismissive, or anxious when they expressed emotion or sought help. Sometimes a brother or sister is so needy or hard to manage that the other child retreats. By elementary school and definitely by adolescence, avoider kids will appear very even-tempered, rarely display emotions, and ask for little to nothing relationally.

Helping Babies and Toddlers

- Encourage (don't force) eye contact: notice when your baby makes the most eye contact. Is it during feeding? when you are changing him? after he has eaten? on his back? in a baby seat? Take advantage of those times. When your baby is alert and awake, take him to a quiet room without too many distractions. Stay in the same spot within the baby's visual range. Use a soft voice and call the baby's name, inviting an interaction. When the baby looks your way, greet him with a smile. If the baby makes a sound, copy the sound as though you're having a conversation. When the baby looks away, stop talking, let him rest, and wait for him to reengage. Play again when he looks back. Notice when he stops responding and is telling you that the game is over. This is not rejection; he's simply overstimulated and needs a break from faces.

- Play peekaboo with your baby when she is five months and older. It promotes many things, including eye contact.
- Stroke and rub your baby, and pay attention to your tone of voice. Some babies are easily overstimulated by loud noise and quick movement. Remember this is a little person getting used to a new world. *Everything* is new and babies adapt at different speeds. If you believe you're not affectionate, keep in mind your baby thrives on touch and needs lots of it. In the first year, there is no such thing as holding a baby too much. But, of course, you need breaks too.
- When your preschooler is receptive (bedtime is usually good), tell her, "I want to say I love you with my eyes." Then blink three times and say, "My eyes just said, 'I love you.'"
- Look for opportunities to comfort and pick up your child when he's hurt or distressed rather than telling him, "You're fine." Say verbally, "People need hugs when they're hurt or sad. Kids need comfort, mommies need comfort, and even daddies need it too. Hugs help take hurt away."

- Get down on the floor and play with your children. Avoider parents are averse to playing and resist this suggestion. But just do it! It's so important to enter your children's world on their level, participating in what they enjoy. When they are verbal, let your children direct the play and tell you what to do. A fun game for preschoolers is to create a role reversal. "I'll be the little girl, and you be the mommy."

HELPING SCHOOL-AGE CHILDREN AND TEENS

Jack, a ten-year-old avoider, got help quite by accident. He was reluctantly dragged to a family session I requested because of his thirteen-year-old sister, Joanie, who was angry and rebellious and had been ruling the family from her tyrannical throne since she was a toddler. Two pleaser parents surrendered to this little queen before she could speak a word. By thirteen she was becoming unbearable to live with. Jack sat quietly with his eyes cast to the floor while Joanie tried to dominate the session complaining about the unfair rules and yelling at her mom to be quiet and not interrupt. And Mom complied.

I could see that from Jack's perspective, emotions were likened to a ravaging flood that drowned the family in a torrent of Joanie's relentless outbursts. Joanie ruled with her disruptive, uncontrollable emotions, and it wasn't a pretty sight.

I told Joanie it was Jack's turn and asked Jack a pointed question, although I was quite sure I knew how he would answer. I wanted his parents and sister to hear his answer.

"Jack, has either of your parents ever asked you how it is living in the house with Joanie?"

Nope, said Jack's eyes, still glued to the same spot on the floor.

"Let me take a guess," I said. "Better yet, let me show you." I stood up and took a lion from my shelf of toy figures and put it on the floor where Jack was focused. I then added a family of three bunnies to the scene. I sat down on the floor to enact the scene. Jack made fleeting eye contact with me.

"Roar!" I yelled, making the lion knock over the bunnies. "Roar! Roar!" The lion trampled the bunnies by Jack's feet. I did this a couple more times and said, "If I were this bunny, I'd want to find a big dinosaur." I went and pulled the dinosaur off my shelf and made him roar louder. "'Enough,' said the dinosaur. 'That's enough! No more noise from you.'" I looked up at Jack. "I think you'd like a dinosaur to move into your house." Jack gave me ever so slight a grin, and his eyes met mine for a brief instant. His sister glared at me, but his feelings had been heard and affirmed.

Jack learned to be an avoider because he experienced emotion as loud, relentless, unmanageable, and exhausting. If having emotions meant being anything like Joanie, he wasn't interested. No one ever asked Jack about his feelings or experiences, so he didn't have words. He just turned off and tried to avoid the queen's tirades. Joanie had been begging for boundaries for years. I worked with Jack's parents to help them learn to accept their roles as parents and with Jack to help him learn to experience feelings as signals to know what he needed. And I spent time validating the frustration and loss for him living with an out-of-control sister. It took time, but they all made progress and Jack came back to life.

"The Soul Words list needs to be a part of every conversation," I explained. "Jack has to learn to put words to his internal experiences." I asked Jack's parents to create more time for conversations, giving him opportunities to self-reflect and talk about his feelings and experiences. I encouraged them to show more interest in what was inside of Jack instead of assuming he was fine.

Here are some things that you can try:
- Make observations and put unspoken feelings to words. "I bet you feel sad and upset because your friends were unkind to you today," or, "When my friends were mean to me in the sixth grade, I felt lonely and confused. I wonder if that's how you feel."

- If you've been too busy, apologize and be more attentive. Let them know how important they are and schedule some one-on-one time. Make it a goal to have a heart-to-heart talk with each child at least one time every week.

- Use games like the Ungame (ungame.com) or read together and talk about what happens in the stories to stimulate conversation that's deeper and self-reflective.

- Make it a point to notice what kind of touch your older child enjoys. Back rubs? Shoulder massage? Hugs? Pats on the back? High-fives? Avoiders have to make a conscious effort to keep touching their kids as they grow.

- Apologize for dismissing, ignoring, or making fun of your child's feelings in the past. Normalize feelings in the present because avoiders have decided feelings aren't good, normal, or acceptable. "It's understandable that you feel mad about not making the team," or, "Girls are hard to get along with in junior high, so feeling confused and hurt about being left out makes sense."

It's never too late! A good friend of mine has two college-age boys. They recently asked her why she was always asking them about feelings lately. She said, "I wish I'd asked more about your feelings growing up. Your wives will need to know how you feel so they can know what you need, so I'm helping you help them!"

We'll expand on this in chapter 13, when we discuss introverted children, but many introverts are assumed to be avoiders since they prefer time alone and entertain themselves independently. Introverts need time alone to rest from a lot of interaction and to rejuvenate so they can engage again. In contrast, avoiders isolate because they are overwhelmed by the emotions of others or because they don't want to display their own emotions. It's important to observe the personality of your child and discover which characteristics are natural and which are learned. We've worked with introverts of every love style.

When it comes to making changes, don't overwhelm yourself or your avoider child by trying too hard and going too fast. Try one suggestion at a time, and keep with it until it seems more natural. Plenty of parents have succeeded with time and continued practice—and you can too!

Ten

The Pleaser Child

Melinda came up to me (Milan) after a workshop and asked for a few minutes of my time. The crowd was thinning, and she'd waited at the front of the sanctuary, her face broadcasting, *Oh please, oh please, oh please...*

We sat down and I said, "Your face is telling me you need some help...pronto."

She smiled and told me she was having problems with her four-year-old, Olivia. "I can't get her to leave my side. It was a total hassle for me to just get to your seminar."

"I'm so glad you did."

Her eyes opened wide. "I'm the pleaser parent—textbook—and I'm scared I've kept her too close. My parents told me to get a job and be out of the house within six months. I don't know how I can get Olivia to stay in day care."

Noticing she had no wedding ring, I asked, "Where's Olivia's dad?"

"We met several years ago and got married within three months, just before he was deployed. After he left, I discovered I was pregnant, and six months later, he told me that he was in love with a woman in his unit, and they were spending time together."

As she teared up, I said, "That's a horrible thing to find out. What happened?"

"He told me he wanted a divorce, and after I pleaded with him, hoping and waiting he would change his mind, his girlfriend in Afghanistan became pregnant. I was hurt and angry, and my parents encouraged me to go ahead and file for divorce. After today's sessions, I realize he's the controller dad living day to day, conquest to conquest."

As most parents would, Melinda's took her in, cared for her during pregnancy, and were with her when she had the baby. They financially supported her as she parented without a dad, let her grieve the betrayal and sadness, and allowed her to come to terms with the reality that she was a single mom at twenty-three. Melinda was a very anxious mom, having been abandoned by her husband. Her extreme attentiveness was a result of extreme fear of another loss. Hoping Olivia would never feel the abandonment she had, Melinda overcompensated and kept Olivia by her side morning, noon, and night. They slept together, played together, and ate together. Being there for her baby gave Melinda tremendous comfort as well.

Though she was deeply loved, Melinda's distress, fear, anger, and emotional pain were being absorbed by Olivia. She felt her mom's anxiety and grief through her actions and demeanor. Melinda had finished a degree in accounting and had earning potential, but she didn't know how to separate from Olivia to find a job and an apartment, and send Olivia into day care and preschool.

Below are some examples of how a child can become a pleaser:

- overprotection or enmeshment by an insecure mother, father, or caregiver
- a critical and angry parent who rejects the child when displeased, possibly leading to anxiety disorders—the anger may be overt or indirect, but can cause distress that leads to social difficulty, panic, irrational fears, phobias, and obsessive behaviors to calm and soothe
- an emotionally volatile or erratic parent, caregiver, or sibling creating an unpredictable atmosphere within the home
- trauma, either chronic or acute—either observed or done to them

One young adult told me she was fine until she saw a very scary movie one night with friends at a sleepover. With her safety bubble popped, her perception of reality changed, and she experienced deep insecurity, making separation from mom and dad difficult. Researchers have observed that severe separation experiences such as death, unavailability, frightening behavior, and parental withdrawal can yield social anxiety.

With further thought, it's easy to see that, even as an infant, Olivia experienced many of these factors because Melinda was drawn into love and romance only to be traumatized by betrayal and disregard. For the two of them to be discarded so callously was traumatic to say the least. As well meaning and loving as Melinda was as a parent, Olivia's insecurity and clinginess was birthed here.

What signs of pleaser tendencies can you look for in children?

IN INFANTS AND TODDLERS

It will be hard to see this love style during infancy. Fearful parents are often very attentive, and babies respond, creating exchanges of mutual delight. As babies grow and develop more awareness during the first year, they will feel the apprehension of an anxious parent or a tense atmosphere in the home. Pleasers are more tuned into children's fear than other emotions.[1]

It's hard for fearful mothers or fathers to separate from their toddlers. A crying child reaching for a departing parent makes a pleaser feel guilty and upset. The parent is also fighting worry that something bad will happen in her absence, so her alarm and agitation is both seen and felt by the child. Just like a sponge, the child begins to absorb the parent's fear. The saying "more is caught than taught" is really true here. Fearful parents try to hide their fear, but overtly and obliquely they give the message that the world is scary and their children are only safe with them. Many pleasers are not aware of how anxious they are until we ask them to notice and rate their anxiety throughout a week. An anxious state is normal for many pleasers, and children sense the anxiety even when the parents are not aware of it.

Stranger anxiety and some separation anxiety aren't unhealthy. From seven months up to two years, children should prefer their mom and protest strangers taking them. That preference for Mom is actually a sign of a good bond. If a parent struggles with anxiety and a child won't separate or go off and explore, a pleaser tendency may be developing. Here are some traits typical of a pleaser infant or toddler:

- acts very afraid and gets panicky when left by Mom or Dad
- is hypervigilant about Mom's whereabouts
- won't let caretaker out of her sight
- doesn't explore or venture away from Mom, but stays in close proximity
- has lots of fears and concerns
- is afraid to sleep in his own bed
- is overly compliant and lets other kids dominate
- is aware and sensitive to the mood of others, so caretakes other children and reports problems to adults

Remember, some fears are totally normal for this age group. The big question is, "Is this child learning to be afraid from a fearful parent?"

IN SCHOOL-AGE KIDS AND TEENS

Olivia will eventually grow up, and if her mom remains fearful, so will she. An angry parent creates a lot of anxiety and insecurity too, and being good to keep the peace becomes the goal. Pleaser kids are dependent on others, and security is assured by other people's presence and approval. Left unchecked, high levels of insecurity and dependence upon others becomes a way of life.

Children can't always put words to this. But they really feel upset if someone is unhappy with them or there is a lot of discord in the home.

Without realizing it, they are living by an unspoken truth: "If everyone is happy, I can relax." Pleasers need to keep everybody smiling. One way to do that is to be the good little girl or boy, to compensate for a family member who's challenging. As constant observers, they are experts at reading the mood, behaviors, and nonverbal communication of family members. As a result of this outward focus, pleaser kids aren't very self-aware and will have difficulty describing their feelings. They might also lie to avoid distressing people or getting in trouble. A pleaser is used to minimizing or living in denial from fear of facing the potential outcome, which is usually anger, criticism, or disapproval.

This self-sacrificing leaves their needs unmet, and they will periodically "hit a wall" and have a meltdown from too much stress. These kids carry loaded backpacks that little shoulders weren't made to hold. Of course, children who internalize negative feelings will draw many incorrect conclusions about life. Like ancient astrologers connecting dots and deriving spiritual guidance from it, pleaser kids can make unrelated comments and perceptions into portentous signs. Irrational fears can plague them.

One anxious six-year-old thought the blinking streetlight outside his bedroom at night meant the nearby nuclear power plant was going to blow up. He was a smart little guy, and he knew those power plants made electricity. He also knew they were terrorist targets. He put the facts together and believed he was in danger. His mom nearly fell off the couch when he expressed these deep fears he fought every night.

Pleasers feel better if they know exactly what to expect, so they can have surprising resistance to change and balk at new things and unpredictable surprises. They put on the brakes when anything seems out of the ordinary. Predictable is good, because they rest and relax in a world that is *known*. Children that are anxious have a high need-to-know factor. Fear of the unknown may make them homebodies. Staying home has another advantage. The pleaser child can monitor the mood and emotional temperature of family members. It took me years to understand why I often chose to stay indoors rather than go out and play in the neighborhood. Now I realize I was afraid of some of the mean kids on the block. Second, I wanted to keep an eye on my mom and keep her happy so my parents wouldn't fight at night. I lost a big part of my childhood because I was anxious, and my parents never realized all this turmoil was inside me. They thought my constant stomachaches were due to appendicitis. An appendectomy didn't resolve the stomachaches.

Anxiety travels with the pleaser child to school and the social interaction on campus. Bullies seem to have radar for this anxiety, and pleasers are the targets of bullies who can make their lives miserable and add to anxiety. Lacking good boundaries, they may prefer adults to peers. One teen I talked with told me that he was more comfortable as a helper in the athletic department than hanging out with his peers. When he was a senior in high school, he was one of only three people in the school to have a master key. The head custodian and the principal were the only others. Pleaser kids and teens are trusted like adults, because in reality they behave like little adults. Think about why little adults don't always socialize easily with the other kids.

Performance or test anxiety is a problem for pleaser kids. Anxious students can tilt in one of two directions, depending on what is valued at home: overachieving perfectionists or underachievers. As a pleaser, I felt overwhelmed and had horrible test anxiety, especially in classes where cumulative knowledge was important.

Pleaser children and teens tend to take on the parent role. They become rescuers and counselors of the downcast, surrogate parents, or surrogate spouses. Parents sometimes boast that their sons are their "little men," and some kids get exhausted providing a listening ear. One of my friend's teens, a classic pleaser, spent hours on the phone each night counseling her distraught friends who leaned on her. When she got sick and missed a semester of school, these "friends" were nowhere to be found. Evidently she picked girlfriends who were takers, but not givers.

A pleaser child or teen typically has the following characteristics:

- likes routine and predictability; balks change, new things, or the unexpected
- is a homebody; monitors the mood and emotional temperature of family members to keep the peace
- is distressed by anger, conflict, or disapproval; tries to fix it with good behavior, counseling, playing peacemaker, and/or with distraction
- rarely gets angry, sets boundaries, or resists more dominate family members or peers; defers to others' wishes or desires; is compliant
- suffers from separation anxiety; is fearful of going away from home; asks parent to come get them
- does not share feelings and has low self-awareness; is more aware of how others feel
- experiences performance anxiety or test anxiety

How can we as parents help kids who are showing pleaser traits? It should be clear by now the first and most important thing is to change the parent who is fearful or angry. Look at the stressors that are causing anxiety in your child and take measures to reduce the stress. While you are making these changes, here are some things that will help your kids.

HELPING TODDLERS AND PRESCHOOLERS

Encourage exploration and give your child confidence to venture off. "I'll stay here on the bench, and you go get some rocks to fill your bucket. Come show me when you have a bunch." Instead of rescuing your kids when they have social difficulties, give them words to learn to fight their own battles. For example, Mom sees Carson grab the truck from her son, Jake. Rather than rescuing Jake, and saying, "Carson, give Jason the truck back. He had it first." Try, "Jake, you had the truck first. Tell Carson, 'Give me the truck back, Carson. I had it first. I'll give you a turn in a little while.'" In the second example, mom is teaching her preschooler words for boundaries rather than solving his problem for him.

Remember, the brain can remold itself with the right input. Here are some of the ideas I encouraged Melinda to apply with Olivia to encourage separation.

Establishing short windows of time for children to play alone helps them accept solitude. "You can play with your toys in your room" usually works. The anxious child needs to monitor everything to reduce anxiety. Moments of safe solitude teach him that his world can stay safe, without his watchful eye tracking every moment.

At one to two years, they may play alone within your sight. By age four they should be able to play alone within your hearing. With increasing separation, they will learn to be comfortable alone to think, pretend, and process.

When it's time to leave your child, make it direct, short and sweet, and act with confidence. Don't sneak out the back door. Though the pleaser child may appear frightened or cry and protest, don't hesitate or delay the departure by going on and on with reassurance. Allowing your child to experience some discomfort will expand her capacity to handle stress, which is a part of life. The more anxiety you show about separating, the more your child will mirror your concern. "Bye-bye, Stacie. Have fun at preschool. Mommy will have a big hug and kiss for you when I pick you up." Turn around, wave confidently, and walk away. Remember, *she does not have your history,* your worries, pains, fears, biases, and phobias. Your children will only adopt your inner fears if you train them to. So be aware and try not to assume they feel what you do.

Some of us try very hard to keep our children happy versus teaching them to *feel and deal* with their distressed feelings. It's easier to distract them because, as parents, it's hard to watch a child hurt. Be aware of the times your unconscious need to avoid negative feelings overrides your child's need to learn to express and deal with difficult emotions.

Even as kids, pleasers avoid expressing or showing anger and defer to others too much. While we want our kids to be nice, they also need to be assertive at times. Anger is usually the reason we say no, set limits, or refuse bad treatment from others. If your children cannot express anger, they will struggle with the assertiveness they need throughout life.

As you teach your children to tolerate and regulate unpleasant emotions, you will see growth and realize how much better it is than overprotection. Constantly eliminating stress and frustration produces a weak child. Allow some frustration and look for every opportunity to help your children process, contain, and regulate their distressing emotions. And as they learn to be soothed by you, over time they will learn to regulate their emotions and soothe themselves.

HELPING SCHOOL-AGE KIDS AND TEENS

The infant and toddler principles work throughout grade school and adolescence. But here are some additional ideas to help your emerging pleaser.

Give Praise and Criticism

A healthy balance of good and bad is the key here. Too much praise is another way of overprotecting your children from the reality that they do have weaknesses. We want our kids to have good self-reflections and self-awareness, and this means knowing both their strengths and weaknesses. Don't praise everything; applaud what they are truly good at. Give constructive criticism to help them face weaknesses, accept disapproval, and realize conflict doesn't have to be devastating.

Allow Natural Consequences

Let them suffer the natural consequences of their actions. This improves logic and helps them think through reality. Soccer shoes or baseball mitts left out in the rain all night get soggy. And more distressing, bikes left in the park may get stolen. Instead of handing out golden parachutes by protecting them, help them develop stronger logic and stress-response mechanisms—and next time, they won't need to be rescued.

Model Boundaries

Children need boundaries. No means no. They need to learn that loving parents don't allow them to control mom or dad. Children become insecure if they realize kids can control the parent. Loving boundaries breed security. They will learn to delay gratification, which cultivates self-control. And then a child can rest and let the parent be the parent, instead of being the hypervigilant caretaker.

Push Them to Take Risks

If we're not expanding and stretching every day, we will automatically do the opposite: retreat and stay comfortable. I recently sat next to a young guy on a plane who was reading *The Art of Talking to Anyone*. I looked over and said, "Hey, do you want to practice on me?" He was quiet for a moment and then said, "I haven't finished reading it yet." Then total silence for three more hours. The dude didn't say another word. I felt like the cannibal who was late for dinner and got the cold shoulder. I'm a professional talker, but he didn't know that. He chose not to take advantage of the opportunity. Chalk up one more for fear and discomfort.

Insist They Stretch Themselves Daily Past Their Comfort Zones

Encourage your pleaser child to disagree with you or other family members, express opinions, and make decisions. High school debate club, Toastmasters, speech classes, assertiveness training, whatever you can to encourage them to learn to push themselves. Help them think about appropriate first jobs. A job in commission sales teaches how to tolerate rejection. Service jobs, on the other hand, only reinforce the servant role and fail to stretch and grow assertiveness.

Let Them Face Rejection

I heard my radio cohost Dr. John Townsend once say, "If someone isn't mad at you, you probably don't have any boundaries." Jesus couldn't make everyone happy, and more importantly, He didn't *try* to. It stands to reason, neither should you. There's a lie all pleasers tell themselves: "I have to avoid rejection and unpleasant feelings no matter what," which leads to, "I have to protect those I love from ever feeling rejected or unhappy." Captain Obvious here: this is an exhausting way to live. Teach your kids to tolerate disapproval and unresolved situations. Some people will never be at peace with you, and you'll just have to accept it. One day, your child might have to work with a difficult person and learn to deal with it.

Model and Encourage Self-Care

Kids must learn to relax and allow others to care for them instead of fixing and rescuing others. Teach your pleaser child to acknowledge her needs, ask for help, go first sometimes, make decisions, and follow through. It isn't selfish to require rest; it's a necessity of life. Pleasers are good givers and lousy receivers. Help your pleaser child learn to ask for help and be the receiver. That's a part of self-care.

Watch for Bullies and Teach Kids to Handle Aggression

Pleaser children and teens can be immature and socially insecure. Pleasers can be Marty McFlys (from the movie *Back to the Future*), lacking confidence, missing social cues, laughing inappropriately, and trying hard to impress others—to no avail. They may end up bullied. Encourage them to find safe friends and resist the tendency to take refuge in adult relationships. These kids can really benefit from some martial arts training so they can experience what it feels like to push back.

Point Out Their Tendency to Minimize and Avoid Difficulties

Pleasers are voiceless and lack opinions where risk, exposure, and the possibility of rejection are involved. They need to learn to stand up for themselves, face the uncomfortable, and challenge when someone disagrees with them. Teach them to ask difficult questions and grow to tolerate difficult answers so they will not struggle so much in the adult world. They will learn to solve problems, accept paradoxes, and live in reality if you help them trade wishful idealism and magical thinking for reality and truth.

• • • • •

Jesus said, "Have you not read…, 'For this reason a man shall leave his father and mother and be joined [cleave] to his wife, and the two shall become one flesh'? So they are no longer two, but one flesh. What therefore God has joined together, let no man separate" (Matthew 19:4–6 and Genesis 2:24). Yes, you are raising your child to *leave* and someday *cleave* to his spouse and kids. As difficult as it may be, we must resist the tendency to continually look in the rearview mirror and see our little dumpling in the backseat with a Happy Meal.

One day when Kelly was a child, we watched *The Little Mermaid* together. In the final scene, as King Triton sadly watched his daughter Ariel sail off into the sunset with her new husband, Kelly began to cry. She buried her head in my shoulder and said, "I'm never going to leave my daddy." At her wedding last year, as I toasted the bride and groom, I recounted the story to her and said, "Evidently things have changed." The ultimate goal of parenting is to launch our children. As sad as it may be, are you saying to yourself, "Three, two, one, ignition"?

Eleven

The Vacillator Child

What are the signs your child may be a vacillator? Below is a list of traits a vacillator child will exhibit at different ages. See if you recognize your child in the list below, then we will discuss these traits and suggest some helpful interventions in more detail.

In Infants and Toddlers

- is typically a very sensitive baby who wants to be held a lot and cries when put down
- alternates between pursuit of attention and angry rejection of the parent; cries when a parent departs, then angry when parent returns; wants to be held but is too upset to take comfort
- is very focused on the proximity and attentiveness of the parent
- clings to a distracted parent, then rejects when parent wants to engage; may seem angry that connection is not under her control

In School-Age Kids and Teens

- experiences school anxiety: may resist going to school; fears losing Mom or being unable to monitor what's happening at home; may worry that Mom will be too lonely without him

- displays emotion or clinginess to get attention; pursues, but then is indifferent or hostile, distrustful of comfort; may test parent by demanding attention when most inconvenient to give it: "If you really love me, you'll stop everything and pay attention to me now"
- may have crushes on authority figures and is preoccupied with getting their time and attention
- has difficulty regulating negative emotions; tends to ruminate, becoming preoccupied with hurt and anger, which maintains and intensifies emotional distress
- as a teen, may act out to get attention from parents while simultaneously expressing anger at them
- idealizes then devalues; thinks the grass is always greener somewhere else; friendships, teachers, coaches are all good or all bad, with little middle ground
- desires extreme closeness; has early involvement with opposite sex; experiences intense connections, then breaks up when intensity fades

Do you see your child in the list above? Don't be alarmed. You aren't a bad parent. Whether we are adults or kids, we all have something that needs changing. Let us help you see how to encourage growth in your child.

Parents often describe the vacillator child as smart and adorable at times and then needy, clingy, frustrating, and impossible to satisfy at other times. Even as small kids, vacillators are prone to anger (or sulking if they are introverts), and this often sets up a negative pattern between parent and child. In reality, these are sensitive kids with a keen awareness of nonverbal communication and the level of attentiveness given by their moms and dads. They're sensitive to mixed messages, inconsistencies, and incongruent behavior in parents that other kids might miss.

Justin was three when his mom, Amanda, called to make an appointment with me (Kay). "This kid is putting me over the edge," Amanda explained on the phone. "He has always been demanding of my attention, but lately he won't let me out of his sight. If I have to nurse the baby or talk on the phone, he just throws a tantrum. If I pick him up, he's still mad. Yesterday he bit me when I peeled him out of my arms to drop him off at preschool. When it's time to pick him up, he ignores me and refuses to get in the car. He won't talk to me all the way home, so I just ignore him. Once we get home, he does things he knows will get him in trouble. I feel like I've lost control."

"I'd like to meet with you and your husband," I explained to Amanda. "Let me get a better understanding of your family, and we will go from there."

At our first meeting, Amanda collapsed on the couch explaining, "Larry couldn't come. His new job has a lot more travel, and he gets called out of town all the time. I've been alone since Tuesday with the kids, and I just had the usual dropping-off battle with Justin, even though he likes going to Grandma's." Amanda's phone rang and she glanced at it. "Oh, I've been trying all day to get a hold of Tina; this will only take a second," she explained. She spoke to her friend and finished with a stressed tone, then returned to me. "I coordinate the moms' group at my church, and it seems someone is never doing their job."

"Amanda, let's start by looking beyond Justin's behavior. What might be driving it? Try to think of stressors in Justin's life. Have there been any recent changes in your family or his health or environment?"

"Nothing unusual; just same old life as usual," Amanda replied without giving it much thought.

"How about your husband's travel, is that new?"

"Yeah, he got a promotion about three months ago. I guess that's a change. He didn't used to travel at all, and now he's gone a lot. It's been hard. I don't get any breaks."

"Perhaps you're a bit overwhelmed without him around as much?"

"Maybe I'm more impatient. I think I'd do okay if it weren't for Justin. He's just so frustrating."

"How has Justin responded to his dad's new schedule?"

"Every morning he asks if Daddy is coming home tonight. But by evening I don't think he really cares. He won't even talk to Larry when he calls after dinner. He cries and pushes the phone away. I send him to his room when he acts like such a brat. It hurts Larry's feelings."

Can you see how much Amanda was simply reacting to Justin's behavior rather than trying to understand what he might be feeling? How often do parents do this? How often do you do this? Negative behaviors like this are often driven by something emotionally distressing.

While she understood her feelings, she didn't understand the importance of trying to understand Justin's world. "You mentioned a baby. How old?" I asked.

"She's five months. I didn't realize how easy they are at this age until Justin got older. Justin used to be so cute. Well, he still is, but his sister is just so much easier."

"Well, she isn't saying no, or resisting you in any way yet." I smiled.

"That's true!" Amanda laughed. "I guess it's all a little harder than I expected."

"I think all parents, me included, would give a hearty amen to that," I said. I proceeded to give Amanda some observations to help her begin to see from her three-year-old's point of view. "I want you to think about all the big changes in Justin's life in the last five months. First, a new baby comes home. He has to share Mommy with a needy, new baby. He no longer has you all to himself. I tell moms it would be like your husband bringing a new woman home and telling you she's going to live here and you can both share him."

Amanda laughed. "I see your point."

"A couple of months later, Larry's gone most of the time. Another big loss for Justin. He doesn't understand why, but then September rolls around and moms' group starts up, and it seems it might take up a fair amount of your time. Is that accurate?"

As if on cue, Linda's phone rang again. She looked at it. "Tina again."

We both laughed as she silenced her phone. I could see Amanda's great sense of humor was a positive trait.

"So from Justin's point of view," I continued, "he's basically lost his two best friends. Of course he's mad about it. But who's going to help him learn how to put those feelings to words instead of just acting out? You can—by telling him you understand how he feels when you have to attend to the baby. Say, 'I know it's hard to share Mommy. You use to have Mommy all to yourself, and you didn't used to have to wait. It makes you sad and frustrated when I have to help your sister first, doesn't it? But in a few minutes, we'll look at the pictures of you when you were a baby, and I'll show you how I used to help you.' If he bites or hits, tell him, 'Justin, it's okay to be mad and tell Mommy you feel mad, but you can't hit or bite when you're mad. Hitting and biting are not allowed.' If he does it again, give him a time-out for two minutes."

Amanda nodded. "Sounds good."

"When Larry calls, you might say, 'You don't want to talk on the phone to Daddy? You wish Daddy was here to play with you, don't you? I miss Daddy too. Daddy, do you miss Justin? Daddy says yes, he misses Justin too.'"

"I've never really thought about his feelings. But it makes more sense now. You're saying I should try to be Justin, imagine what he's feeling and make some likely guesses about what his feelings are."

"Exactly," I said. "It makes Justin feel seen and understood. It also teaches him words for his feelings. Now just one more thing. I want you to really notice how preoccupied you are when you're around Justin. He sounds like a smart kid who's tuned in to how present you are with him. He may feel somewhat abandoned and invisible, even when you're around. Being busy sometimes is okay. Just make time at some point in the day where you're completely his. Help him understand when that time is and to wait for it and keep it regular. It will help him adjust to these losses."

I worked with Amanda and Larry for several months but never

needed to see Justin. His parents reported a big change in his behavior after implementing my suggestions. If they keep up the good work, Justin's vacillating style will reduce in frequency and intensity. Young children need to feel seen and understood and that they have some control to make connection happen when they need it, not just when the parent decides it's time. When parents just react to bad behavior, or take it as personal rejection or a sign of their inadequacy, an escalating negative pattern is often the result. Reactivity fuels reactivity. Understanding and validation always reduces it. I simply taught Amanda how to recognize what Justin's behavior meant and to let him know his feelings were valid and understandable.

HELPING THE VACILLATOR CHILD

- Instead of reacting, ask what the feeling or need is under the behavior. Make a guess and ask your child for clarification: "I can see you're really upset. I wonder if you're sad because Mom and Dad were fighting this morning."
- Notice indirect communication and ask for words of explanation: "You've been quiet and withdrawn this morning. I'd like to understand. Instead of showing me your feelings, describe what's going on inside with words."
- Look for ways your child may feel alone and abandoned and ask about his feelings during these times: "How do you feel when I go in my room and shut the door?" "My work is taking a lot of time; how are you handling that? I'm guessing you might feel unimportant."
- Offer times of connection she can count on and give her some control. "I'd like to take you out for dinner, just the two of us. You can pick any night next week except Wednesday. What night do you want to go?"

- Notice your level of preoccupation. How present are you when interacting with your child? How often do you make your child wait for time and attention?

- Teach your child to get sad, not mad. When your child is mad, say, "I can see you are really upset. I'll sit quietly with you until you can calm down. I want to listen and understand what you feel. Let me know when you're ready." *Always refuse to engage with a yelling child.* If he gets mean or verbally abusive, say, "I love you, but I won't sit here and listen to this. We will talk and hug when you calm down." When your child is ready to talk, use the Soul Words list and help him put words to the more vulnerable feelings: "I feel sad because my friend is mad at me and I don't know why." Hug him and don't try to fix it.

- After an upsetting episode, make it a point to initiate a time of repair and resolution. Ask about and listen to your child's feelings and experiences during and after the conflict. Seek to understand it from her perspective. Make apologies if you were out of line, and validate her feelings whenever you can.

- Help your child recognize his tendency to see situations and people as all good and then all bad. When he idealizes someone or something, help him take a realistic look at potential disappointments. When your child devalues a person or situation, help him by looking for the good there. Polarizing good and bad is like living life by an electric on/off switch, one or the other. Vacillators need to build in a dimmer switch so they have a range of responses. This is one of the most important things the vacillator child needs help with.

- Help your child with her rejection sensitivity. Vacillators feel rejected when others need space, have other interests, or differing opinions. Vacillators desire to be special and exclusive, to prevent feelings of abandonment or rejection. Vacillators need to give others the freedom to be different without taking it as personal rejection.

- What bad habit have you modeled that you need to apologize for and change? Make it a point to do this.

It would be helpful to read about the vacillator in *How We Love* to better understand your child. Then look through the corresponding workbook chapter, especially the list suggestions for living with a vacillator. And be encouraged! Change may not happen overnight, but if you take it slow and just keep going, eventually you can override your child's vacillator tendencies.

HELPING SCHOOL-AGE KIDS AND TEENS

As vacillators get older and enter the junior high and teen years, their reactivity and anger can cause havoc in a home. Often, the family starts being extra careful not to set them off. Kendra was thirteen when her parents called for help after they discovered inappropriate e-mails with an eighteen-year-old boy. After interviewing the parents, I determined Kendra was a vacillator. While both her parents loved her, they described her as a drama queen whose moods ruled the family. While many thirteen-year-old girls could fit this description, it had been a pattern since Kendra was a toddler.

Other family dynamics that create a vacillator style were also apparent as family therapy progressed. Kendra's mom, Connie, was also a vacillator. The family pattern of interaction that repeated over and over was intense episodes of arguing and reactivity between Connie and Kendra or Connie and her husband, Chris (an avoider). Yelling, name-calling, and hurtful words were common. Finally, everyone would go off to their corners, and over several hours to several days, the fighting pair would just get over it and resume relationship as if nothing had happened. There was no resolution. Reactivity without resolution is a common theme in homes with vacillators, so family relationships are either really good or really bad, without much middle ground. Intensity is a part of the fighting stage (which is a connection of sorts), and then denial of the bad episode is part of the good phase.

What's missing from a family like this is any sort of true repair or resolution after a conflict. No one feels understood, listened to, or validated, and wounds aren't tended to and mended. They're put out of sight and ignored. No apologies from Connie, though she required them from Kendra and Chris after a blowup, and double standards like these only add to the unresolved hurt. Connie apologized indirectly by taking Kendra shopping or buying her something, and she didn't realize her guilt led to rewarding Kendra's reactive behavior.

Kendra was now looking for intense connections outside the family. She idealized this eighteen-year-old stranger as the "love of her life," describing their interactions as exhilarating. She admitted she was very preoccupied with the next encounter. Hiding it from her parents made it even more exciting. Kendra is beginning to replicate her family patterns, mistaking intensity for intimacy and being easily let down. Volatility is just around the corner as reality sets in.

I'm not much for therapy with adolescents. But family therapy with teens, where the dysfunctional communication patterns can be addressed and the family can learn to listen, validate, and resolve, is often very helpful. Older kids who are vacillators need essentially the same thing as younger kids. For real change to take place, parents have to be willing to see their contributions.

Kendra was mad for a good reason. She learned reactivity from her mom. Kendra could remember being eight years old and deciding to fight back with hurtful words when her mom was rash and unkind. Most all vacillator kids have experienced some sort of abandonment. Being ignored after a fight is very painful to kids and leaves them feeling alone, unseen, and misunderstood. Parental withdrawal for any reason leaves kids guessing and waiting for it to end.

Vacillator kids need consistent connection they can count on and consistent boundaries, especially when they're angry. In the *How We Love* workbook, there's a section for the vacillator with suggestions for growth. An important goal for the vacillator is to get sad, not mad. Express hurt, not anger. Connie and Kendra eventually learned to use anger as a signal to stop, get the Soul Words list, and express more vulnerable feelings.

Connie began to own the effects of her reactivity and listen compassionately to some of Kendra's childhood memories of feeling alone and scared when her mom was mad. Connie's sincere apologies and increasing ownership of her own contribution lessened Kendra's anger considerably. Both parents also acknowledged the effects on Kendra of their marital fights, which was very healing.

The family realized they communicated more through behavior than words. Instead of asking for time or attention, Kendra hoped her mom would guess what her moods meant and do the right thing to make her feel better. When this didn't happen, Kendra got mad and picked a fight. Learning to ask, "What's the feeling and need underneath this behavior?" was important for this family.

Twelve

Controller and Victim Children

C andi fumbled through the bathroom medicine cabinet for the bottle of aspirin. Her pounding headache wasn't being improved by three-year-old Caleb, pounding on the door screaming for her. He'd missed his nap when Candi's Bible study group ran late, and now he was in one of his moods. She'd spent all afternoon paying bills, but a few would have to wait, and she was scared to tell her husband they were short. Somehow that was always her fault.

"Leave me alone, Caleb. Can't you see I'm in the bathroom? Go find you sister. You're driving me crazy. Clare, for once could you be useful and get your brother out of here?"

Six-year-old Clare lay sprawled across the couch, her eyes glued to the blaring screen. Suddenly the bathroom door flew open, knocking Caleb to the ground. His fit rose to furious screams, and Clare sat up and gave her mom a terrified look as Candi bolted toward her and grabbed her arm.

"You've been home from school for two hours, and all you've done is sit there and watch that stupid TV. I told you to come get your brother, but do you do it? *No!* Of course not. I have to do everything around here."

Clare sat motionless in a hypnotic trance, staring at her shoes. Caleb raged down the hall, swinging at his mom. Suddenly, Candi heard the warning sound that made her chest tighten—the garage door being opened. "Oh no, your dad's home early. Clare, quickly pick up these toys or Daddy's going to get mad. Quick."

Clare sprang from the couch and began frantically dumping toys into the laundry basket. Candi swung Caleb up on her hip and ran into the kitchen, grabbing pots to create the illusion of dinner being prepared. "Quiet down, Caleb. It's okay, baby. Stop crying. Sh. Daddy doesn't want to come home to a crying baby."

Leon entered and headed straight to his chair. He dropped into it and yelled down the hall, "Candi, I'm home."

Clare obediently gave her dad a kiss and then backed down the hall and disappeared into her room. She grabbed her bear and wrapped herself in her bedspread, organizing all her other stuffed animals in a protective circle around her. The rest of the evening depended on Dad's mood. Most likely her parents would fight, and her dad would yell at her mom. Clare's stomach hurt. She wondered how bad it would be this time. She whispered to her bear, "If Daddy yells, we can put our heads under the pillow and sing. Nobody will find us." She began to count her animals over and over to distract herself from the ticking bomb beyond her bedroom door.

Candi handed Leon a drink and put Caleb down. "Where's my kiss?" Leon demanded. Candi obediently leaned over and kissed him. "Your turn, Caleb," Leon said as he held out his arms to Caleb. "Come give Daddy a kiss."

"No," yelled Caleb, glaring at Leon.

Leon laughed. "You little tough guy. Get over here and give Daddy a kiss."

"No," repeated Caleb, kicking the chair where Leon was sitting.

"Is that the best you can do, little man?" Leon said. "Are you going to give Daddy a kiss or do I have to come get it?"

"No," Caleb said again, and he picked up a toy car and tried to fling it at Leon's head, but Candi caught his hand.

"Caleb!"

"Let him go," Leon rumbled, glaring. In a flash, he grabbed the boy's shirt and dragged him down the hall. "You need to learn a little respect, tough guy." Leon pushed Caleb into his room and slammed the door. "Come out, and you'll get the whipping of your life," yelled Leon. Caleb opened the door, screaming with defiant rage.

"Go rest," coaxed Candi as she pushed past Leon into Caleb's room. "I'll take care of Caleb."

"Those kids are brats because you don't make them listen," Leon yelled as he went back to his chair. "I don't want to see that kid for the rest of the night."

This is a chaotic home. Leon and Candi attend church, but their difficult upbringings have left scars. Behind their closed door, Mom and Dad switch back and forth between the roles of victim and controller.

Candi's unexpressed anger at Leon often leaks out on the kids. She's often depressed and overwhelmed as Leon's expectations are high, and he gets very angry when his rules are broken. Leon's favorite line is, "God made me the leader; why can't you accept that?" Candi switches from controller to victim when Leon comes home. The children see her as both frightening and frightened. She is afraid of Leon and tries to appease him, victimized by his emotional abuse, which can turn violent if he's had a hard day at work. He also drinks to take the edge off, which can lead to more aggression.

Leon is afraid of only one person: his dad, who runs the family business. Leon is the victim around his dad, stuffing his anger daily as his dad storms around the office lashing out at Leon for anything that goes wrong. When Leon comes home, he's fed up and angry, and slugs down a few beers to calm down.

And so the cycle continues.

Leon and Candi love their kids. But they're teaching their kids exactly what they learned in their families, and they have no good experiences or models to draw from. Both parents are highly reactive, and it doesn't take much stress to set them off. Both have a lot of unprocessed grief from their own childhood experiences that they've never addressed.

Since Clare's personality is more timid, she deals by trying to comply, retreating, numbing her emotions, and creating an imaginary world. She's learning to surrender, avoid conflict, and dissociate: the traits of a victim. Dr. Bruce Perry, a specialist in childhood trauma, reports that girls more often cope with trauma by internalizing and dissociating.

Caleb is more strong-willed and copes by fighting back. Following trauma, boys more often show signs of hyperarousal, hyperactivity, impulsivity, and vigilance, notes Perry. Continued chaos will cause Caleb to be in a persistent state of fear, and over time he'll become more reactive and "will very easily be moved from being mildly anxious to feeling threatened to being terrorized."[1] If nothing changes, Caleb will get more impulsive and hostile as he grows up and likely become an angry, reactive controller.

Of course, depending on personalities, in some cases the male may become the victim and the female the controller. But what creates a *chaotic* home containing either victim(s), controller(s), or both?

First and foremost, the parents did not get what they needed as kids to help them become secure adults. So it's accurate to say that these are adults who are still kids on the inside trying to parent their own kids. Sometimes it's hard to tell from behavior and responses who the kid is and who the adult is.

Controllers and victims come from families with severe marital discord between parents, whether or not divorce occurs. Stepparents or stepsiblings with whom there's hostility, distrust, or a lack of connection can contribute. Mental instability of a parent or a sibling can keep the home in an unpredictable state of discord. Job loss, financial stress, and multiple moves may add to the stress as well. And sometimes things happen outside the home that turn a kid's world upside down.

Sometimes trauma interrupts bonding or causes a child to become a controller or victim. Any adoption is a trauma of sorts, as it requires a separation. Trauma can begin in the womb as well, if a mom uses drugs or alcohol, or is chronically stressed. Foster care and orphanages may not provide all a baby needs to bond and develop. Even if the care is good, the baby suffers loss once again when moved to her adoptive parents.

Bullying can be another source of trauma. Children and teens can be very cruel and unrelenting. Most of the time, tormented youngsters internalize their pain, and no one knows what is happening until it's too late.[2] Parents, don't be naive. Always be on the lookout for abuse between siblings and peers.

Sexual harassment or molestation can also greatly affect a child's ability to trust and bond. Our daughter Amy was around six when a friend, whose house she was playing at, pushed her into the bedroom where her parents were having sex. The dad exploded at the two girls standing in the bedroom and Amy was terrified. She didn't have words to describe what she saw and didn't tell us what happened, but we began to see a change in her behavior. She'd wet the bed and have nightmares, waking up at night crying. She refused to have anything to do with me (Milan) and only wanted Mom to tuck her in bed and hug her. I felt rejected and tried to do things with her, which only made her more resistant and distant.

Six long months later, in casual conversation, her friend's mother revealed the incident, and in one moment, all of Amy's behavior made sense. Kay remembers holding Amy, trying to help her make sense of what she saw and her reaction to pushing her daddy away. Amy burst into tears and sobbed in Kay's arms for a long time.

The symptoms soon abated, but they left their mark. It took time for her to trust again. Her world had become unsafe in one volatile moment. She was victimized, and for a time became victimlike in her behavior. When you see a child revert to extreme shyness or regress developmentally, don't give up until you discover the source.

Abusive situations can be another source of stress for children. When our kids were small, a lady who lived below us baby-sat a group of toddlers. Kay had a clear view of her backyard, and once all the drop-offs were complete, the toddlers were shoved outside and the sliding door was shut. They cried at the door to no avail. They may have had loving, attentive parents at home, but they were traumatized daily in the day care. The children were too young to tell anyone what was going on, but an anonymous report ended this woman's career as a baby-sitter.

In Infants

What signs does a small child exhibit as a controller or victim? In abused, neglected, or traumatized infants and toddlers, a chaotic home will produce symptoms that exist on a continuum of mild to severe. And controller or victim tendencies will become more apparent during school and teen years.

- maintains poor eye contact with limited responsiveness; an apathetic distant look or trancelike state can be signs of early dissociative symptoms
- cries inconsolably; has a weak cry or has difficulty being soothed
- often has a frightened, wide-eyed look; is easily startled and/ or goes rigid
- has eating and digestive problems; fails to thrive and gain weight
- is indifferent and lacks reciprocal smile response

In Toddlers and Preschoolers

- is anxious, clingy, hypervigilant (on guard), and overly observant about new settings and strange people; has severe separation anxiety and displays panic when left by parent or caretaker
- appears apprehensive around the parent

- has contradictory behaviors; approaches parent, then appears disoriented and avoids parent
- experiences night terrors, poor sleep patterns, bedwetting; has more than age-appropriate fear of the dark
- will hide and isolate self; is easily shamed and embarrassed
- has eating and digestion issues, often refusing to eat or overeating; youngsters from abuse or impoverished backgrounds may hoard and hide food, a sign they don't trust their basic needs will be met
- exhibits bizarre soothing behaviors; rocking, scratching, head-banging, tapping, and chanting
- displays outbursts of anger, meltdowns, tantrums, and aggressive behavior
- suffers with developmental delays

Extreme neglect and mistreatment can result in profound problems or delays, which are very resistant to treatments. Fear is the predominant feeling these kids deal with, and without safety, an infant or toddler cannot learn to trust.

In School-Age Kids and Teens

By the time Caleb and Clare enter school, they will have lived all their young lives in an environment with too much stress. Their brains are literally organizing and developing in response to a chaotic environment. Yelling, fighting, violence, unpredictable behavior, and sudden mood changes develop different coping mechanisms. Victims deal with high levels of anxiety by freezing and moving into an internal world to escape. Controllers become highly provoked, and the fight-or-flight response kicks in, making them impulsive and aggressive.

As these kids grow, their tendency to lean toward a victim or controller will become more apparent. Some kids take abuse passively until teen years and then explode in violent combat with the dominant parent. Other kids, like Caleb, fight back and resist from an early age. Here's what to look for as these kids get older.

Learning Problems and Disorganized Thoughts and Speech

For chaotic children and teens whose brains have been organized around "fright without solution," their ability to store and retrieve information efficiently is compromised. Chronic anxiety makes learning difficult, if not impossible. When anxious and overwhelmed, kids have difficulty remembering instructions and may experience dizziness, nausea, or panic. When a victim gets anxious in school, she will daydream and space out, whereas controllers will be fidgety, impulsive, and reactive. Both will have great difficulty focusing.

Coherent verbal expression can be difficult for chaotic kids, as their thoughts may be scattered and disjointed, randomly jumping from topic to topic in an erratic way. Victims will mumble or speak softly, perhaps robotically, while controllers are more likely to chatter incessantly to try to gain attention or control. Even handwriting can appear chaotic, messy, and disorganized. Often I will receive letters from *New Life Live* radio listeners, and I can tell the person is a chaotic controller or victim by how my name is addressed on the front of the envelope.

Poor Socialization

Controllers and victims can struggle with socially inappropriate behavior. Chaotic children and teens are highly insecure and have not learned social skills at home to help them fit in and relate to their peers. Therefore they are impressionable and easily swayed by others' opinions and actions. The controller's exploitation of others' weakness is developed early in childhood. The victim's weakness is obvious to peers, which invites bullying, teasing, victimizing, and often sexual exploitation.

Lack of Empathy

Chaotic children do not experience empathy or comfort from their parents. There is no tender response to the stress and anxiety these kids endure. Their chaotic home teaches them that adults are stress makers, not stress relievers: parents are necessary for survival but are dangerous and unpredictable. Since children must receive comfort and empathy before they can learn to give it, controllers are aggressive, without remorse or sympathy for the pain they inflict. Victims distract, count, space out, and go into their internal world when someone is upset.

Traumatic Play

I (Kay) treated a woman who grew up in a violent home. She remembered beating her dolls and punishing them in cruel ways. She often acted out scenarios of escape and dramatic rescue with her stuffed animals. Kids reenact their trauma in play, trying to master and make sense of their experiences. Sometimes they assume the role of the powerful perpetrator to feel some sense of relief over their helplessness. In extreme cases there may be fascination with evil, fire, gore, knives, weapons, or cruelty to animals. Violent video games are another way to numb out and become the conqueror of evil or the executor of malevolence.

Lying and Stealing

Controllers and victims learn early on to lie in order to avoid harsh punishments. It's an adaptive response and can become such a habit that a bold-faced lie will be maintained in spite of obvious contrary evidence. Both types of kids will struggle with eye contact, unless they are lying. Intense, concentrated eye contact is often part of telling a lie. Stealing is a way to have what you want immediately, without depending on anyone else.

Addictions

Controller and victim kids have a lot of pain in their histories. This makes them an easy prey for addictions of all sorts. All addictions are an attempt to find relief through elevating a depressed mood or soothing agitation. Addictions provide distraction and relief from pain. If controller/victim kids don't learn people can be a source of relief, they will most likely turn to addictions to find it. Many *New Life Live* radio callers and clients share stories of becoming addicted to drugs and alcohol at an early age. Sadly, many were introduced to it by their parents.

UNIQUE SIGNS OF A CONTROLLER CHILD

Many chaotic kids will challenge the dominant parent and fight back no matter what the cost, even from a young age. Some kids comply until the anger builds and begin to fight back as teens. They will exhibit some behaviors that are different from the child who is becoming a victim.

Manipulative and Superficially Charming
Some more extroverted kids may learn control is possible through charm and deceit. These are the con artists in the making, who use their magnetic personalities to lure their victims into their control.

Anger, Fighting, and Bullying
Realize this: controllers start out as victims. As they grow up, they master their world by becoming controllers themselves, displacing their anger on others who are weaker. Anger is a powerful feeling and distracts from any vulnerable feelings that are uncomfortable and unwanted. Controlling kids and teens may vent their anger on younger siblings or neighborhood kids who are weaker.

Lawbreaking: Destructive to Property, Self, and Others
With consciences numbed and impulses unchecked, controlling teens think nothing of stealing, shoplifting, lying, vandalizing, cheating, and creating the chaos to which they are accustomed. In their homes growing up, the rules were not fair, and now as teens, they don't play by the rules.

High levels of adrenaline are normal in these kids, and risk-taking elevates adrenaline, which feels normal. Adrenaline rushes themselves thrill, distract, and medicate. For many controllers, the shiny badge of the law is the first boundary with consequences they have ever experienced.

Sexualized Behavior

Controller males become sexually active very early and, with the onset of puberty, can quickly become addicted to sex as a pleasurable mood-altering activity. Masturbation, pornography, and sexual exploitation of others may become a routine part of daily life.

Unique Signs of a Victim Child

Boys and girls who survive childhood trying to be invisible may cope by detaching, numbing, distracting, and spacing out. As school-age kids and teens, their paths will take a different turn from the controller.

Detached

This is the primary defense of the victim. Anxiety always precedes disconnecting. I worked with a male who grew up in a chaotic home. He remembers often retreating into a book or talking with his imaginary friends. He told me, "I realize I spent much of my childhood in my room in a fantasy world where I could control the events and tune out reality." When a child or adolescent "goes away" in this manner, they often have poor observational skills and have difficulty focusing on the present.

Low Common Sense

Victims are accustomed to danger, so their alarm system is broken. Their response to danger growing up was to stay physically present and escape mentally. When faced with a threat outside their home, they cope the same way. Abused children are taught to disregard their needs, and hence are more vulnerable to abuse outside the home as well. Victims often retain a childlike demeanor even into adulthood, so they are easy targets for predators to pick out.

Victims don't have good judgment about who to trust. As teens, they are quick to jump fully into relationships and untested alliances with others where trustworthiness is never questioned. The inability to assert themselves, have opinions, or hold their ground keeps victims in a place of excessive dependence upon others.

Low Self-Esteem and Anger Turned Inward
The victim tries harder than the controller to please her parents, even though it's an impossible task. She feels angry at herself for "not getting it right," and her sensitive temperament makes her more prone to believe the unkind remarks her parents make. She's likely to struggle with anxiety and depression throughout life as a result of her chaotic childhood. She may even resort to cutting or hitting herself. Self-mutilation can become addictive as it releases endorphins that alleviate a depressed mood.

Overly Compliant and Can't Set Boundaries or Make Decisions
A lack of confidence makes the teenage victim dependent, needing someone controlling to make decisions and take charge. They offer little to no resistance when pressured, which can give rise to excessive servitude or revictimization. Do not interpret this type of child as ideal. If you are not getting any pushback when you push a child or teen, something is wrong.

Promiscuous or Fearful of Sex
Female victims may realize early in life that sex gets the attention of men. In some cases teenage victims may dress provocatively to get attention. Others may go the opposite direction—refusing to embrace their gender and sexuality by hiding behind baggy clothes and gaining weight, with the hope of repelling attention.

Anxiety-Based Disorders

Adolescent victims continue to experience high levels of anxiety. Compulsive organizing and cleaning or obsessive behaviors such as rocking, pacing, picking at their skin, pulling hair, nail biting, excessive exercise, ticks, and unusual mannerisms may all serve to relieve anxiety and give some sense of control. Since victims internalize their stress, they may also struggle with health problems, eating disorders, social anxiety, and depression.

First, Help Yourself

Whether you are a biological parent, grandparent, stepparent, foster parent, adoptive parent, or guardian, our hearts go out to you. More than anything, patience and time are required to turn this around. If the cause of chaotic attachment is "fright without solution" or safety, then the cure must require the opposite: *safety* with *solutions*. Sounds simple, but for a person raised in a chaotic home, it's just words on paper. How can parents give something they know nothing about?

If you relate to controller/victim kids and your parents exhibited some of the same behaviors, you may now know that you *can* and *must* have empathy for yourself first of all. Please take this to heart. To help yourself and your kids, begin to come to terms with the effects of your traumatic childhood. If you don't have empathy for yourself and what you went through, you cannot see how you hurt your children in the same way. You need the exact same thing your child needs: safety with solutions.

The rest of these suggestions will help, but remember to first focus on developing your memories and sharing your early struggles with someone you trust. Airlines instruct parents to put their oxygen masks on first in the case of emergencies, and then on their children. Why? Because you may pass out due to lack of oxygen, and then you're both in trouble. In the same way, to help your children, you must make sure you have help and professional support to find the healing and strength you need to become a great mother or father. You can't help that your childhood was difficult, but you can help how you respond. You need to be responsible and honest with yourself now that you're a parent and accept help to face the challenge.

Find a mentor, classes, and groups to help. You can't undo a chaotic background without guidance. Find a family with great kids, share your background, and ask for help. Older moms and dads you respect can help advise you. Make yourself accountable to them and let them mentor you on your journey as a parent. Seek out classes on marriage, parenting, and family. The purpose of small groups within a Christian community, or recovery programs in local churches, is to help move you in a positive direction as a parent.

You need a new "family" that will help you continue to grow up, so you can become a better parent. Community centers offer classes and services as well. If you have an addiction, join a group and get a sponsor who can be supportive of your journey toward sobriety. Read our first book, *How We Love,* and apply yourself to the workbook section designed to help you grow.

No matter the age of your children, there are things you can do that are essential to help reverse the effects of a chaotic home. Let's look at these first, and then later we will discuss what can help prevent the child from becoming a controller or victim. Whether you have a toddler or teen, the comfort circle near the end of the book is your guide. Consider it the universal antidote for all emotional wounds. Also, reread the growth goals for the controller parent at the end of chapter 6, which will help you to keep focused on making the most important changes at each stage in the process.

Another important step is to learn to be present. To be present is the opposite of being absent. Abandonment may be familiar, but successful parenting demonstrates availability to the child. Your child needs to know that you will never abandon him and you aren't too self-absorbed to see and know him. This includes attentiveness when you're with him, instead of being checked out, dismissive, neglectful, or reactive with him. Promise you'll be there and earn his trust, day by day. Eventually, he will trust you, and security will be developed. When you are detached, or angry and reactive, you cannot be present. Notice when your chest tightens and try to breathe.

Find comfort and security for your own anxiety. To help children process their thoughts and feelings, you have to first know how to do this yourself. Security develops every time you talk your way around the comfort circle with someone close to you. Security comes from higher levels of self-awareness. This in turn leads to bonding, safety, trust, and healing. Then, every time you console your child and provide comfort, you help her make sense of her world. It's a confusing world to adults, let alone to a child. When we reassure, reframe, and address issues truthfully, explain as best as we can, confess, and apologize when necessary, we eliminate shame and bring relationship into the light where there is healing for all.

Finally, become a protector of your child. No baby or child can feel safe or learn to trust in a fearful environment. Finding a shelter or safe house may be an important first step. If you are a parent, your child deserves to be protected from violence and harm.

You can also protect your child from anxiety by creating predictability and routine. When Fred Rogers died, I listened to the tributes of adults who sought refuge in the orderliness of his daily routine on *Mister Rogers' Neighborhood*. He was kind and calm and created a highly structured and predictable routine in his shows. According to researchers, this is the kind of thing that yields healthier emotional functioning.

The other part of protecting your child is in reducing power struggles at home, with your spouse and with your child. This means you should avoid parenting systems that require "first-time obedience." Instead, give children options and allow them to make decisions: "You have a choice: you can take a long bath tonight or a quick shower in the morning before school. Which would you prefer?" Power struggles and excessive discipline will get you nowhere fast. We highly recommend the book

Parenting with Love and Logic as your guide. *Parenting Teens with Love and Logic* has wonderful tools for parenting older kids. *The Connected Child* by Karyn Purvis, David Cross, and Wendy Lyons Sunshine is also very helpful.

HELPING INFANTS

Silvia came to see me (Kay) after she heard me speak at a Mothers of Preschoolers meeting. She asked to see me privately, explaining she felt unattached to her four-month-old baby daughter, Megan. I asked Silvia to bring the baby to our first session. When Silvia arrived at my office, the baby was sleeping, and Silvia left her in the carrier. As we talked she told me sad stories of her chaotic upbringing. Just as we began to talk about Megan, the baby began to stir. "I don't know what's wrong, but I don't feel close to her," Silvia explained. "Maybe I don't have a mothering instinct. Megan is such a little manipulator, and it makes me angry. You'll see; the queen bee is waking up."

I watched Silvia's anxiety rise as she tried to get Megan back to sleep, bouncing the car seat and fiddling with the pacifier. "No matter what I do, it's not going to be enough to make her happy," Silvia complained. Megan began to cry, and after trying to talk over her for a few minutes, Silvia lifted her out of the car seat and began bouncing her baby on one knee. Megan continued to whimper. "See? I can't make her happy. Whatever I try, she doesn't like it." Finally, Silvia put the baby back in the seat and pulled a bottle out of her diaper bag and held it for Megan, who happily gulped it down.

I handed Silvia a list of soul words. "How do you feel when you can't seem to satisfy Megan?" I asked.

"Angry," Silvia said without looking at the list.

"Use the list to see what else you feel," I encouraged.

"Helpless, hopeless, afraid," Silvia said.

"Silvia, I think the past may be intruding on the present. You told me a little while ago you could never make your mom happy. Did you feel helpless, hopeless, and afraid when you were a little girl and tried to make your mom happy to no avail?"

"Every day, until I got smart enough to quit trying," Silvia replied.

"Could it be that Megan makes you feel the same way and dredges up those old feelings? You described your mom as someone who was hard to please and always wanted things her way. That's kind of like a 'queen bee,' isn't it? You never felt close to your mom, and if Megan's a stand-in for your mom, bringing up the same feelings, you conclude you can never feel close to her either. I think this may contribute to why you feel so much stress as a new mom. It's hard to enjoy Megan when you are stressed and feel little-girl feelings inside." Silvia sat and stared at me, then at Megan. I sat quietly, letting her soak it in.

"Wow, I just felt this total shift happening inside me. It's like I'm seeing Megan for the first time, without the mom glasses on," she said.

Silvia continued to work with me, separating the past from the present and learning to recognize and lower her anxiety. She began to relax and realize Megan was just trying to communicate what she needed. Without help, Silvia's past could have profoundly affected her ability to connect to her child. Silvia's fear about not being able to "do it right" prevented her from being able to love and enjoy Megan. What will parents, like Silvia, from chaotic homes have to do to become good parents to infants? Like Silvia, you first have to help yourself.

- Make a list of anything and everything that might make you feel tense, insecure, or fearful in your role as a new parent. Your baby cannot thrive when you are constantly stressed, afraid, and overwhelmed. Make every effort to remove, change, or eliminate these stressors.
- Realize your baby's crying may be triggering unresolved pain from your childhood. Use the Soul Words list to help you discover what feelings are created and how those feelings might relate to your experiences as a child.

- Parenting produces feelings of uncertainty and anxiety in *all* moms and dads. It's normal to feel overwhelmed. Remember, feeling overwhelmed is the story of your childhood, so it reminds you of painful times when you were helpless as a child. Try to separate the past from the present, and remember that you can reach out for help in ways you couldn't when you were little.

- If you use strong negative words to describe your baby (like Silvia did), your baby is probably triggering old childhood feelings. Infants don't know how to manipulate, control, or be selfish. They are trying to let you know what they need.

- Get help and training to learn to understand how babies communicate.

- Feelings of anger and rage at your baby or toddler are almost always related to your chaotic background. Use the Soul Words list to determine the painful, more vulnerable feelings under the anger.

- Let yourself cry and grieve for your difficult experiences as a child.

- Babies need a lot of holding, cuddling, rocking, and soothing. Try not to let your baby cry it out. Make eye contact, smile, and talk softly to your baby.

HELPING TODDLERS AND PRESCHOOLERS

- Make it your goal to be present and calm rather than detached or reactive. Take five deep breaths when you tilt in either direction.

- When your toddler resists you, remember that is a normal part of development. Don't scream, yell, tease, or provoke your toddler.

- When you check out or scare them, tell them what happened and apologize. "I'm sorry, I wasn't paying attention. Tell me again." "I got too angry, and you don't deserve that; I'm sorry."
- Get help to understand what appropriate expectations are for the age of your child.
- Many times toddlers refuse to come, resist affection, or don't listen. Don't take this personally. You may overreact if it reminds you of rejection or dismissal when you were little.
- Notice when your toddler is scared. She may freeze, stare, or watch you with wide, frightened eyes. The pupils in her eyes may be extra large and dilated, or extra tiny. If you place your hand on her chest, you will feel a fast, pounding heart. Soothe and comfort your child and talk about what scared her, even if you think she is too young to understand.

HELPING SCHOOL-AGE KIDS AND TEENS

Should you happen to have taken on a chaotically attached child or teen midstream, continue to talk through your childhood and anxieties using the comfort circle, as well as all the infant and toddler suggestions listed above. Don't assume you have a teenager; instead, regard the new member of your family as fifteen going on five.

Keep in mind that your child's entire life has been organized around trauma, abuse, and neglect, and without some drama going on, he will feel nervous and unsettled. He is used to daily high doses of adrenaline, and without it, he might pick a fight or act out to feel normal again. This is why an authoritarian combative approach may only add fuel to the fire. Instead, remain present and engaging, but take the softer approach. Sit on the floor, avert your gaze, and say, "Wow, that was interesting. Your behaviors tell me you are really upset. What are your feelings right now? I'll be quiet and wait for your answer."

Validate Their Anger and Pain

Controlling, aggressive kids often have very good reasons to be angry. Remember, when they were little, they were very afraid before they became angry. No one helped them with that fear and terror. Validate the hurts and traumas that have contributed to their anger and acting out. Offer empathy and comforting words, even when your child denies the hurt. Talk about the pain under the anger, and make guesses as to what the feelings underneath might be.

"I notice everyone in the family is really irritating you tonight. I can see you're angry, but under that you probably feel sad, because your dad promised to show up to your game and he didn't come. Maybe you are afraid your dad will never make you a priority. I would love to talk to you about that, if you want to." The controlling kid will most likely dismiss this and walk away, but he'll think about it. Slowly, you're teaching him to pay attention to the deeper feelings. Seek your child out in a quiet moment, and ask again if he wants to talk about it.

I know a family who adopted a teen from a chaotic background. She has dramatic episodes of anger and unkind words about every three weeks. Afterward, she crawls into bed with her adoptive mom, and they have some of their best talks. She is learning there is a lot of grief underneath all that anger.

Don't Engage with a Yelling Kid

Controller kids are masters at provoking anger in others. Don't take the bait. Keep breathing. Gently and softly say, "We never get anywhere when we are both angry. I'll be glad to talk to you when you calm down." Then, be quiet. If you are consistent, he will eventually believe you won't engage in a war with words. If the controlling kid gets violent or dangerous, call the police. Sometimes he needs to know you are not the final authority. One teen we know made a big turnaround after he spent a week in juvenile hall. It was the hardest decision his parents ever made, but he learned there are consequences that extend outside the home for out-of-control behavior.

Major on the Majors, Minor on the Minors

If you have five pages of rules, you'll stay in constant battle to enforce them. The most important goal is to get to the pain and fear under all the anger. It's the cause of the anger, and until the pain is acknowledged, embraced, and released, the anger will serve as a defense to keep the pain locked down and buried.

Notice When Your Victim Child Spaces Out

This can be surprisingly subtle and hard to detect. Withdrawal, downward eyes, difficulty articulating thoughts and feelings, or eyes that seem to look through you, can all be signs your child is retreating. Lower your voice, use a gentle tone, and say, "You seem like you're closing down. I want to make it safe for you to stay here with me and tell me what's upsetting you." Touch her gently (if she can tolerate touch) and say, "It's okay to stay here with me."

Ask her to describe the physical sensations of "leaving." We have often heard it described as feeling lightheaded or dizzy, floating, or like seeing things on a movie screen. Some say they have tunnel vision, and others have trouble thinking. Many times the victim has never articulated these sensations and associated them with feeling stressed, afraid, or overwhelmed. It has become so automatic that the victim sometimes doesn't realize it's happening. Help your child understand this is how she learned to cope with too much stress when she was little.

If your behaviors as a parent are highly reactive, you will have to manage your stress better, or your child will have a good reason to retreat.

Help Your Victim Child with Assertiveness

Victim kids don't have any pushback. Give them words, encouragement, and support to say no, set boundaries, give opinions, and make decisions. For example, you could say, "You had the TV remote first, and you just let your brother grab it out of your hands. It's okay to say, 'Caleb, don't grab the remote. I'll give you a turn when my program is over.' You say the words, and I'll support you." Victim kids need help and support to speak up. Don't fight their battles for them. Instead, role-play or have them say the words out loud.

Help Him Acknowledge and Express Anger

Somewhere in the past the victim child has experienced anger as threatening, dangerous, and overwhelming. Victim kids turn anger inward toward themselves, and they need to learn anger can be expressed outwardly in appropriate ways. They may not understand anger can be helpful and constructive if kept within reasonable bounds. Have your child practice expressing anger in appropriate ways.

Help Your Child Grieve

Victim kids have painful histories, but they are often too shut-down to connect to the feelings of those events. Often, there was no comfort or tenderness for the difficulties they faced. Make time to go around the comfort circle, and use the Soul Words list to help your child process painful events. Watch carefully for his tendency to close down when you are helping him in this way. Go at a pace he can tolerate, and sit quietly and hold him if he cries.

Teach Your Child to Ask for Help

Many times the victim child hoped for help and no help was given. Now, she doesn't expect it. It may not even occur to her to ask for help. This is another area where she needs help and practice. Look for times when your victim child is struggling on her own, and have her practice asking for help from you or others.

● ● ● ● ●

Remember that victims and controllers can switch from one style to the other, so if you notice controller or victim tendencies in your child, all these suggestions for growth will be appropriate. With victims, remember, it was feelings of fear and even terror that caused them to withdraw, detach, and move into an internal world. If this has become a well-developed method of coping, it's going to take time to draw them out into the open where they can learn to trust, acknowledge their pain, and learn what comfort feels like. Because they internalize their pain, it's tragically easy for them to view themselves as bad, flawed, unlovable, and thus deserving of what they get. No child can come out of hiding when it's dangerous to do so.

It's easy to see why chaotic homes tend to repeat generation after generation. But change is possible. If you are caring for a child raised in this kind of home, you can be the transitional caregiver. Help from you can affect generations to come.

You can break the cycle. And if not you, then who?

Unique Children

Thirteen

The Introverted Child

We've asked thousands of people, "How many of you who are introverts felt known, understood, and accepted by your parents when you were growing up?"

Less than 5 percent of introverts in our audiences can raise their hands to that one. The overwhelming majority feel that their parents did not know or understand them. This should be a wake-up call to all parents with an introvert in their family. We *must* do better with these kids.

But what are introverts? And why do so few feel known and understood by their parents?

Basically, introversion describes a number of common temperament preferences, primarily, how a person refuels and gathers energy in life and interactions with others.[1] The word *shy* is often used to describe an introvert. In her book *The Introvert Advantage,* Marti Laney makes an important distinction between *introversion* and *shyness.* She says:

> Introversion…is a healthy capacity to tune into your inner world. It is a constructive and creative quality that is found in many independent thinkers whose contributions have enriched the world. Introverts have social skills, they like people, and they enjoy some types of socializing. However, party chitchat depletes their energy while giving them little in return.
>
> Shyness is social anxiety, an extreme self-consciousness when one is around people.… It is not an issue of energy; it is a lack of

confidence in social situations. It is a fear of what others think of you. It produces sweating, shaking, red face or neck, racing heart, self-criticism, and a belief that people are laughing at you.

If an introverted child is continually pushed or criticized for being introverted, he or she can become shy, inhibited, or afraid. If extroverted children are shamed, criticized, or humiliated, they also can develop shyness.[2]

Introverts commonly:[3]

- feel drained from a lot of interaction; prefer a few close friends and feel lonely and sometimes overstimulated in a crowd; gain energy from private time and need space to be alone.
- have a strong internal processing preference and verbalize only necessary information; gain insight and come to conclusions independently; listen and observe more than talk and participate.
- enjoy meaningful, in-depth conversations about internal feelings and experiences with carefully chosen people.
- become anxious when drained of energy from activities and/or interaction.
- guard feelings—are more private and less likely to show their feelings and reactions.
- watch, wait, and observe; are slower to get involved.

Temperament researchers estimate only 25 to 30 percent of the general population is introverted, so often there's only one introvert in a family of extroverts. Since extroverts outnumber introverts, introverts often feel there is something wrong with them, and "if they were normal," they would be more social. While introverts want to be seen, known, and understood, they're not going to tell you about their desires unless you ask and wait patiently for an answer. It requires patience to ask what they feel, and sometimes you have to wait for an answer, as opposed to extroverted kids, who answer before you finish the question.

Our first grandchild, Reece, is an introvert. He enjoys people and is well liked by his playmates. He can seem reserved, but he is not shy. At family gatherings I (Kay) can watch him wear out, and although he has a lot of fun with his cousins, he's often the first to ask to go home. He knows when he needs some downtime.

At times Reece is very affectionate, wanting to sit on someone's lap or just cuddle. At other times he's reserved and reluctant to be hugged or kissed. If he has had some special alone time with Nana or Poppy, when we see him a few days later, he may run up with an excited greeting and hug us. If we haven't seen him in a few weeks, he's more reserved and less engaged at first. He needs time to warm up, and we give him room to be himself.

If your child is an introvert, there are things you can do to help your child thrive.

- Don't overschedule. Introverts need time to recharge, and too many activities are overwhelming. School is more taxing for an introvert, and she often desires alone time, not more activity after school.
- Extroverted parents get frustrated with an introverted child when they take him to a birthday party or preschool. You might say to him: "Some kids are extroverts, and they like to go play right away. You are an introvert, and you like to watch what the kids are doing and decide who you want to play with. I'll stand with you while you watch and check things out."
- When the family is gathered, don't let the extroverts talk over the introvert and interrupt. Teach extroverted family members to wait respectfully for the introvert to process, then talk. Include introverts in the conversation by directly asking them for their opinion.
- Make it a goal to have at least one in-depth conversation with your introverted child every week. Be sensitive to the

timing and avoid noisy, distracting locations. Bedtime is often a good time. You have to learn to be good at asking questions to draw out the introvert. They often do not elaborate unless you ask for more information. Pick a subject of interest to your child and find out what he thinks. Many times he has a fantasy world he doesn't discuss unless you ask. Ask a question and then *wait* for him to process his answer.

- If your introverted child shares a bedroom with a sibling, give your introverted child a private spot in the house she can go to when she wants to be alone. Teach your extroverted kids to respect the introvert's need for space and alone time.

- Give verbal appreciation. "You are a great observer. You notice things other people don't notice." "You have some interesting thoughts and ideas that you don't often tell people. I love to hear them."

- Write notes to your introverted child about his strengths and positive attributes. While all children like this, introverts appreciate written words and often reread notes or cards in quiet moments.

- Plan birthdays that suit your introverted child. Large parties in noisy places are often not enjoyable to an introvert. Give your child choices for celebrating that takes her temperament into account.

Take time to get to know your introverted child. His depth of understanding, insight, and observation is marvelous. Don't miss out on the treasures inside your gifted child.

Fourteen

The Free-Spirited Child

The free-spirited child is fun, spontaneous, adventuresome, impulsive, unstructured, carefree, and adaptable. Enjoying the present moment is the motto of this type, and no one is better at turning work into play or finding a way not to work at all.

As toddlers, these good-natured kids love to roam, explore, build, and create, and are curious about anything new. These kids are on the move and rarely complain until some structure or limits are necessary. As lovers of freedom, they find being constrained at odds with their temperament. More than other types, free-spirited kids use their body and sense of touch and movement to learn about the world.

Generally, this type would be a joy to parent if it were not for school. The classroom contains everything the free-spirited child dislikes. They find structure, rules, sitting and listening, reading, preparing and regurgitating information boring and useless. Most often these children are *kinesthetic* learners, learning by watching and doing, and they have an acute awareness of their body and physical world.

Since the school system doesn't cater to this learning style, it's important for a parent to know how to compensate. When learning a new skill or topic, this type wants to do it *hands-on*. They prefer to jump straight in, manipulate, maneuver, move around, and operate immediately. Taking something apart and putting it back together is preferable to reading or looking at diagrams about how it works.

To this type of child, the thought of sitting and listening to someone talk is exhausting and torturous. In such circumstances, these kids will fidget and want to get up and move around.

Here are some signs you may have a free spirit on your hands:

- wiggles when asked to sit, taps feet, plays with small objects, or swings legs
- might be considered hyperactive because he finds it difficult to sit still
- learns through movement: does well as a performer, athlete, actor, or dancer; works well with her hands, repairing things or making art; coordinated and has a strong sense of timing and body movement; often excels at sports

INTELLIGENCE NOT MEASURED BY TESTS

When John was thirteen, we moved into a new house. The phone jack in the bedroom he shared with his older brother wasn't working, so John opened up a working phone jack in another room and studied what wires went where to confirm no parts were needed. When his older brother got home, he noticed the phone working, and John informed him he'd fixed it. His brother didn't believe it until I confirmed that no repairman had been in the house.

This is the intelligence of these learners. They can often immediately figure out how things work without receiving instruction. Whenever we move any big item in or out of the house, we ask John for his advice on how to maneuver it. He has an uncanny awareness of what will fit where and can often see the easiest way to do any task. I can't count the number of times I've heard John say, "Not that way. Try this; it will be a lot easier." And he's always right.

In the Winter Olympics and X Games, one of the big events is the freestyle ski jump. If you've never seen this, you owe it to yourself to check it out. The ramp shoots skiers downhill (some face backward) and it abruptly stops, sending the skier airborne—twisting and flipping and ultimately landing with a jolt. I joked with Milan, "How many of these kids do you think loved school?" We guessed none. Most likely, all were kinesthetic learners—even the name "freestyle" fits them. John is an excellent surfer, skater, and snowboarder, and being an introvert, he prefers individual sports.

One thing you'll see over and over on report cards is: "Does not work to potential." We heard this in teacher conferences for as long as John was in school. Milan and I could retire wealthy if we'd had a dollar for every time this was said about him.

The truth is, *the school system* does not utilize this kid's potential. Most schools are set up for auditory and visual learners, and free-spirited kids end up feeling like they don't measure up, don't fit in, and aren't as smart as other kids, which is very sad. After some very bad semesters of school with rigid, structured teachers, we began to better understand John and his learning style and asked for teachers who were more spontaneous, energetic, and flexible.

We wish we could have understood sooner and made more effort earlier in John's life to teach him about his temperament and learning style. Eventually, we did help him understand his talents would only be understood and appreciated by a few teachers, and that his intelligence was not measured by report cards or the school system. We sympathized with his dislike of school and expressed confidence that he would discover his potential when he was doing activities he loved and learning in ways that fit his style.

We also attempted to help him understand that life requires some structure and conformity. Adults have to pay bills, balance checkbooks, pay taxes, live on a budget, and keep records. They must do tasks that are mundane and unpleasant, and require consistency and paperwork. School would at least prepare him for these realities.

By the time John was a junior, he was miserable. He had had enough of school. After much prayer, debate, and soul searching, we did something controversial: we gave John the choice to graduate early by testing out. I have never seen a happier face on a kid in my life when John opened his letter announcing he had passed the test and obtained his high school degree.

For the next ten years, he lived and traveled in the mountains, Hawaii, and Europe. If you ask John, he will tell you it was the best decision we ever made to allow him to be himself and learn through discovery, curiosity, and adventure. We're not saying this is the right decision for all free-spirited kids. But we do feel it was the right decision for John.

Like most free spirits, John's current job is outdoors and hands-on, and he has variety from day to day. A great dad and an accomplished guitarist, he still participates in all the sports he loved growing up. Your free-spirited child needs to know you understand him and appreciate his unique gifts and abilities. While it's a challenge to teach this type to plan ahead or do anything that requires repetitive routines or schedules, these skills are also important to life as an adult. Foresight, planning, and delaying gratification will never be areas of strength, but free-spirited kids do need to learn these are their shortcomings that will hold them back if no effort is made to address them.

The free-spirited child has the capacity to truly enjoy life and find pleasure in the moment. This is a gift she can share with the family: to stop and smell the roses. When John was sixteen, we asked him to be in charge of a family adventure. He took us all to Mexico for the day (just across the border in Southern California), and our adventure ended with a fabulous lobster dinner in a local restaurant. We went places we'd never have gone if not for our explorer leading the way.

As young adults, free-spirited kids are often late bloomers and need to roam before they settle down and find a niche in the adult world. They need to financially support themselves in these ventures as a step forward in learning to manage money. They do well in careers that offer variety and require adaptability.

How can you help free-spirited kids?

- When toddlers, let them roam as much as possible and expect them to get dirty, touch everything, and push every button.
- Give them opportunities to utilize their kinesthetic skills. For example: athletics, drama, arts, and music.
- Give them something to (safely) take apart and put back together. They love to see how things work.
- Don't be alarmed if they dislike school. Let them move while they memorize flashcards or spelling words. Putting learning to song or movement helps them retain the information. Teach them to see the words or phrases they are trying to master in their heads.
- Homework will be a battle zone. A lot of it is busywork, which they find almost intolerable. Allow breaks, give rewards, and be happy with a C or B.
- Make sure they know they're smart and help them realize school does not measure their kind of intelligence.
- Most free-spirited kids don't love to read unless it's an adventure story or area of interest.
- Help them learn skills that don't come naturally. For example: planning, budgeting, organizing, and consistency. Never place expectations on them to love these skills.
- Let them travel whenever possible. Adventure is like food and water to a free spirit.
- Expect them to be late bloomers.
- Don't rescue them financially or in other ways if they get in trouble through their lack of planning. Let the consequence be the teacher.

The free-spirited child can help you enjoy and live life to the fullest. Enjoy her zest for life and learn from her ability to play and enjoy the moment.

Fifteen

The Determined Child

(Kay) call the determined child "leadership in the rough." I can hear some of you saying, "I'd rather have a follower!"

These kids pop out of the womb wanting to be in charge. Once they're verbal, they can make a case for getting what they want with astounding clarity, insight, and persuasiveness. It's going to take more time than most need for these kids to learn to control their whims, will, and emotions.

One of my friends has a bright, determined daughter who was reading by age three. When she was nine, she read a parenting book that was lying around the house. She then proceeded to direct her mom on how to parent her more effectively using the techniques she had just learned. Be advised: if you have a determined kid, you might want to hide this book.

Persistence is the middle name of these kids, and they're on a mission to wear you down, no matter how long it takes. Early on, they develop the art of pestering, like a woodpecker pecking an insect out of a tree. They drill your ears relentlessly with what they want or don't want. While determined kids are more prone to anger when they meet limits or resistance, not all angry kids are strong-willed. Unfair rules, inconsistency, favoritism, unclear communication, harshness, and lots of criticism can make any child angry.

A consistently angry child is often a big red flag that something is wrong with family dynamics. (Anger and frustration can also come from underlying processing problems or developmental issues, and this chapter isn't meant to address these problems.) Many of the angry kids I have seen in my office are angry for a good reason. They are reacting to something unhealthy in the family system. Many times (but not always) it's a reactive, unavailable, inconsistent, or pushover parent that is the source of the problem. Fix the parenting, and the kid is far less angry.

We see a common pattern develop between determined kids and parents. You might have a two-year-old or teen, but the pattern will look the same. I call it the Lose-Lose Loop, because both parent and child are defeated in this downward spiral, and it continues until the parent breaks the loop. It goes like this:

- kid misbehaves
- parent reacts and gets angry
- kid gains power from causing parent's reaction and continues behavior or amplifies it
- parent becomes more reactive when kid gets the upper hand and may begin to secretly or openly dislike the kid for making her feel powerless and inadequate or angry
- kid feels this and decides negative attention is better than none, and power is better than defeat, so continues to misbehave
- parent feels justified for not liking this kid and has more negative feelings toward him
- kid has no more motivation to behave, so continues misbehavior

If you have a more feisty, intense kid, you're probably familiar with some form of this loop. At times it can feel as though every interaction with your child is negative. The focus becomes problem after problem after problem. And while this loop is more likely to happen with a determined kid, it can happen with a child of any temperament. Some kids are not strong-willed, but if they have less impulse control, it's going to take longer to learn self-control.

If you had a reactive, angry parent or a passive, overindulgent parent, you're more likely to get trapped in this loop. Why? First, reactivity breeds reactivity. If you were trained to react impulsively and a lot of reactivity was normal in your family growing up, it will feel normal to be reactive with your kids. Similarly, passive parents like pleasers and victims train kids to not pay attention. You'll simply feel overwhelmed and wonder how to respond to the challenges and deal with a determined kid by minimizing, ignoring, and excusing bad behavior, which only communicates that there are no limits.

So how does a parent get out of this loop?

1. Hunt for the Good Things

First, remember who your determined kid is underneath. Stay with it until you have a list of at least five things you appreciate about her core temperament and personality. It might be challenging, but it's a necessary first step. For help, look at baby pictures, review fun times and happy memories, and use the list of positive descriptive words at the end of the book in the Parent's Toolbox.

2. See the Positive and Speak It

Now you'll put your good-hunt to use. Make an observation about anything your child does or enjoys. Then verbalize to your child how that observation fits the positive traits you've already listed. This will also require you to show an interest in *your child's world* to meet on his territory. Don't worry if you're rebuffed at first. Keep trying, and make every effort to seek out the kid you enjoy within that activity, whatever it is.

- "You really love that video game, don't you? I'm impressed by how you focus and how good you are at it. What's your highest score/highest level?"
- "Your football coach gives you quite the workout. I'm proud of how you're so dedicated to the hard work."
- "I can see you're frustrated, but you're using a lot of self-control right now not to hit your brother."

- "You are so happy and funny when your friend Ryan comes to play. I love to watch you enjoy your friends."
- "That is such a tall block tower! Most kids would have given up before it got that tall. You are a great builder/so determined/impressive."
- "You're good at relaxing after school. I need to get better at relaxing. Maybe you could help me figure out how to put my work aside better."
- "I see the way you are helping your sister, even though she did not ask very nicely."
- "I saw you try a cartwheel out in the yard. You're so brave at trying new things. And you'll have that down in no time."
- "I really like that shirt you picked out. You look great in blue."
- "I loved the way you handled that. You made such a good choice there. I'm amazed by your self-control."

Catching your child in good behavior will be easier after you spend time thinking about his positive traits, so don't skip this step. For the Lose-Lose Loop to be broken, your child needs to experience your enjoyment of him. Remember, you are the parent, so it's your job to stop the negative cycle. Make it a goal to observe and comment on the good whenever you find yourself in the negative loop. Talk about the present moment with phrases that begin *I see/hear/notice, I love/like, I appreciate/am thankful for, I'm excited/thrilled about, It's nice/helpful when.*

3. Trade Your "Button" for Thinking Time

Don't give your child the pleasure of a reaction when she misbehaves or tries to push your button or pulls you into the loop. Instead, show that your button has disappeared.

Don't lecture, moralize, remind, threaten, count to ten. Just calmly and swiftly send the consequence. You can minimize the difficulty of having to be overly creative with your consequences by keeping it simple and consistent. Make the consequence *thinking time.* When your child disregards your request or a family rule, calmly and gently say, "You need some thinking time. Take a seat." It will be easiest for her to sit down right where she is, but you can direct the child to sit in another place if that seems more appropriate. How long? Generally, one minute for every year old is a good rule of thumb. As thinking time becomes more regular, you can also get your child a clock to watch the minutes herself. With a two- and three-year-old, you might say:

- "Whining means you need some thinking time in the kitchen chair. I'll tell you when thinking time is over."
- "Hitting is not okay. You need some thinking time. You can stand there or pick a place to sit here in this room. I'll tell you when time is up."
- "That tone of voice means you need thinking time. Take a seat."

If you direct him to another location and he refuses to go, say, "You can go by yourself to the chair for some thinking time. If I have to take you, you will get more time to think." If he won't go, lead (carry) him to the chair, sit him down, and say, "I'll tell you when you can get up."

If he gets up before time is up, put him back, saying, "Now you'll need three minutes." Don't get angry or reactive, otherwise you are in the loop. The better you can control your reaction and tone of voice, the better you model the self-control you are trying to teach.

Don't give up and don't lecture or threaten. Your determined kid will resist and might put up quite a fight getting angrier because you are setting a limit. You can always say, "I'll give you time to calm down in your room, and then you can sit for thinking time." If it takes an hour, it's time well spent. If you cannot get a three-year-old to sit, what will you do when he is thirteen and as tall as you are? Security is built by consistent limits. The most miserable kids are those who constantly act out and have a mom or dad who rages or acts helpless. A feisty kid will test your consistency. Help him believe in this line, and that he can trust it, and you'll help your child learn limits are a part of life.

If a child doesn't learn certain behaviors are unacceptable, she'll struggle all her life with self-discipline, resisting temptation, delaying gratification, and treating others with respect. If she makes a mess in her room during thinking time, impose another few minutes in the chair, and then ask, "Would you like to play the clean-up game or have more thinking time?" If she breaks something, impose more time and say, "We will have to sell one of your toys to get some money to fix this. Which one would you like to sell?"

A reminder is fine for a two- or three-year-old. By four and five years old, they know the rules, so don't explain, remind, lecture, or count to ten. Just send the consequence. Once your child knows the rules, don't even say which rule he broke. Just send the consequence. Tommy hits his brother and Mom or Dad says, "Tommy, sit and take some thinking time until I call you."

"Why? What did I do?" whines Tommy. "Jason hit me first. What are you going to do to Jason?"

Don't explain, don't lecture, don't remind, don't moralize, just calmly enforce the consequence. "Your time will start when you are sitting and quiet." Do not engage and reinforce negative behavior with your attention. Sending a consequence is *not* the time to listen to feelings. "Why did you hit your brother, Tommy? What are you feeling?" Those are questions for another time. Whatever the feeling, hitting is out of bounds. Send the consequence. Save the feeling talk for later.

Your child may be acting out because of deeper issues, and you do need to consider the stresses your child is under and the possible reasons for her bad behavior. This is extremely important and is discussed earlier in the book. A consequence for bad behavior is also important to help your child learn limits and self-control bit by bit. It takes time.

4. Set Them Free
Once you get compliance, you are in charge, and your child will feel secure in knowing the limits of what's unacceptable behavior. Once she's

served her time, set her free with a positive tone of voice and without lectures, reminders, warnings, or explanations. Smile and be positive.

- "Thanks for thinking, Trace. Let's try again."
- "Roxanne, I think you're ready to play again."
- "Stacie, feel free to come join us any time you like."

With determined toddlers, leading them away from the place or thing that's off-limits and giving them a new activity may be sufficient. More determined kids may need more containment. Use a portable crib or gated area and say, "Oops, that's dangerous," and put them in the enclosure. After a minute take them out and let them play, and when they do it again—"Oops," and back in the playpen. Ignore protests and don't make eye contact when they're fussing and crying to get out. No need for them to stop crying: toddlers and preschoolers don't have that much control over their emotions. When you take them out, smile and say, "Let's try again."

A few days working on this and your toddler will quickly learn *freedom* means staying within the limits and keeps you from screaming. Better yet, it allows you a few minutes to catch your breath and maybe go to the bathroom! When your child has a bit more control, introduce sitting for thinking time.

For older kids who refuse a consequence, remove privileges until the consequence is taken. "I'm not going to my room." Mom answers, "It's your choice when to take the consequence, but no privileges until you take your time." What are privileges? Anything they like: the next meal, toys, friends, electronics, snacks, phones, makeup, car keys. Teach them that a lack of control "steals" their privileges. For teens, thinking time may include a talk. "Now that I know you lied, our trust is broken. Take some thinking time and give me a plan for rebuilding trust."

Your determined child has the potential to be an outstanding leader, but he must learn to be a follower also. Consistently enforcing fair, firm limits provides security to a determined child. Give your leader opportunities to make decisions and choices, and then hold him to his decision. And if you could use some additional help, we recommend *Parenting with Love and Logic* or *Parenting Teens with Love and Logic* by Foster Cline and Jim Fay.

Sixteen

The Sensitive Child

Dallas and Carolyn made an appointment with me (Kay) to discuss problems they were having with their six-month-old baby, Camden. "We haven't slept through the night yet, and that would be fine if he was happy during the day. He's fussy a lot and wants to be held most of the time. We've only started feeding him finger food and you'd think we were offering him dirt clods. He cries if anyone else tries to hold him, and he won't have a thing to do with my mom. Maybe we do give in to him too much, but sometimes it's the only way to get some peaceful moments."

"Does he startle easily?" I asked. "Is he sensitive to loud noises?"

Dallas and Carolyn looked at each other and smiled. "When I make coffee, I take the grinder in the other room and wrap it in a towel," Dallas said.

"How about bright light, like going out on a sunny day?"

"He cries at camera flashes, and he fusses if the sun is bright, but I figured all babies do that."

I told them I suspected they had a sensitive child. Sensitive children have a more delicate nervous system. Senses are more easily stimulated. Noises are louder, fabrics scratchier, lights brighter, smells more noxious, tastes and textures more intense.

Reactions and emotions are more extreme as well. Highly sensitive kids can even notice subtle changes in others' moods and react with deep sadness, fear, or distress. When he's older, Camden may be far more impacted by violence and intense movies, but he also might be more creative and deeply moved by art or music.

It's far easier for highly sensitive children to get overwhelmed by interactions and events that other kids could more easily handle. Because their nervous system is more sensitive to stimuli, they get uncomfortable more easily, physically and emotionally. Change in routine and schedule is more difficult, because unpredictability is stressful for sensitive children. They need a perceptive parent who understands their unique makeup.

One of the best things you can do is try to put yourself in your sensitive child's shoes. "Imagine being Camden," I said to Carolyn and Dallas, "and entering a room where it sounds like everyone is yelling, the TV is on full blast, you feel the itchy tag at the back of your neck, and the top of a zipper is poking into your chin. Smells are strong and the lights are like bright floodlights hurting your eyes. It's all too much and you start to cry. Mom picks you up and bounces you around, increasing the stimulation. Now you wail. This makes Mom anxious, and she feels overwhelmed and inadequate. You feel her arms tense up, and her voice gets a bit frantic. 'What's wrong?' You have no way to communicate. You cannot talk. You get passed to Dad, who decides you want a kiss. A scratchy beard rubs across your cheek and it hurts. You scream louder. Grandma takes over. She is sure you're not getting enough milk nursing and is determined to get you to accept a bottle. Now a nipple is being pushed into your mouth. 'Come on, eat, baby. You'll feel better.' Now you scream with rage. It's easy to see this becomes a no-win situation with both caretakers and baby feeling frustrated."

Carolyn looked at Dallas. "Now I'm feeling a little sick."

I smiled. "It's simply going to take him longer to get used to the intense world. You're not spoiling him. He just needs more time to adjust. Understanding his sensitivity will help you take it easier and have confidence."

If you feel you may have a sensitive child, here are some ideas to help.

- See if your baby is calmed by a quieter, more dimly lit environment. Some children nurse or engage socially in a quiet, peaceful room.
- Remember, babies are never *trying* to be difficult. Help your child regulate the level of stress she feels by helping her be less stimulated and overwhelmed. Be patient and don't compare your child to the "easy baby."
- If your baby seems to have difficulty with touch, try skin-to-skin contact without a lot of rubbing, stroking, or patting. Firm, gentle pressure is often better tolerated than light, tickly touch.
- Use cotton fabrics for clothing, bedding, and pajamas.
- Introduce foods slowly and expect reactions to new textures, tastes, and smells. Be patient and go slowly. Don't push it. Just offer finger foods and enjoy your own meal with him.
- Some babies sleep better with white noise like a fan or air filter that blocks out other noises. For some kids even music is too stimulating.

A baby who does not readily engage, smile, coo, and keep eye contact can make a mom feel rejected and inadequate. Allow more time to accomplish these developmental milestones. Your baby is not rejecting you. Let him rest and look away to calm down.

If your child seems to fit the characteristics above, we recommend reading *The Highly Sensitive Child* by Elaine Aron. Children with sensory integration problems and some kids on the autistic spectrum may have some of the traits just mentioned. In her book, Dr. Aron helps to differentiate between sensitivity and deeper problems. Lots of good articles can be found on the Internet on "sensory integration disorders." Read up on this topic if your child seems overresponsive or underresponsive to touch, sound, or light, or has balance or coordination problems.

I worked with a mother whose son was diagnosed with sensory motor integration problems and recommended she place him in a therapy program involving desensitization techniques to tune down his nervous system. He also learned coping skills for times when he was overstimulated and exercises to improve integration between his senses.

His mom was thrilled with the results. "I took him to a birthday party, and for the first time in his life, he enjoyed it. He's aware now when he is getting overloaded, and he takes a short time-out away from the other kids and breathes and soothes himself. I've actually learned to take better care of myself by doing the same thing. We started calling them BCS moments—breathe, calm, and soothe. Now we've nicknamed them BCs. I can tell him, 'Hey, buddy, take a BC.' Or, 'I'll be right back; I need a BC.' And we know it's a reminder to get away and relax everything."

As sensitive babies grow into preschoolers, school-age kids, and teens, they retain their sensitive natures. Things still affect them deeply. While we accept these traits more easily with girls, boys may have a harder time and need more support. These boys probably won't gravitate toward rough team sports and may cry easily because they feel things deeply. If parents, especially dads, react without understanding, this can be very detrimental to the development of a healthy self-esteem. Sensitivity needs to be valued and celebrated, not dismissed or shamed. What woman wouldn't love to marry a sensitive man?

These kids often have gifts in the arts and also excel in professions like counseling, social work, and nursing. Keep your eyes open for these strengths, and give your child opportunities to express their sensitive natures in creative ways.

- Think of the number of stimulations your baby or child is receiving. Notice what overwhelms him and protect him from too much arousal. Work on helping him manage overstimulation when he's old enough.
- Give her more time to adjust to change and new situations.

- Help him understand the positive aspects of being sensitive and ask him how he thinks others are feeling and responding in different scenarios. Help him realize the extraordinary insight he has and affirm this gift.
- Protect her from intense media—news broadcasts, movies, and video games.
- Never shame him for his tears. He will likely be teased enough. Boys and girls need support and understanding for their strong emotional responses.
- Fighting, anger, marital discord, or sibling conflict is traumatic for all kids, but especially this type. Reassure, comfort, and draw out your child's feelings after such events. Help her see and hear the process of reconciliation whenever possible.
- A sensitive child often holds stress in his body. Ask him where he feels things in his body or ask him to draw a picture of different feelings in his body.
- Teach relaxation and breathing games to help relieve stress during difficult situations.
- Remember the highly sensitive child is not trying to be difficult; she just feels things deeply, physically, emotionally, and spiritually.

Above all, learn to enjoy your highly sensitive child! He will make a difference in the world by caring for people and changing injustices. Help this child become aware of his gifts and the many ways God can use them. Celebrate his sensitivity!

Seventeen

The Premature Child

My (Kay's) first three weeks of life were spent in an incubator after my twin and I were born three weeks early. After a thirty-six-hour labor and a difficult forceps delivery, my mom received a blood transfusion to save her life. She went home without her baby girls and became depressed, and I eventually came home to an anxious mom who described me as a "glum baby" who never smiled. She became convinced that something was wrong with me, comparing me to my more responsive sister.

She was right. Something was wrong with me. The difficult start impacted me more deeply than my sister.

I avoided eye contact and was fussier, which made my mom anxious. My mother's nervousness made it harder for me to feel comforted by her. The vicious circle impacted our relationship from the start. At eight months I tried to crawl into my sister's crib, fell, and broke my collarbone. My mom told me that for a month, I cried if anyone tried to pick me up, so I lay motionless with a somber expression. It was a difficult first year.

There are some good books on this subject discussing the challenges (and joys) of raising premature babies. Early trauma has an impact and requires extra effort and patience to work through. Developmental delays are common. Fortunately, you can help your child make sense of her experience by linking current symptoms to the past.

Many parents think a baby can't remember her first few years so it doesn't impact her. Yet much research is showing this is not true. Children retain these memories *implicitly,* and they become wordless, emotional memories.

I met some parents who had a three-year-old son who was born too early. They came to speak with me after a general class on parenting. "We're worried about our son. He seems to have no fear and does dangerous things," they explained.

"Like what?" I asked.

They looked at each other and laughed. "Which story should we tell?" the mother asked. "How about the time he was two and he crawled between the bars over the second-story window and dropped to the ground? Another time, he talked the baby-sitter into letting him crawl out on the roof. He told her he did it all the time."

"He rides his bike down the five stairs in the front yard," the husband continued, "crashes, bleeds, and doesn't even cry or stop playing. He just keeps going."

"Seems like he has a high tolerance for pain," I said. "This may seem like a strange question, but did he experience any birth trauma? Was he premature, or did he have medical problems early in life?"

They looked at each other, wide-eyed. "Yes, he did. We adopted him when he was born. He was six weeks early and weighed little more than three pounds. He also had gastroschisis (gas-tro-SKEE-sis), where the intestines protrude from the abdomen. He had surgery and was in intensive care for six weeks." Debbie sighed.

"That explains his high tolerance for pain," I said. His first experience of the world was one of high levels of pain. He lived, but he had no choice but to endure and learn to defend against it. Even the best mothering can't take away this survival mechanism he has, and pain will always be more normal for him than you and me.[1]

Preemies are usually restless and impulsive, have sleep difficulties and bad dreams, and alternate between anger and clinginess. Because these kids can't describe their early trauma, the memory lies dormant until something triggers the feeling they had in those first months or years. They don't remember with their heads but with their bodies and their emotions.

When the parents, Debbie and Scott, came to see me in my office, they brought three-year-old Nate, who played on the floor as we talked.

"He can't remember what happened to him as an infant," Scott said, "so why does it matter?"

At just this moment, we all happened to be watching Nate play. He picked up a syringe from the medical play set and stuck it into the foot of the doll. Debbie and Scott gasped in disbelief.

"They were constantly sticking his heel to draw blood in the hospital. It's like he doesn't remember with his head, but he remembers with his body and heart," said Debbie.

"I would not have believed this if I didn't see it with my own eyes," Scott said. "Nate's making a believer out of me. Maybe his early experiences are still impacting him."

Implicit memory begins at birth. Before babies can talk, they take in information through touch, facial expressions, voice tones, and eye contact. Good and bad experiences create responses in a baby's body, and these sensations and experiences begin forming the hard-wired encoding a child will carry for life. "In other words, what we don't remember with our minds, we remember with our bodies, with our hearts and our 'guts'—with lasting implications for our thinking, feeling, and behaviour."[2] These primary messages impact everything we do—how we think, feel, and act. Though Nate had no conscious recall of being an infant and having blood drawn from heel pricks, he remembered.

If this is the case, what must this mean for premature babies? Any comfort experienced is insufficient to stop the pain. Even Mom's presence may be confusing. *Is she the cause? Is she the one who comforts? Why does she stand by while people hurt me?* Babies and toddlers who experience repeated painful procedures may have difficulty trusting adults and developing socially.

Today, most hospitals are protective of infants and children. Yet as a parent, be aware and help your child by reducing pain and potential trauma in situations if your child is to be hospitalized. Premature babies and those who suffer medical interventions early in life may struggle later to bond and connect with their parents. For most babies, born full term, distress is manageable and more easily soothed.

Be sure to also take care of your feelings and reactions. The stress of having a child who's born too early or is sick churns up a lot of feelings. Be aware and honest about your emotions and share and release them with your spouse or parent. What is shareable is bearable: sit with your spouse and take turns listening to each other. Offer comfort and pray for each other. Find a friend or support group if necessary, where you can be honest and find comfort.

We all deal with stress in different ways. Some get anxious, others live in denial. These were my parents, Mom and Dad, respectively. When my sister and I were about four months old, my mom tried to share her concern with my dad. He laughed at her and told her there was something wrong with her for worrying. Neither could be honest with each other or be supportive, so the problems continued. My mom grew more anxious, and I grew more detached, while my dad pretended nothing was happening.

If you have a premature baby or child, or have had to hospitalize your child, you may need to work on rebuilding trust, not because you did anything wrong, but because of the difficult circumstances. Pay attention to the symptoms you're seeing and respond calmly and decisively. Most kids will have residual effects that show up after a hospitalization. Some kids are born with a more resilient temperament and will recover more quickly. Be aware of sensitivities, and don't panic if you notice some of the following symptoms. If you're seeing something that isn't quite right, you have options about how to resolve the problem.

Premature babies or ones that have had to be hospitalized may

- avoid eye contact and seem off in their own world.

- not reach out to be picked up.
- reject efforts to calm, soothe, and connect.
- not seem to care or notice when left alone.
- wake up upset and screaming.
- not coo or make sounds.
- not follow with eyes.
- rock to comfort themselves.

These are signs your baby needs extra love and care. Don't give up or take his resistance personally. Your baby doesn't dislike you; he just has problems trusting and feeling safe. Talk to your baby in a calm, soft voice. Reassure him, even if he doesn't seem to take it in. Experiment and try to determine what's soothing to him. Music? Singing? Rocking? Swaddling? Swinging? Vibration? Often less stimulation is helpful. It will take some time for your baby to trust your love and comfort. The most important thing is to be patient and don't give up.

Toddlers may exhibit

- separation anxiety and may want a parent within sight, even at night.
- nightmares and sleep disturbances, including night terrors, when falling asleep.
- excessive worry about the safety of family members or their own safety.
- resistance to going to school or other activities that take them away from home.
- control issues. They are often easily frustrated and argumentative and don't like change. They demonstrate "you can't make me" attitudes.
- tantrums and anger problems. Anger may be expressed directly in tantrums or by acting out, or through manipulative, passive-aggressive behavior. It is not always obvious why they are angry.

- regression—by showing a need to return to earlier developmental stages again. For example: there may be problems with potty training, language, and sleeping through the night.
- repetitive play of traumatic experiences. This is their way of trying to work though the trauma.

What should you look for and how can you help?

REGRESSION

Medical trauma often causes regression in toddlers and preschoolers. Never punish your child when she regresses, but patiently help her regain the skills. Listen and watch any reenactments of trauma during play, and see how she is processing the experience indirectly.

PLAY WITH THEMES OF TRAUMA

Kids who have had trauma often use imaginative play as a way of working through difficult emotions. Play with your child and use comforting words and thoughts. "The baby is so scared and the mommy is sad because she can't take the pain away, but she knows baby will get sicker if the doctors don't help. Mom is happy too, because she knows the baby will get better."

SLEEP PROBLEMS, REPETITIVE NIGHTMARES, OR DISTURBING IMAGES

Many kids with early medical trauma have sleep problems and nightmares as a result. If your child can recall his dreams, or especially if he has a repetitive dream with imagery or feelings representative of the trauma, help your child by making a story that changes the dream (or adds an ending to the dream with a more positive, calm, empowering outcome).

LINK THE PAST WITH THE PRESENT

You can best help your child if you can see the world from her perspective from birth onward. No matter how old your child is now, she may still be showing aftereffects of early trauma or may be having implicit memories from her early experiences without realizing it. A big part of healing is being able to make sense of one's feelings and reactions. Kids need to hear the story of their birth and how it might have felt to be in their place.

Tell your child the story of his birth and make observations how it might have felt to be a little baby (or toddler or preschooler) in such circumstances. If your child had difficult early experiences, start by writing what you know and remember about the time from his perspective. Imagine being the child and write what happened. Use the Soul Words list and write some feelings and sensations she must have felt. Babies have the same physiological response to stress and pain we do: stress hormones are released, and respiration, heart rate, and blood pressure rise.

How will you know if your child is experiencing unconscious recall (implicit, wordless memories) of her difficult beginnings? These kinds of memories are most likely to come out in stressful situations. When your child is feeling overwhelmed, current situations may evoke bodily sensations and feelings that your child experienced in the hospital. Your child won't realize it's a memory. The goal of helping your child make connections is to deepen her self-awareness and help her grow and heal. Make guesses as to cause and effect. For example, "I wonder if you need so much control and power because when you were a little baby and in the hospital, you had no power. That was a hard time for you. Let me tell you the story about that time and see if it makes sense to you."

If you are accurate, your child will likely experience grief or other strong emotions but will feel relief by the end of the talk. If you are off base, it's still a good experience for your child of having a parent listen and care about what's in her heart.

Body Memories and Overreactions

Strong feelings or exaggerated reactions that seem out of proportion to the present circumstance can be an indicator of implicit memories. Grant was thirteen months old when he was burned in a kitchen accident and hospitalized for weeks of painful treatments. When he was eight, his mom was called to pick him up from school. He'd almost fainted during science class.

As they drove home, Grant was highly agitated and told his mom, "You have to get me out of class when it's time to study science. I'm never studying science again. It was horrible."

His wise mom was alarmed at his level of agitation. "Tell me what happened, so I can understand," she coaxed.

"We are studying muscles. There was this huge, gross chart that was a picture of a person with just muscles, no skin. I almost threw up. I couldn't look, so I put my head down on the desk, but I was so dizzy. Then my arms got stiff, and I couldn't move them for a while. I hate science and you have to come get me when it's time for science. Please!"

His mom, who recognized the possibility of implicit memories, made the connection. "Grant, I wonder if those pictures of muscles reminded you of when you were little and in the burn ward. That's what burned people look like, raw and red. It seems like when you saw the picture, your body felt what it was like for you when you were little and in the hospital: nauseated, agitated, and confused. Even your stiff arms make sense. The doctors had to splint your arms so you couldn't scratch or hurt your wounds. They were straight and stiff for a while."

Grant burst into tears and cried for a long time. His mom was able to comfort him and help him make sense of his strong feelings. She reminded Grant of how much it hurt her to see him suffer as a baby. Now, Grant is thirteen and in the seventh grade. Recently, he had the same reaction and almost fainted again during a dissection unit in science. This time, Grand understood why he was feeing faint and the reason for his feelings, and he excused himself and calmed himself down.

DIFFICULTY WITH CALMING AND REGULATING EMOTIONS

Regulating emotions and calming down after upsets can be difficult for kids who had early medical trauma. In Jonna Jepsen's book, *Born Too Early,* Josephine talks about her five-year-old daughter, Jaqueline, born at thirty-two weeks. Josephine describes how her daughter reacts when she gets upset:

> Her whole world collapses during these moments [of distress].
> I still find this very difficult to observe and to help her. In this
> situation only consolation, more consolation, and big hugs seem
> to help, even though it can be difficult to reach her as she often
> switches off completely and only focuses on the thing that has
> just happened.[3]

When a child's "whole world collapses," she either is in desperate need of sleep or perhaps is mixing the past with the present. This wise mom has learned to keep on comforting, as distraction has no effect during these times. It will take many more experiences of comfort for this little girl to gain the ability to self-soothe because of her difficult start. Her mom might recount the story of her birth to her, saying, "Jaqueline, I think sometimes when you get hurt now, you are crying tears for the little baby you were, who couldn't get all the comfort you needed when you were in the hospital. Maybe that's why you need extra hugs." This would increase Jacqueline's self-awareness and help her understand her feelings and reactions.

ANGER AND CONTROL ISSUES

I include one more personal case history from *Born Too Early,* because it portrays something many parents experience. Pernille writes about her six-year-old daughter, who was born nine weeks early. Although she describes her daughter as having a lot of fear and separation anxiety, she also says, "At home she seeks conflict beyond belief, yet at school she uses all her energy in cooperating." In trying to prepare her daughter for a visit to the doctor, Pernille recounted her birth experience and showed her daughter pictures of her early hospitalization.

> At first she became angry, really angry, over the fact that I could have left her in that glass case, and when I explained that it was a question of whether I wanted her to live or to die, she totally broke down. I do not believe I have ever experienced so deep a grief in anyone. It was a frightening experience, and it made me realize that the body remembers its traumas.[4]

Many kids with early trauma are angry and don't know why. Helping link the past to the present helps these kids get to the grief under the trauma. It may take more than one time of making these connections to help your child process through his difficult beginnings. Pray for wisdom and get help for your emotions as your own grief or anger may be reactivated as you help your child. Even if your child is now an adult, you may be able to make connection that will help him make sense of his feelings, reactions, and behaviors.

• • • • •

Premature kids grow up and need the same thing all kids need: predictability, firm limits, attention to feelings, reassurance, and repair after misbehavior. I have focused in this chapter on implicit memories, because so few people write on this subject. I know hearing about my first year helped me understand and accept myself and gave me more insight into where I needed healing. My prayer is that more parents can help their kids process through the aftermath of these difficult circumstances and make sense of their reactions and feelings.

The Healing
Journey for Parents
and Children

Eighteen

The Gift of Insight

M any parenting methods focus on winning the battle for control and teaching children to obey. While consistent limits help children feel secure, we need to respond in a way that isn't only about consequences, but about what's behind the behavior.

No matter what your child's age, give some thought to what's driving the misbehavior. What stresses is your child facing? What recent changes have occurred? How is her health? Is she tired? How is school? How about her friendships? sports? How does your child act when he is stressed? Does he get angry? withdraw? fight with a sibling? eat? sleep?

You get the point. Every kid is different. You can say, "I notice when you're upset, you do *this*. I'm wondering what's bothering you. Let's see if we can figure it out together." While you're thinking about it, consider how you handled stress as a kid. You probably do the same now.

I (Kay) remember a family who came to me because their sixteen-year-old son was acting out. He was argumentative and hard to get along with. He had just been in a car accident caused by his speeding. His parents grounded him for two months, and his driver's license was suspended. Now he was even more belligerent.

I discussed with his parents every stressor they could think of. When we finished, we had a list of fifteen stressors, one of which was his dad's tendency to be critical. Both parents realized they had not sat down and really thought about all their son was facing in his daily life. They showed him the list later that week and asked him to rank the stressors from highest to lowest. He added several things to the list they hadn't even considered. They asked about feelings and expressed concern and care for things he was dealing with. They came back the next week and said, "We gave him a consequence, but almost missed the opportunity to connect to his inner world. Thanks for helping us connect in a meaningful way."

When you look below the surface at what might be driving your child's behavior, you're teaching your child the vital skill of self-awareness—having insight into himself. We often ask kids, "Why did you do that?" We all know the usual answer: "I don't know." And that's often the truth. Kids need help to look inside and understand stressors, motivations, reactions, triggers, and their God-given temperament.

When John was in fifth grade, he began to choose some questionable friends whose characters seemed a bit shaky. I noticed he often seemed remote and quiet after being with a certain friend. As an introvert, he tended to hold his feelings inside.

I waited for a good opportunity (always important with an introvert) and told John, "I notice when you play with Will, you often come home and keep to yourself. I wonder why that is." John was quiet and reflective.

"We have fun. I like Will because he's funny." He paused for a while and I waited. "He's kind of bossy. He always wants his way, and if I don't go along with it, he says he won't be my friend anymore."

"Wow, that could be hard to hear. You really enjoy him, but you don't like his threats to stop being your friend." I waited some more.

"Today he was kind of mean to me," John continued. "He was making fun of me, and Scott was there too. He always does that when Scott comes over."

"How did you handle that? What do you say or do when Will is mean?"

"I don't know what to do. I just try and ignore it."

"How does it make you feel when this happens?" I asked.

"Mad, but I don't want to tell him or he won't be my friend."

"It makes sense that you're mad, John. But when you hold it inside, he gets away with being mean. You still have a friend, but when you come home, you're sad. It's still bothering you."

"Yeah, I'm never mean to him. I don't see why he does that."

"John, you're not mean. In fact, sometimes you're too nice. An important part of friendship is respect. If you never stand up for yourself, Will won't respect you. He may like you, but he'll think he can treat you any way he likes. Try this: let's practice some things you could say to him when he acts this way. I'll be Will and I'm being mean to you. You say, 'Knock it off, Will, or I'm out of here. And next time, I won't want to play with you.'"

We practiced this until John could say the words confidently, and with some gusto.

"Now, he probably won't believe you until you do what you say you're going to do," I said. "The first time he's mean, give him your comeback, and then leave if he doesn't stop."

Two days later, John came trudging through the door with a slight grin. "I did it." We then practiced his next line for when Will would come to ask him to play again: "I'd like to play with you, but last time you were mean. I don't feel like having a mean friend. I'll play with you again when you agree not to be mean."

Sure enough, Will came around a couple of days later. John performed flawlessly, although he was afraid Will might never play with him again. To his surprise, Will apologized and said he wouldn't be mean anymore. John had to set the boundaries a few more times, but Will eventually learned to play nicely. And John learned how to speak up and respect and protect himself.

The process followed this progression:

1. Know how your child behaves when he's stressed. Each child is different.

2. Instead of reacting to your child's behavior and forcing her to change, use the Soul Words list to think about what's causing the stress. Go to your child and make observations about her behavior, and offer some guesses as to the stressor or reasons she may be reacting this way.
3. Ask him to pick three feelings. Ask what circumstances, people, relationships, events, or pressures may be causing the feelings and difficult behavior.
4. Validate her feelings: "Your feelings make sense to me."
5. Teach or problem solve, only after you have really listened to your child's heart.
6. For extra credit make observations about your child's temperament and her strengths and weaknesses, if applicable: "You are a kind, sensitive person, and it can be hard for someone so nice to say no when she needs to. Let's practice ways you could say no when your friend is doing something bad."

For those with sensitive or introverted kids, it's okay if they reject an offer to talk. Let it go for a time, but keep offering. Eventually, they'll know you're serious. And once you're "in" and they trust you, you can insist a bit more. Just remain sensitive to their world, and don't force them to talk on your timetable.

With more outgoing, decisive, headstrong kids, it's better to push back. Our oldest son was the opposite of John's temperament. His tendency was to push back when stressed. When he was in high school, the whole family was getting annoyed and reactive to Kevin's knee-jerk reactions. And he refused to talk. So we decided to match his strength with our insistence.

"Kevin, we know things are bothering you by how you're acting. You're pretty reactive and edgy. We're concerned about letting you drive under the circumstances, so you can have the car keys back after we talk. Not until then. Let us know when would be a good time for you."

Wow, was he mad! But he wanted to drive. Reluctantly, he agreed to talk. We asked him to make a list—to pick three soul words in each category of his life at the time. The category headings on the list were: *School, Friends, Church, Family, and Football.* He wrote down his words, and as we started to discuss why he chose them, his self-awareness skyrocketed. We talked for over an hour. At the end of the conversation, he actually said, "Wow, I really didn't know all those things were bothering me. I feel much better." Milan and I smiled. "Can we quote you on that in the future?"

The gift of insight is about raising a child's level of self-awareness. When you, as a parent, open the door to her inner world, you help her look inside and understand what makes her tick. Relief is spelled I-N-S-I-G-H-T. An explanation, a clarification, a resolution, or a needed skill are all possible outcomes when you help a child develop her insight by learning to articulate feelings and needs.

Think this could come in handy in adulthood? You better believe it.

We want our kids to walk into adulthood knowing their God-given temperament and the strengths and weaknesses that go along with their personalities. Kids who only hear praise and words about how great they are enter the adult world unprepared for more realistic and accurate feedback. Some of the contestants on *American Idol* are a great example. They have all been told they're great singers. And then out come noises that make Randy's eyes pop, and he says, "Wow, dude. You can't sing, baby. That was bad." And the contestant just can't believe it and goes off determined to prove himself all the more.

Such blinding lack of self-awareness is shocking, but when the truth has become impossible to hear, healthy feedback is not an option. We may be afraid to see our kids realistically, because somehow it's a reflection on us and our parenting. And the reality is, they are extraordinary in many areas, but they need help in others. No parent is perfect, and none of us raise perfect kids.

Good insight means our kids leave home knowing their strengths and weaknesses, aware of the good and bad within themselves and others.

Critical parents who don't allow mistakes or any weakness do damage in another way. Some kids leave home feeling they're so flawed they can't see their strengths or take a compliment.

Are you prone to seeing your kids as better or worse than they are? Do you tend to react to their behavior, or can you help them grow in self-awareness? If you have grown children, tell them about any new insight you have as you read. Tell them what you wish you could do differently if you could do it all over again.

Each of the love styles has difficulty with self-awareness. Look at the Awareness and Reflection Skills chart in the Parent Toolbox at the end of this book to see how each love style struggles with self-awareness and awareness of others. The more you develop the ability to self-reflect and share what's going on in your soul, the more you can pass this important skill on to your children.

As you use the six steps detailed earlier in this chapter to help your child, also use the points to journal or talk about the stressors in your life. Learn along with your child. The gift of insight and self-awareness is the primary gift that all others build upon, benefiting your child in every relationship he will ever have.

Nineteen

The Gift of Comfort

One weekend we were baby-sitting our four-year-old granddaughter Penelope for an overnighter. In the morning I (Milan) was brushing her hair, and she started to tear up, so I said, "Honey, you have tears and you look sad. Tell me what you are upset about."

She said, "I miss my daddy."

I looked at her big brown eyes and said, "Well, I don't blame you. Come sit on my lap and tell me what you miss the most."

She slowly slid onto my lap and said, "When he takes me on his surfboard."

I told her how special that is and what a good daddy I knew he was. I quietly rocked her for a minute or so, and then she got up. She looked at me and said, "That was a bonding moment."

I laughed. "Yes it was." And we decided to do some coloring.

Whether four, fourteen, or forty-five, all of us should know so well how to express what we feel and receive comfort like my precious granddaughter. But I know how much of that is what she's been taught, how she's been encouraged to feel and experience life for all that it is.

I could have analyzed and problem-solved and pulled out the kid's clock. "When Mickey's big hand is on the twelve and his little hand is on the three, you will get to see your dad." Or, "Let's make a chart and do a countdown." Or I could have dismissed her feelings, saying, "Don't worry, we will have fun today."

I did none of this…and yet she was content. Somehow, there was resolution that satisfied her. All I did was comfort her and listen to her emotions. Remember the mats you had rest time on in preschool or kindergarten? Remember that word, MATS. Comfort involves just four little steps:

- **Mention** what emotion you see.
- **Ask** more about how they feel and validate it.
- **Touch**—offer your lap, share a hug, cover a hand.
- **Stay** until the emotional need changes or is filled.

They will see you differently. They will love you for it. They will feel resolution. It will be a "bonding moment."

Comfort and the Brain

Life is stressful. Even in the womb we are exposed to the stress hormones surging through our mother's body. We can't remember the shock of being squeezed into a cold, bright, loud world and discovering the knot of hunger or rumblings of indigestion. We need comfort from the moment we are born, and our brains are shaped by receiving it. Comfort provides relief as we help a distressed baby to calm and physically relax.

Over time parents provide repeated experiences of moving from stress and tension to calm and composed. You might think of it as constructing a comfort-and-relief highway in the brain. The more the highway is used, the more lanes the brain adds. The more lanes there are, the easier it is to calm down after stressful events. This child learns to bounce back after feeling sad, scared, or agitated. Once the highway has been around awhile, and it's nice and wide, the child learns to self-soothe. And even when Mom or Dad isn't immediately available, the child can easily find the road to relief—calming down and recovering from stress.

Your baby's brain and nervous system are learning a lot about how to manage stress during the first years of life. "When a mother soothes her hurt child, by stroking and talking sweetly to her, she is helping the child's brain turn down the volume on its pain."[1]

Likewise, if the baby is left in high states of stress, with no relief, there is a very narrow lane for comfort. It doesn't get used much. Stress and tension remain high, and it's very hard to find that little narrow road that leads to relief. In fact, the superhighway is carrying messages of distress, pain, and anxiety without relief. For this child, stress will be harder to manage, impulses and emotions harder to control, and self-soothing will be difficult, if not impossible.

Without enough comfort, these babies and toddlers don't know what it feels like to calm down, bounce back, or feel better. It's easy to see how this scenario sets up a greater susceptibility to seek relief though addictions later in life. A highly stressed person needs relief, and all addictions provide relief without the need for relationships, but, of course, there is a price to pay, because all addictions also have negative consequences.

"Those who are nurtured best, survive best."[2] A comforted child learns people provide relief and can be trusted to help. Early experiences shape how our child sees the world and what the people in it are like. Asking for and receiving comfort involves relying on others to help and knowing how to manage emotions. These are the essential tasks for successful relationships.

Our ability to create strong relationships depends on whether we can regulate our emotions. Many experiences of comfort teach us to do just that.

As I did with my granddaughter, separation between the comforting phase and problem-solving or resolution phase is critical. But we don't have to be superparents. Some mistakes and disharmony are actually good for babies, strengthening them to tolerate some uncertainty. In fact, "experiencing disconnection is the only way that infants can learn to value moments of connection."[3] Over time babies actually learn they have a part in making connection last, the power to make their parent pay attention and engage with them.

As mentioned previously, during the first year, babies manage their interaction levels by looking away when they get overwhelmed. The more sensitive (or tired) the baby is, the more she will need time to regroup for more interaction. By five months, babies sometimes look away to establish some autonomy, testing their ability to end or initiate interactions. Some avoidance of eye contact is not rejection, it's just a baby's way of saying, "That's enough for now."[4]

EARLY EMOTIONAL MEMORIES

During the first two years of life, Mom and Dad are building a memory scrapbook in their baby's right brain, where emotions, facial expressions, and musical tones of emotional speech are processed. In essence, parents are creating *emotional memories* that will shape internal feelings of safety and trust or, in cases of trauma, feelings of uncertainty and fear, which eventually turn into defenses to protect the child from the painful feelings.

Do we remember what happened during the first two years of life? Not consciously, but right-brain memories do get reactivated from those early years all throughout our lives. To adults these right-brain memories feel like strong surges of emotions and feelings in the body (good or bad) that may seem to come from out of nowhere.

These right-brain memories are called *implicit*, which mean "embedded, hidden, or unspoken." We can't speak about them because conscious recall and words come from the left side of our brain, where language comes from. Babies don't use their left brain nearly as much until after two years old, when they start to talk. "It turns out that the vast majority of memory is implicit, and it is these memories that shape our emotional experiences, self-image, and relationships."[5] Every parent with a baby or toddler needs to read that again. This collection of stored experiences truly is *essential emotional* memory. Building a scrapbook of nurturing memories in your baby's right brain is the programming that will last a lifetime.

Memories of early caretaking become the emotional backdrop for all our later lessons about relationships and even self-awareness. "Despite our lack of [awareness of] these experiences, they come to form the infrastructure of our lives. We experience these early lessons as the 'givens' of life, rarely noticing their existence or questioning their veracity. We seldom realize that they are influencing and guiding our moment-to-moment experiences."[6]

These wordless, emotional memories come to life in adulthood in positive or negative ways. Good experiences during the first two years cause feelings of trust, safety, and positive emotions about connection. When things go wrong during the first two years, these emotional memories are felt in adulthood as a surge of distress. A dear friend of mine (Kay's), now in her fifties, was hospitalized at eighteen months old, when she and her mom were both diagnosed with tuberculosis. She has no conscious memory of this time, but she has been told that her mom was transferred from the hospital to a sanitarium for several years.

She could not yet talk and suddenly found herself alone in the hospital. Weeks later, she finally came home to find her mother absent. Throughout her adult life, departures have been traumatic for her, flooding her with agitation and a sense of foreboding. In addition, when she's sick, she sometimes feels like crying and curling up in a little ball, convinced no one can console her.

Once we were able to link these current feelings to her early experiences, the feelings made sense for the first time. Her right brain was triggered by departures (reminders of abandonment) and by illness (being confined to a bed). She recalled her early trauma with strong feelings, body sensation, and negative beliefs. At first she found it hard to put words to these sensations; they were wordless, emotional memories formed during the first two years of life when she couldn't talk.

Because so much of what we believe about relationships is formed so early, we encourage moms to stay home and be available to their infants. This is why parenting styles that are overly rigid, especially in the name of God, and put too much emphasis on schedules versus comfort and on control versus connection can have lifelong consequences. We're not saying schedules are bad, but comfort is also important. Nurturing, responsive contact, enjoyment of your baby, and minimizing stress should be high priorities for both mothers and fathers during these early years.

FILLING THE SCRAPBOOK

Comfort is not just about calming a crying child. It's about deeply observing your child at any age so you get to know her while finding pleasure in her unique qualities.

Do you find your children delightful, amusing, enjoyable, and entertaining? Maybe not at five o'clock in the morning, but kids know whether they are being enjoyed or simply tolerated. To be enjoyed means you have value. But being tolerated produces a core of shame. And it all gets put into the memory book.

When we are adults and someone is interested in us and takes the time to get to know and enjoy us, we feel secure and loved. Babies and toddlers feel the same way. To be noticed, wanted, and deeply understood is comforting. It's about responsiveness: "I see what troubles you, what you enjoy, value, desire, and need, and I respond."

Our adult right brains have a scrapbook of how our parents experienced us. Just imagine; what facial expressions did you see? Try to visualize each of your parent's eyes. What do those eyes communicate without words? How about voice tone? Do you think it was engaging and eager, or irritated or indifferent most of the time? How were mistakes handled? We make a lot of them between one and two years old.

As you go through your day with your kids, try to think about what you're adding to the scrapbook today—and every day. Whether they know it or not, they will carry it with them for a lifetime.

If you have older kids, you still have a chance to fill that scrapbook with soothing, pleasant, satisfying memories. Perhaps circumstances prevented you from giving all you wanted to provide for your baby. Maybe your attachment injuries from childhood were a hindrance. Fortunately, the brain is moldable and can be rewired with healing experiences later in childhood or even adulthood.

Personally, I've traced many of my reactions and core beliefs as an avoider to my first year of life. My spiritual life, my husband, and my friends have helped me replace those old distressing emotional memories with *curative* ones that have been very healing. And the more I healed, the better parent I became. I acknowledged why I became an avoider, what I had missed, and I went through the uncomfortable process of learning to accept comfort as an adult. And now I know how important comfort is because it has changed my life.

Once again, it's never too late. The greatest fact of life is that redemption is *always* possible. You can be delivered from mistakes and pain. I've seen God's redemptive work in my life in so many ways, and I'm praying you'll experience the same deep gratitude I have.

WRITING THE STORYBOOK

Right around two years old, the left brain gets on board and toddlers turn into kids who talk. And talk. And talk and talk and talk. Parents of extroverted kids may find themselves searching for games that keep them quiet. "Let's play the giraffe game and see how long you can be a giraffe. What do giraffes say? Oh, I guess they don't make any noise."

With language, parents help a child learn to name a feeling and associate it with a need that can be met. "You're sad because your friend has to go home. Come get a hug." "Aw, you're grumpy because you just woke up. Let's have a snack and read a book." "You might be upset because Daddy has to work late and you miss him. Let's hug for a while, and then we can make Daddy a great big card to say how much we love him."

These phrases are like a *mini story* that explains life to your child. We feel certain things because of definable forces, and we can respond to them in comforting and proactive ways. They involve interactions with our internal worlds, giving words to what's happening in a child's mysterious heart.

Stories like this give your child the first experiences of self-awareness and self-reflection. You must introduce your child to making these associations so she can learn to do it for herself. You'll have more energy for mini stories at different times during the day, but at bedtime you can often weave them into a longer story of a paragraph or longer. "Today, Emily and Mom went to the park. I think that was the best part of Emily's day. Emily was sad when we had to leave, and Mom gave her a hug. Then she had pizza for dinner and Emily loves pizza. Now we're snuggly in bed, and soon we will all go to sleep. Tomorrow will be a brand-new day for fresh adventures."

Self-awareness and the ability to self-reflect are essential to successful adult relationships. We have a simple important saying: "If you don't know what you feel, you won't know what you need."

For a child, such short stories are especially important after an upsetting event. When you forget to pick up your child from school, and he doesn't want to go the next day, tell him a mini story. "I know you felt alone and scared when I was late to pick you up. What else did you feel? And now you don't want to go to school because you're afraid it might happen again. But today, I'm going to set the alarm on my watch so I'll be sure to be here on time. You'll see me standing by this tree today when your teacher brings you out. Here's a hug and I'll have another one when I see you soon." A story like this, with the four MATS elements, makes your child feel seen and understood, and lets him know his feelings matter.

As your child grows, you can ask him questions to prompt him to tell his own story. "What was the best and worst part of your day?" "If you had one wish, what part of your day would you change?" "Your teacher seemed really grumpy today. How did that make you feel?" "Your girlfriend seems to be mad at you a lot; how are you handling that?" By the teen years, you can ask him what he needs. "I know you feel horrible about losing that game. Is there a way I can help or is there anything you need?" Every conversation helps your child learn to assess his inner world, understand his feelings, and communicate his personal experiences.

Comfort doesn't mean we should never say no or correct a child. Security is built on firm, consistent limits. And it's not comforting when there are no boundaries. We can acknowledge a feeling and still hold a line. "You lost dessert tonight because you chose to hit your sister. And I can see how mad you are, but name-calling is off limits. You can take a time-out now or miss dessert tomorrow night too. Which will it be?"

Comfort is one of the most important gifts we give our children, because it teaches them that people are our main source of help and relief. With this firm knowledge, your child will understand that God comforts us as well (see 2 Corinthians 1:3). What's more, your child will be far less prone to use addictions of all kinds to find relief. And when she leaves home, she will know how to manage her inevitable stresses well and ask for help from others when life becomes difficult and overwhelming.

Twenty

The Gift of Power

D oes your child have the power to influence you? Can she offer ideas to change your mind or show her point of view?

All children need to know they have the power to influence others, and as a highly influential and respected adult in your child's world, you have the power to affirm that in her. With the security of firm, consistent boundaries, a child can be trained to confidently affect decisions and outcomes.

Even babies say, "No more!" with body language, refusing a bottle, pushing away, or crying. Toddlers protest by running away, refusing to come, or slithering when you pick them up. And one of the first words a toddler learns is, "No!"

By responding to these early communications with descriptive words, your little one will learn she is seen and heard. For example, the baby pushes the bottle away and you say, "You're telling Mommy no more milk." And when you can't comply with a toddler's request, let him know you hear and understand. "You want me to put you down, but it's not safe. I keep you safe from cars." The protest may continue, but your child knows you understand his request even when he doesn't get his way.

Older kids need to exercise the "no" muscle too, for when it's time to launch. Like every other ability, the ability to consider options and persuade others is only developed through practice. And the more opportunities, the stronger the ability.

Your child gains the gift of power in four ways when you remember to PLAY:

- **Provide** choices.
- **Listen** to their opinions.
- **Ask** their opinions.
- Say **Yes** to requests to pretend and role-play.

POWER DECISIONS

Giving choices helps children learn to make decisions and live with the consequences of their choices. At first the choices are simple. "Do you want to wear the red coat or blue sweater?" "Do you want to start your homework with math or your book report?" Yet over time children can consider more complex options. "Would you like to try dance or art classes?" "You can decide which three friends to invite." "You research which car in this price range seems like the best option, and let's talk when you have some facts gathered."

Asking for ideas, opinions, and reasoning gives your child a chance to articulate critical thinking and develop the skill of persuasion. Many adults don't do these things well because they are skills that must be taught and encouraged. Some kids will be more naturally gifted, and you may know a preschooler who's already showing great proficiency at persuasion. Bear in mind that pestering is whiny, repetitive begging, and that kind of behavior needs a consequence. The skill of persuasion requires critical-thinking skills and the ability to articulate differing opinions.

To help kids develop thinking skills, ask questions:

- "What do you think would motivate you to brush your teeth and get your pajamas on quicker so we have time for a story?"
- "How do you think we could help Mr. Nelson since his wife is sick?"

- "Which skateboard do you think is best? Why is that?"
- "Why do you think Billy is being so quiet?"
- "What are three good questions to ask a new friend so you can get to know him?"
- "If we go for ice cream now, can you give me a plan for how you'll be in bed by nine o'clock?"
- "Why should you have that cookie before dinner? Give me three good reasons."
- "Tell me your exit plan in case that party gets out of hand. How will you know if it's time to go, and what will you say?"
- "Can you give me a list of pros and cons about buying that now as opposed to later? Let's talk when you have your ideas on paper."
- "If you were in my shoes, how would you handle this problem?"
- "What do you think it will take to rebuild trust between us?"

Notice these are not telling statements, they are questions that invite thought about solving problems, planning, analyzing, and voicing ideas. The critical next step is to *listen* to your child's reasoning and offer feedback that's encouraging, yet honest. When you do this, it shows your child that she has the power to influence you and allows her to feel confident that she is learning to figure out the world around her.

POWER PLAY

Pretending and role-playing are great ways to have fun while teaching a variety of skills. Preschoolers love to try on different roles as firemen, animals, and even parents. Kids become influential in these pretend roles and take on decision-making power.

For young kids (and even for older ones), healthy power is learned through make-believe. Initiate play with role reversals. "I'll be the child and you be the mommy or daddy." My four-year-old granddaughter Roxy loves playing Mommy. When she cooked me a hot dog the other day, and I cried because there was no ketchup, she decided to "go to the store." Before she left the room, she put a pretend cell phone on the table in front of me and said, "Now, don't touch this phone while I'm gone." I looked at the phone, up at her, and back at the phone. "Okay, Mommy," I said. She started to leave and then jumped back in. "You are going to touch that phone, aren't you?" I tried my best not to laugh, but it was so cute, and for the next hour she fed me, hugged me, made me nap, read me a story, and bossed me around. She was experiencing the feeling of power and control in the role of Mommy. It was a *hoot*!

If you have young children or grandchildren, play is how you enter their world. Po Bronson and Ashley Merryman reported the wild success of a preschool and kindergarten program called "Tools of the Mind" for their book *NurtureShock*. The program emphasizes extended play sessions as the primary learning method. "With the teacher's help, the children make individual 'play plans' [of what roles they will play]. They all draw a picture of [or write about] themselves in their chosen role.… Then they go play, sticking to the role designated in their plan…for a full 45 minutes." The results showed standard test scores jumped from the sixty-fifth percentile to the eighty-sixth percentile.[1] What are these kids learning through this prolonged play? Planning, prediction, sustained attention, impulse control, cooperation, taking turns, symbolic thought, organization, self-direction, patience, and several other essential skills.

Play is vitally important, and role-play is a central focus of young kids. Take time to enter your child's world and *play*. You'll be surprised how much fun you can have.

Role-playing can also be used when your child is struggling, to help in making friends, standing up for himself, saying no, setting a boundary, or confronting a problem. Pretending offers him practice in a safe place so he feels prepared to face his difficulty.

You will know your older kids have learned their lessons well if they can make good choices and exercise influence and take control in positive ways. As a senior in high school, our fourth child, Kelly, could stand up for herself better than most adults in their thirties. One day, she came home from school and announced at dinner that she'd gone to the principal's office. She'd transferred out of her math class because of her teacher's rude behavior toward her. Our eyes began to widen as she explained, "About two weeks ago, I confronted him after class. I waited until the other students had left and asked, 'Is there a problem between us, or have I offended you?'

"He stammered and said, 'No, well, no, I can't think of anything.'" Evidently, Mr. Nealey wasn't used to being confronted maturely by a student!

"I gave him three examples of being singled out as the recipient of his rude remarks," Kelly continued. "He said he was just teasing, but I didn't appreciate his sense of humor.

"So I said to him: 'Mr. Nealey, I don't appreciate your teasing, and I'd like you to stop.'

"To this, he said, 'That's fine. Let's start over.'

"He was fine for two weeks," Kelly said. "Then today he started up again, so I picked up my books, told him I was transferring out of his class, and went to the office. I just wanted you both to know."

Milan and I looked at each other. And slowly we grinned. Apparently, she was well on her way to not needing us anymore.

The next night, her math teacher called our house and said, "Your daughter and I had a conflict. She handled herself in a very mature way." I thanked Mr. Nealey for the call and said, "We trust her judgment. Apparently, she's worked through the problem, and we support her decision."

These are vital skills for any healthy adult. How can you grow to be successful at empowering your kids? Kids are empowered when they leave home for the adult world if they have good critical thinking skills, can say no and set boundaries, and make wise decisions. Each love style will have a different challenge.

Avoider parents will have had little help learning these skills and are used to evaluating and making decisions on their own. So, you'll have to train yourself in PLAY to provide kids choices, listen, ask their opinions, and say yes to role-playing. They need more help than you probably got from your parents.

Pleasers would rather rescue their kids, minimize conflict, or fight their kids' battles for them. Pleasers also often give in to pestering, which teaches children to get what they want by whining. Since pleasers have difficulty setting boundaries or making decisions, it's important to think about modeling these skills. As pleasers learn to lean into conflict and accept the reality of rejection and anger, they improve in helping their kids do the same.

Vacillators go the opposite direction. They exert power by being overly angry or withdrawing. And neither models healthy boundaries or self-assertion that works toward resolution. Vacillators often feel they know best and can have a difficult time listening to differing opinions without getting defensive. It's important to seek out your children's ideas and give them some influence. Engage with them in an activity of their choosing and be curious about their ideas and opinions, especially when they differ from yours. You don't have to agree to listen.

Controllers need to stop overwhelming people with aggression power and learn to soften their approach. Kids must learn that having power is not a scary thing, but that it can be a good relational skill. Work to share the power by truly listening and allowing others in the family to have a voice. Having sympathy for the child you once were, and coming to terms with your suffering, makes this possible.

Victims model passivity by tolerating the intolerable: allowing their spouses to be the power brokers in their families. This gives a loud and clear message to the kids: one person gets all the power in this family, and it's not you or me. Kids who have been controlled and dominated end up insecure about making decisions, unable to speak up when they should, and susceptible to being controlled as adults.

Once again, your growth is the first step to raising kids who leave home empowered to live in an adult world where not everyone is nice, protective, sincere, or kind. It's never too late to learn to be appropriately assertive rather than passive or aggressive. We all have a different journey to get there, but healthier uses of power are possible with the proper balancing from every type of parent.

Twenty-One

The Gift of Frustration

I (Milan) was driving to the *New Life Live* radio station one morning, and I listened to an interview with Lakers superstar Kobe Bryant on KNX 1070 Newsradio. He said he attributed his team's success to the fact that since training camp, Coach Phil Jackson had taught them to talk among themselves on the court and solve their own problems—no matter what another team threw at them. Bryant went on to point out that this is why Jackson sits quietly on the sidelines. This story illustrates precisely our goal of parenting—to train our children to be able to solve their *own* problems in life, no matter what gets thrown at them.

I think we can all agree life is stressful. How can we prepare our kids to solve their own problems and manage stress well by the time we launch them?

IT ALL STARTS IN TRAINING

Home and the early years are children's training camps. The right amount of frustration and stress will build strength into their lives. While frustration may not seem like a wonderful gift to give your children, if it's age appropriate and leads toward resolution, it will improve their abilities to cope later in life. Frustrations should be kid sized to match the size of their shoulders, beginning with light pressure when they are toddlers and eventually becoming heavier on toward eighteen.

Allowing kids to feel some stress is good while we can still step in and help. With the knowledge of effective stress management, parents can help their children not be overly stressed or too coddled.

The key for parents is in *regulating* the frustration while guiding the process of learning to manage stress.

A child is born without skills for dealing with fears, disconnection, and confusing sensations. These various coping mechanisms are built up gradually, with experience, through modeling and direct training from parents. An infant is soothed and finds comfort when swaddled and held close to the mother. As the new mom and dad are attuned, make eye contact, nurture, laugh, feed, talk, and coo to the child, his little brain feels safe, and the anxieties settle down.

For the first year, parents are the primary regulator of their child's stress. Many episodes of distress followed by soothing will train the child (and the brain) how to recover and return to a state of calm composure. For the next eighteen years, parents gradually allow the child to build tolerance for frustration, so she can eventually handle difficulties and her shoulders are able to successfully carry more of the stresses life brings.

If this process is accomplished well enough, the developing child will gradually learn to *self-regulate*. She will manage stress well and calm down easily after an upset. Calm people can face and solve problems more easily than highly reactive people. Sadly, there are many people who come into our offices as adults who have never learned to self-regulate. Often their parents have erred in one of two directions.

The Understressed Child

"Can you type my paper, Mom?" "Can you get me a drink?" "I need a clean shirt." "I know my room's a mess, but could you make my bed anyway?" For Dean, a freshman, his pleaser mom is his live-in maid. Since he was born, Dean has given the orders and Mom has been a *wonderful* mom.

Or is she?

When children are overprotected, they are *understressed* and can't handle frustration, find solutions, and calm down. Some parents believe love means never having to hear, "I'm struggling" or, "I'm in pain." So they protect their children and keep them from any stress or problems. But protection from pain isn't love. Only natural consequences raise strong children who have tested their abilities to withstand difficulty. Fear-based children won't have a lot of confidence in their abilities.

Another problem of being overly attentive is that indulgence creates a sense of entitlement. Parents, be adult enough to tolerate your kids' disappointments and anger over not having their way all the time. Overly solicitous parents send the message, "You need my help because you are incapable of doing things on your own." Pleasers, vacillators (when not angry), and victims may all tend to want their children to be overly dependent on them. Pleasers and victims lack boundaries and vacillators tend to alternate between overprotection and withdrawing in anger, which leaves kids confused.

THE OVERSTRESSED CHILD

Lacy's experience growing up could not have been more opposite to Dean's. When Lacy was six, she was left to baby-sit her two younger siblings while her parents partied. Her angry dad created enormous stress, and Lacy was left to deal with daily chaos. By high school she was expected to pay for almost everything she needed, including medical supplies.

Lacy's dad was a controller. Avoiders, controllers, and angry vacillators are parents who are likely to do the opposite of Dean's pleaser mom. Insensitive to the pain they're inflicting, parents of overstressed children don't recognize how too much frustration creates "fright without solution," stress without relief. Being left in a high state of distress causes children to need extreme coping mechanisms that block out the anxiety. As a result of feeling overwhelmed much of the time, they learn not to *manage* stress but to *escape* it. Instead of a process of gradually working toward dealing with stress, they're overloaded from the start, and anxiety may become normal.

Anger without resolution is always damaging to kids. Some parents, most notably controllers and vacillators, often get into states where they become angry at someone in the family, and after a blowup, they withdraw. Left without an adult to help settle them down and regulate their emotions, kids end up extra stressed.

PROVIDING HEALTHY FRUSTRATION

So how much stress is too much? Babies vary in how much they can handle. Some fall apart without much provocation and some seem to go with the flow. As a general rule, the more help babies get, and the more often they are soothed, the better they can calm themselves down later on. So don't worry about spoiling a baby. Schedules and routines are fine, as long as a baby isn't overly stressed. Overall, the less a baby is frustrated, the better.

With toddlers and preschoolers, alternate between applying the brakes and stepping on the accelerator. Some toddlers and preschoolers seem to have the pedal down constantly, and you do a lot of chasing with this kind. In perpetual motion, these kids are on the go, and they get frustrated and feel stressed when you rein them in and set limits. Other kids seem to have the brakes on. Cautious, observant, careful, and guarded, they need prodding and encouragement to try new experiences. The toddler with the pedal to the metal is going to feel frustrated when you try to slow him down and teach him limits. But the preschooler who's pumping the brakes will feel anxious when you try and prod her to explore, join in, or try new things.

The goal here is to pay attention to *your* kid and allow him to experience moderate frustration, whether reining him in or pushing him forward.

Last time I was in the store, my head automatically turned when I heard the wailing child behind me. My eyes fell on a three-year-old sitting in a shopping cart, and I couldn't believe what I saw. At least fifty pounds overweight, he was just starting to wind up, and within a few moments, I knew the fire-engine scream would release. But my big clue about what was going on was the terrified look on the parents' faces. As a former lifeguard, I've seen panic-stricken faces, and though there was no water nearby, they had that same look. They swiped things off the shelves faster than a dog licking peanut butter. Anything to head off the inevitable. Of course, the inevitable happened, and I quickly chose another lane.

This kid was screaming to be reined in. But the parents were too afraid. And a child who's in control of his parents knows nothing of how to manage his frustration. Pleasers, avoiders, and victims are conflict-averse and hate confrontation, so early on, the goal will become to appease, distract, and avoid rather than set limits. A firm, "No, we are not buying that," would have likely caused this three-year-old to throw a fit. But he did that anyway! So let him, and remove him from the store!

Three-year-olds don't have much, if any, control over their emotions. So don't tell them to stop crying. They can cry and still learn an important lesson: we don't always get what we want in life. And another lesson: Mom's no means no. Think about the alternative. If this little guy can hold his parents hostage, imagine what he'll be like at sixteen. Think he'll tolerate anyone telling him no?

What if he's five or six, instead of three? It's fair to expect a little more. "Mom said no and you may cry if that upsets you, but yelling, screaming, or hitting is off limits. You'll sit on the time-out chair when we get home if you continue."

Then there are kids like Isaac, a four-year-old with the brakes on. I watched his mother do a masterful job with him at a birthday party for one of my grandkids. "I know you like to watch before you join in Isaac, so I'll sit here with you on the edge of the pool and we'll watch awhile." After ten minutes she said, "What do you want to try first, the pool or the bounce house?"

"Neither," he whined. "I just want to sit here with you."

"Well, I want to have fun," said Isaac's mom. "So I'm going in the pool." Isaac whimpered when she left, but she swam nearby and played with the kids. After a while she came over and took Isaac into the pool, without asking him if he wanted to swim.

"It's cold," Isaac complained.

"Good thing it's a hot day," Mom said cheerfully. "It feels good once you're in a few minutes." Sure enough, in minutes Isaac's frown had changed into a wide grin. Soon he was playing happily. His comfort level was stretched without completely overwhelming him. I took the time to compliment her on her sensitivity and how she coaxed Isaac to discover his fears were exaggerated.

With School-Age Kids and Teens

In Southern California, elementary school children study the old Catholic missions that dot the landscape. These missions were placed in key population areas and were a vital part of the religious and cultural development. Kids generally build models of these missions out of sugar cubes, Popsicle sticks, and various things from the yard.

Yet every year at open house, it's no challenge to figure out which third graders have overprotective parents. While her kid was off playing with other girls, one such proud mother stood vigil over their project with a first-place ribbon, beaming with pride. I walked by and said, "Nice job."

"Thanks!" she said, completely oblivious to the fact that she'd undermined the entire goal of the project.

What happens if you do your kids' work for them? Will they end up able to manage stress and pressure well as adults? And if they do manage to perform, will it be with high levels of anxiety, looking to others for reassurance?

Ask yourself this question. Am I doing things for my child that she could easily do for herself? Am I allowing enough frustration in my school-age kids to teach them to cope with stress and frustration? Do I ever allow them to fail, so they know mistakes are not fatal or final? Do they have a little bit more responsibility than they did last year?

With adolescents, strive to help your teen make decisions. David's dad liked to brag that his fifteen-year-old son had a 4.0 in all his honors classes and was selected for the all-star baseball team for the second year in a row. He was sure that with a pitching coach, David would do even better this year. The kid *was* truly amazing, but what David's dad was missing was that his poor kid was stressed to the breaking point. Sleep deprived, grumpy, anxious, and prone to angry outbursts, he had way too much to handle, and he was crumbling under the weight of his dad's high expectations.

Is your teen challenged without being a stressed-out, nervous wreck? Are you slowly increasing the weight of responsibility and stress?

Sometimes this means letting your teen decide how to handle a problem. I got a call in the middle of the day from my son when he was a junior. "Dad, I've got a big problem on my hands." They were not words a parent likes to hear, but I took a deep breath and asked him what was up. "Dad, do you remember the team party last month where the mom served beer and the players and coaches were there drinking? Well, the lid is off, and I'm in the middle of it. The athletic director and the principal want me to tell them who I saw there."

My gut response was to rescue him, go to the principal's office and persuade them to give my kid a break. But I resisted. He wasn't a little boy anymore. He was seventeen, going on eighteen, and soon would leave for college.

Kay and I listened as Kevin stewed over his conviction to not be the team tattletale. We told him we'd support his choice and reassured him that despite any threats by well-intentioned adults, this problem wasn't fatal.

The next day, the principal and athletic director pressured him, but Kevin stood his ground. He explained his moral dilemma, reiterating that he'd done nothing wrong, and that this was his final answer. He told them he was prepared to take whatever punishment they wanted to give him for not cooperating, and they finally dismissed him to go back to class.

Games were forfeited, consequences were enforced, and, as a result, the team finished last in the league. Some time later, both the principal and the athletic director contacted me directly to say Kevin handled himself well. He was stressed, but he handled it.

With the correct amount of stress for each child, he will mature toward adulthood well. Work with your child as he gets older to manage his stress levels. Also, try to remain aware of his confidence level: is he too confident or not confident enough? The best approach is to be a stress regulator as you teach your child to *comanage* his stress and frustration with you, growing in his ability as his own regulator.

Twenty-Two

The Gift of Confession

One caller to the *New Life Live* radio show had been struggling with guilt about an abortion she had at sixteen. She told us she had prayed about it over and over, but to no avail. The guilt remained and it seemed to be getting stronger the older she became. We asked if she'd ever told anyone other than God. She was quiet and then said no. We shared a verse with her that says, "Confess your sins to one another, and pray for one another so that you may be healed" (James 5:16).

Confession is a gift because it provides *freedom* from sin, shame, and embarrassment. After Adam and Eve disobeyed, they were afraid and covered themselves and hid from God. When we hide, it slowly eats away at us. The psalmist wrote, "When I kept silent about my sin, my body wasted away through my groaning all day long" (Psalm 32:3).

Undisclosed sin is like the Dead Sea, toxic without an outlet. And life is extinguished. But when we confess, we create an outlet for the toxic contaminants, and it brings refreshment and freedom to our hearts. In his confessional psalm, David asked God to "restore to me the joy of Your salvation" (Psalm 51:12). When we lay out our guilt to God and confess to others, the distress that eats at us vanishes, and we can feel the joy of our restored relationships. Confession is like letting ourselves out of jail.

Confession Is a Gift to Others

Kay and I have asked a question to thousands of people as we travel and speak: "How many of you had parents who apologized to you for their mistakes or ways they hurt you?" We estimate that only around 10 percent had parents who owned up to their shortcomings and gave them apologies. This is a major problem we don't want to duplicate with our kids.

How did your original family handle apologies? Were mistakes owned regularly? seldom? never? Did your parents require apologies from you but never gave them? Did your parents overapologize or say they were sorry a lot but never changed? Did you try to apologize to an angry parent and get rebuffed? What were your love lessons about confession? Most likely, you're still following the rules you learned.

We asked the adults in the audience who did have a parent who genuinely apologized what they experienced from that.

"It was life changing for me."

"I saw my parents as more human and vulnerable."

"It brought us closer, and the apology erased my resentment."

"It gave me more respect for my dad."

Not once have we heard a negative experience with parents owning their mistakes. Confession is a gift to your kids, no matter how old they are. They may be toddlers or grown adults, but it will liberate them, and it will free you as well.

The Facade of Strength

None of us are perfect, so we all wound and are wounded within relationships. Most of us think we are fine, especially when we're alone. If we could be honest with ourselves, we'd see them, but usually our wounds become most visible when we enter relationships. Relationships expose our wounds. Many can't allow others to see their mistakes, and so create a false self—a facade of competency. Like the wonder of Main Street at Disneyland, it looks amazing for a few moments, but after a while we realize it's fake. While we may not feel angry or lied to by Walt Disney, it's easy to feel that way with people's fake fronts. It makes you wonder what sort of garbage they're hiding back there.

How many people strive to get others to believe in the false selves they themselves so desperately want to believe in?

Not only is this exhausting (take it from me), but sooner or later your spouse and kids will see your weaknesses anyway. Ask your adolescent and he will tell you exactly what your weaknesses are. Sooner or later the truth comes to light.

A caller to the *New Life Live* radio program told us her husband had died nine months earlier, and he was the hero to the family. Yet as she cleaned out his office and opened his computer files, they were filled with porn sites and explicit e-mails to prostitutes and call girls. "I'm deeply betrayed and filled with anger. My kids are still mourning the death of their hero, and I want to dig him up and scream at him. Should I tell the kids? I feel so alone." I told her I believed that at some point the adult children needed to know the truth. I felt deep sadness for this family, but when the facade falls, the garbage is exposed.

How much different it could have been if this man could have owned his addiction, confessed to his wife, and gotten the help he obviously needed. There were understandable and fixable reasons for his runaway lust. But to stay on track and make progress, he would have needed accountability, that is, regular, honest confession. At some point his sons could have greatly benefited from his story of healing and an explanation of how porn works on the brain and why addictions develop.

And now it was too late.

Another consequence of facades is that we'll have to blame someone else or defend ourselves when confronted or criticized. In reality, we're broken, the world is broken, and nothing here works right. We're all under the curse of sin, and failure is a part of life. Blaming and defensiveness send the message, "I'm perfect and others are the problem." How much better to admit our failures and enjoy the grace we'll receive as a secure platform of future success?

We must model how to be human and admit our failures to our kids. To show your real self, relax, and teach your children to accept their humanness, you must come to accept your humanness first.

WHAT ARE THE BENEFITS OF CONFESSION?

First, we can fulfill God's commands. God calls us to confess in James 5:16. Many other scriptures talk about what we should be doing in relationship. We like to call these "one another" verses: We're commanded to *love one another.* But how can we if we don't tell each other the ways we haven't been loved? We're told to *serve one another,* but how can we do that if we're ashamed to express a need? We're ordered to *encourage one another,* yet is this possible if we fail to share where we're discouraged? God insists that we *comfort one another,* but can we if we don't know where we're distressed? He says to *bear one another's burdens,* yet if we don't know where the load is heavy and tell someone, no one can help us. And God is clear that we must *confess to and pray for one another,* yet this becomes quite impossible if we won't face our guilt and shame.

Since we're not like God and can't read minds, the only way to see each other's souls is to risk revealing ourselves to one another. This requires exploring our hurts, laying aside pride, revealing our wounds, sharing the pain in our hearts, admitting our needs, and asking for help.

A second benefit of confession is that you can help your family live in *reality.* Your confession as a parent demonstrates to your kids the most realistic view of self and others, which is essential for health and vitality. When Mom and Dad are both good and bad with strengths and weaknesses, making good choices and bad, kids learn that confession reveals truth. When this happens, we are able to integrate the good and bad parts in ourselves and others, which results in far less shame and embarrassment.

Throughout their development, your kids will understand mistakes are expected, forgivable, and valuable, creating immense emotional freedom.

Confession also brings comfort to wounds. Sometimes it's as hard to confess and admit our mistakes as to confess horrible things we've endured at the hands of another. A couple came into my office seeking marital therapy because they were having control battles. If he wasn't in charge, he became threatened and very angry. As I had them explore the details of the past, week after week, a story finally came out that provided an answer.

To me, it was an all-too-common story, but to the wife, it was new. The husband revealed a history of abuse and torment by a bully who hovered and reveled in the fear he caused through a mere glance or sneer. Much to the wife's surprise, it wasn't a schoolmate or a kid next door but an older sibling who was jealous, aggressive, and meanspirited. The avoider dad minimized his son's feelings and was inattentive and totally unaware of the horrible abuse going on in his own home.

Though my client was explosive toward his wife and children, he took a while to confess the worst part. "When my parents left the house, my brother would tell me, 'Go run and hide, and when I find you, I'm going to hurt you.' After the chase and the beating were over, he would threaten me and say, 'If you ever tell Mom and Dad, I will smother you in the middle of the night. They'll never know how you died.' I believed every word he said."

This went on for *several years,* and my client suffered from insomnia, anxiety, poor grades, bedwetting, and separation anxiety. The clueless parents believed he had ADD and a learning disorder. He was shamed by his dad and coddled by his mom. Like Esau and Jacob, the parental favoritism caused a huge divide in both the family and the marriage. Finally, one day he was big enough to kick the brother away and hurt him in return. And the abuse began to subside.

I asked his wife to hug him as he told the story, and she cried with him as he sobbed about the pain he'd endured for so many years. Almost immediately, his explosiveness and rage began to diminish, thanks to the nurturing and grieving he was able to process with his wife. Confession had opened the doors of healing. His healing will filter down to his parenting.

Avoiders will understandably have trouble with being independent and self-sufficient, growing up in performance-based homes where mistakes were unwelcome. As parents, avoiders feel admitting mistakes shows inadequacy and weakness. They can't imagine the relief of being allowed to be human.

Pleasers minimize problems rather than wading in. How can pleasers confess or believe other family members should own up if they make excuses for them rather than acknowledging their shortcomings? Pleasers overapologize to keep the peace and don't tend to require apologies from the spouse or kids, even when they deserve one. "Your dad doesn't mean to yell; he's just had a hard day." Pleasers let family members off the hook, and they don't naturally model or teach confession well.

Vacillators tend to see everyone else as the problem. Often on a mission to extract confession from others, they have great difficulty owning their mistakes. When vacillators do look at their faults, they tend to go to the "all bad" place and feel miserable, which sends them back into blaming mode. Apologizing for angry outbursts and hurtful words is a good starting place.

Controllers see confession as demeaning. Punished unfairly as kids, they've often experienced enough humiliation and shame to last a lifetime. It's difficult for controllers to feel genuine remorse, as they rarely have seen it. It's also difficult for controllers to imagine the freedom and relief confession can bring. But when controllers are willing to admit how damaging their anger is, and accept comfort for the pain that fuels the anger, it is truly a miracle to behold.

Victims apologize for anything and everything to avoid another explosion. They are often made to apologize for things they are not responsible for. Trained in childhood to accept blame, this is a natural role for the victim to assume as an adult. Confession doesn't mean being responsible for another's actions or feelings, but for your own.

What If My Child Won't Apologize?

- You may have an angry kid who gets the blame for everything. Harsh, unfair, or inconsistent parenting (or constant focus on a kid's weakness) can backfire. A child's refusal to apologize might be a sign that something needs attention in the family system.
- You may excuse the child too much and give in when you meet resistance.
- Ask yourself how well you model these traits in your life: humility, ownership, confession, remorse, forgiveness. More is caught than taught.
- Don't expect a child to make amends when she is still very upset, agitated, and distressed. Give her time to calm down first.
- You may have a strong-willed kid who resists compliance. Don't give up. (See chapter 15, "The Determined Child," for suggestions.)
- You may be a parent that demands respect in a disrespectful way. Sooner or later the injustice and double standard makes a child or teen angry.

What If My Child Apologizes Too Much?

- This is a sign of pleaser or victim tendencies.
- You may model apologizing too much, and they're following your example.
- Your child may be afraid of your anger and wants to appease you.
- Your child may fear emotional or physical abandonment and is trying to win you back.

Then, Forgive

Mindy, a thirty-year-old client, was a pleaser for good reason. She was afraid of her mom's anger because it meant days, weeks, and in one instance, a full month that her mom would not speak to her. When she felt her mom withdrawing into one of these silent tantrums, she would frantically write notes of apology and slip them under her mom's door or put them in her purse. Her mom never acknowledged her efforts at reconciliation, and Mindy suffered with horrible anxiety, which became a problem in her marriage. Kids need to know their mistakes can be forgiven, and reassurance must be given that they are loved and accepted.

Confession liberates your family to live in reality, be human, and know that mistakes are not fatal or final. It's truly an amazing gift. When forgiveness is offered, it is balm to a hurting soul. You can give this gift to your children, even if your spouse is not willing to go along with you. And someday, their spouse may thank you.

Twenty-Three

The Gift of Laughter

When I was a young pastor making a meager salary and paying for our children to attend Christian school, even something like eating at McDonald's was out of the question. So, if we weren't invited to lunch or dinner, I'd make lunch for Kay and the kids, and we would sing my version of the old ad jingle: "McMilan's is your kind of place (clap, clap), a hap, hap, hap-happy place..."

Having fun was something that I could do without a lot of money. I served them all kinds of things—grilled cheese, burritos, pizza, German pancakes, spaghetti omelets. I once made barbecued beef sandwiches that were so salty, I tried to rinse the meat under the faucet. When they ate them, the water ran down their arms to their elbows. Even the neighborhood kids would come over and want to eat and sing the song. And sing we did.

Not too many years ago, we ran into one of the grown kids from the old neighborhood, and she said she wanted to bring her child over someday to sing the McMilan's song. Fond memories were made, and my kids are fully grown with their own children now, but if I'm in the kitchen and I start singing McMilan's, they all sing along and clap on cue. I'm a better cook these days, but they still look for opportunities to make fun of my runny barbecued beef sandwiches.

As with all issues, having the proper amount of laughter in a family is a matter of finding balance. As King Solomon said, "[There is] a time to weep and a time to laugh; a time to mourn and a time to dance"

(Ecclesiastes 3:4). What was modeled for you: weeping and mourning or laughing and dancing? Were your parents playful, and were they playful with you? If not, it won't feel natural to be playful with your kids. But fun is a very important part of the bonding process.

The importance of play between parent and child has been well documented. Studies show that children who play with their parents are more able to balance work and play later in life. In fact, there are several things being taught when you play with your kids, among them that *enjoyment* is central to a fulfilling and productive life.

THE FAMILY FUNNY BONE

All children are naturally playful, yet some have their *fun factor* killed off by the parent's emotional state. When Mom and Dad sulk instead of smile, or pout and withdraw instead of play, there's not much room for fun.

Parents who don't ever play with their children often don't know how to play themselves. Their motto is "life is work and play is pointless." For many in this camp, play is avoided. Perfectionists and workaholics speed along at a breakneck pace, and moody-broody parents learned a while ago that play was for other people. Children learn early that approval comes with performance, and I see clients all the time with ulcers, anxiety, depression, and compulsive traits who can trace their problems to their frantic lifestyles during their formative years.

For some, immense pressure to perform creates an all-work-no-play mentality. Parents with addictions don't play either. We had a radio caller who told us about his twenty-year battle with pornography. It had been all consuming, and even when he was with his kids, his mind and hormones were elsewhere. Now that he was recovered, he was realizing how much time he had lost with his kids. He cried and mourned, "It robbed us of precious time that can never be recaptured."

Some parents play too much. Some grown-up children buy themselves expensive toys, feeling they deserve to protect their own pleasure. Other parents buy their kids anything they want and never set boundaries, maybe to appease a guilty conscience.

The goal is finding a balance between caring for yourself and getting help for your wounds, but also entering your children's world to play at *their* level, not yours. When parents can do this, they create an atmosphere that allows the family funny bone to develop. And wonderful family fun and bonding is the inevitable result.

How Do Different Love Styles Play?

Avoiders can be fun when they choose to engage, but often turn fun into work and mastering the game at hand. They can push kids for mastery too and make them practice extensively until their game is perfect. Of course, this ruins the fun. Avoider parents aren't easily pleased and may drive away from the Little League game quiet, dismissive, or correcting mistakes.

Pleaser parents generally bring laughter and fun to the family and will work to turn just about any occasion into a fun moment if it will please the kids and spouse. If it doesn't, pleasers may struggle to have fun and be spontaneous. Yet often pleasers can be found having too much fun, with too many smiles and too few boundaries and consequences.

Vacillators are very fun parents *if* they're in the right mood. Their laughter and playful side is intermittent and cyclical. When they're preoccupied, they're no fun. They'll eventually cycle back to a lighter state, see their children again, and want to engage. Sometimes the timing of vacillators is insensitive and intrusive, and they barge their way into the child's world, uninvited and expecting a grand welcome. If the child then declines to go along with it, vacillators may get angry.

Controllers can be fun, but their playfulness is unpredictable. When they're in the right mood, they can have a good time, but often at the expense of others. Lacking empathy, they can be sarcastic, laugh and make fun of others, and create humor at the cost of another's feelings. They can lack good judgment, because their awareness of themselves and others is low. When they engage, they can tease unmercifully and be quite unaware of going too far. They can easily drive a child to tears.

Victims struggle to be present and have fun, as they are quite preoccupied with their safety and protection. When they do engage, they do so impulsively and unpredictably, which keeps the child in a confused state. Like the controller, they can laugh inappropriately and shame others who are weaker and helpless.

What Constitutes Play?

Play is not defined as activities done in isolation, such as computer games. Too much isolation leads to poor development socially, as these skills are shaped by playing and interacting with peers. Of course, playing alone quietly is important as well, to learn to be alone and care for oneself. But it's important for a child to play with others at a peer level, to explore and figure things out together.

Play is where enjoyment is mutual and laughter happens together *with* others and not *at* anyone. There is nothing demeaning or shaming about healthy play. Teasing is often at another's expense and can easily cause anger or hurt feelings.

The anxious core within each of the love styles can make it difficult to enjoy play for anyone with attachment issues. Just like with other parenting tasks, personal struggles can overwhelm our ability to engage and enjoy others. To find your funny bone again, you need to take care of yourself, so you can be less self-absorbed and pay attention to your kids. Counselors, psychologists, and psychiatrists are trained to find the areas of weakness and identify the patterns and help you create the shift toward becoming a healthier parent.

Taking time for yourself and enjoying your own playtime is vital to getting your body's natural mood elevators flowing. If you tend to work too much or go too fast to play, think about places in your day that might use a little balancing of playtime—you don't want to be a dull boy or girl, after all. It seems many people running around these days are rather worn out and quite dull.

In the Old Testament, God required observance of the Sabbath day for rest. One day a week, no one could do any work. Travel was for short distances only, and there were several other rules that prevented people from making money or generally getting ahead on the Sabbath. So, with nothing else to do, play would have become part of the equation. Moms and dads undoubtedly played on those days. God knew they needed to.

Parental health develops healthy children. But sometimes we need to be reminded.

PARENTS TEACH FUN

Like other abilities, laughter and fun is caught more than taught. But it's even more taught than defined by love style.

My dad could be so fun. My mom was a fearful type, so father-son times were Dad's chance to satisfy his longing to explore new and different places. When I was little, he'd surprise me by whispering in my ear and asking if I wanted to get up early and have a snow day. I'd be so excited as we got ready. I always felt safe with him on our adventures.

I remember going to baseball and football games in downtown LA. We'd often eat in Chinatown or "Little Tokyo" at a restaurant where no one spoke English. Dad would smile at the waiter, say a greeting in his language, and then say, "Bring us what's good." I'll never forget the time they made sukiyaki on our table and I first tried octopus. Afterward we'd walk to a Japanese candy store. To this day, whenever I use chopsticks, I think of being with my dad.

We'd go on night drives, just to get out of the house. He'd have me sit close and steer the car while he worked the pedals. I remember him letting me get behind the wheel of his '51 Studebaker when I was twelve.

I worked the three-speed column shift. I could hardly see over the steering wheel, and when I popped the clutch, I went over a curb and hit a bush. It scared me and I wanted to quit, but he laughed and made me back it up and try again until I could shift into all three gears. While I was driving, he'd cheer me on while delivering a physics lesson on all the mechanics of the car. I still love driving *and* the physics my mechanical-engineer dad taught me.

Of course, we never told Mom.

He always found new and different things to do by looking in the newspaper. From Little League to Boy Scouts to pinewood derbies, he'd read about it, and we'd be there on opening day. He taught me how to use all the tools when the house or car needed work. And one day when I was in college, we both stayed home from work and spent the entire day under our house fixing a plumbing leak.

He let me play jokes on him as well. One day we were fixing the washing machine, and I said, "Hey, Dad, look in the water hose. I think it's plugged." Just as he did, I hit the start button and he got a surprise. He laughed and laughed. At a family gathering, I got him with the old smell-this-pie trick, and he wound up with a whipped-cream-topped nose. He'd always cuss a little and then have a good laugh.

The things you do with your kids don't need to be elaborate or even something outside of what you'd normally do. Kids bring fun with them wherever they go. Let them join you in your chores, and look for ways to make work into play.

FUN WITH KIDS

My kids remember many, if not most, of the fun things we did together as a family, and they've started doing them with their kids. Here are several:

- Driving to school, I'd wiggle the steering wheel and say,
  "Oh no! The car is out of control! It has a mind of its own.

I don't know where it's going!" Then I'd turn into a
driveway and come to a stop in front of a doughnut shop.

- One Fourth of July, I spent three hours filling water
  balloons and loading them into buckets in the back of my
  Ford "Exploder." I waited for the kids and, at just the right
  moment, I opened the back and hit one of the kids with a
  balloon. Within a nanosecond, everyone headed to the
  buckets, and all those balloons were gone in sixty seconds.

- We'd use buckets of warm soapy water to wash the cars and,
  at some point, I'd say, "Hey, I forgot to take a bath today."
  I'd sit on the driveway and start lathering up with the big
  sponges. The kids would gasp and start to giggle, and pretty
  soon we were all taking baths on the driveway (with our
  clothes on, of course!).

- During the hottest months, I'd walk out on the patio with
  a bucket filled with squirt guns and start shooting. The
  squirt-gun wars would last for hours, and sometimes end
  up in the house. And we never told Mom. (Hi, Mom!)

- We'd play "kisses make the horsie go," and there could be
  two or three kids on my back at any given time.

- We'd ride waves at the beach on boogie boards, over and
  over and over again. Last weekend, I helped my six-year-old
  grandson catch a wave, and my son John looked over and
  smiled. "That was déjà vu." John now surfs waves that are
  way out of my league.

- We spent countless hours with our electric guitars playing
  along to U2's *The Joshua Tree*. Kevin went on to lead worship
  at youth group, and John now plays at open mike nights at
  a local restaurant. Recently, we went to a U2 concert and
  shared a smile remembering our jam sessions.

- Kay was in graduate school part-time when Kelly was five.
  Every Monday night we'd turn on the football game, and

I'd tell Kelly, "I really want to watch the game." Then for the next three hours, we'd wrestle as she'd jump up, close the doors on the television cabinet, and pounce on me to hold me down so I couldn't get up. We'd have arm-wrestling matches, and I'd lose after making lots of straining noises. And when she was tired, I'd carry her upstairs to bed.

- When John was in fifth and sixth grade, Kay would pack dinner and we'd go to the BMX bike races. His older brother and I were his pit crew, fixing flats and making adjustments to his bike. His room was loaded with trophies.

- I was Amy's chauffeur to volleyball games, soccer games, the mall, and the movies. She was my "Sweet-tart" (tart the first hour after she woke up and sweet from then on) and went in a blink from a little girl in pigtails to an elegant woman. When she needed a new bathing suit, I'd take her shopping and any suit had to pass the strict Daddy Test. She learned she had power as a woman and how to handle it responsibly. We still smile about those shopping trips, and at thirty-four, she still calls me Daddy, though she doesn't run her bathing suits past me anymore.

- I used to do short triathlons when the kids were little, and when Kevin was twelve, we did one together at the local university. We look back fondly on that time as one of the most wonderful bonding times in our relationship. I still smile remembering running across that finish line to-gether—him slightly ahead of me.

- The other day, I wrestled with my two-year-old grand-daughter. She'd get on top of me, and I taught her to say, "Tap out, Poppy," and then I'd give up. Someday she'll learn what that means, but until then, she knows it makes her giggle.

FUN WITH PARENTS

What goes around, comes around. If you dish it out, be prepared to take it as well. The best parent-child relationships happen when the child feels free to play with the parent. Here are just a few of the many things the kids did to me:

- They'd plot wedgie attacks together. When I least suspected it, they'd pounce and drag me to the ground. Most of the time, their strategy was for two of them to get me down, and the free one would grab my underwear and pull as hard as he or she could.
- After a run I'd take a shower, and I've had many a bucket of ice water on my head as the heartless fiends sprung out of nowhere. I would shriek like a third-grade girl, and they would laugh and run, which would start the chase around the house.
- Kelly and her grade-school friend pounced on me one day. The shy fifty-pound girl from up the street bravely held me down while Kelly painted my toenails with clear glitter nail polish. I went along with it, and they walked off in victory, having carefully hidden all the polish remover. The evening went by, and I forgot about it until the next day when I spent most of my kung fu lesson curling my toes under. When I told the girls, they howled with delight and told everyone at school.
- Fishing through my briefcase for a stick of gum, I found that Kelly had chewed all twelve pieces and neatly put them back into the pack.

The gift of laughter is about enjoying play, and every family will have their own style. Practical jokes, satire, dry humor, or make-believe, your kids will learn to play the way they're taught. Like any other area of growth, you can choose today to become an improved parent in the fun department.

Do you want to be bonded to your children? Do you want them to tell stories about growing up and have laughs available for a lifetime? Do you want to see them play the same games with their kids as you did with them? All you have to do is start today, and make it a point to enjoy life and bring enjoyment into their lives while you can.

You have more power over them than you know. Use it wisely and make investments into fun and laughter.

And by the way, spaghetti omelets are *really* good.

Twenty-Four

The Gift of God: The Perfect Parent

Jenny sat next to her husband, Jim, her arms folded tightly across her chest. "I'm so upset. Jim and I had a hard week, and then yesterday's sermon at church really annoyed me. I didn't even want to go since it was Father's Day, and for once the pastor at least acknowledged we didn't all have great dads. But then he went on and on about God being our perfect Father. I'm sorry, but that doesn't make up for what I missed. I can't relate to having a personal relationship with Christ and feeling all warm and fuzzy about it. Most of the time I feel like I'm invisible to God. How am I supposed to know He cares? My parents took us to church my whole life, but I sure don't admire their marriage. What good did it do them?"

I (Kay) considered what she was saying. "From what I know of your history, Jenny, your feelings make perfect sense. For a child, parents are the first picture of God. His love, grace, mercy, kindness, and justice become tangible and real through experiencing those qualities with others, especially parents. Though your parents were Christians and took you to church, they weren't able to demonstrate love in a way that made God come alive. Is it fair to say you experience your heavenly Father as disinterested and too busy to give you time and attention?"

"Yes, exactly. It seems so obvious now that you say it, but I'm an avoider with God too, not just with Jim and the kids. Wow, that explains a lot."

"My hope for you and Jim is that together you can learn to experience a love that gives each of you a clearer picture of God. Then you can parent differently. Jenny, remember last week when Jim held you and comforted you about the painful memory with your dad? Though it was awkward, you took a risk to let Jim love and console you. As you cried and looked into his eyes and heard what he said to you, his hug and his gaze was a taste of what God's love is like. You didn't get that as a kid, but your marriage can become a place of healing. Together, you can learn to deeply know each other, comfort each other in the places of deepest hurt, and challenge each other to cultivate the unique talents and abilities you each possess."

Jenny's eyes scanned mine. "So giving my kids a clear picture of God means I need to work on not avoiding emotion—since they have to *feel* a loving connection with me first and not just hear me say I love them."

"Yes, that's it exactly. How you love your kids gives them an understanding of God they can directly feel. And your marriage provides another picture of God. Say Brittany and Jason had watched Jim holding you last week. What do you think they'd have felt?"

"Well, I was upset and crying. Wouldn't it scare them?" Jenny asked with some alarm.

"They get upset every day," Jim piped in. "I think crying is normal to them. Just not for you and me."

"That's true," said Jenny, "but they're kids, not adults."

"We never get too old to be upset and cry, Jenny," I continued. "What if Jim said to the kids, 'Mommy is sad, so Daddy is going to hold her until she feels all better. She's not sad about you, Jason, or you, Brittany. She's sad about something that happened a long time ago. Mommy will feel better after Daddy holds her for a while.'"

"So you're saying to do this in front of the kids?" asked Jim.

"Well, what would they learn about their parents and God that you didn't as kids?" I asked.

"Lots," said Jim. "Maybe that it's okay to express sadness and to need comfort. That Mom and Dad know how to help each other."

"That arms are for hugs, not hitting," Jenny added. "That Dad can be tender and loving. That Dad cares about Mom and her sadness."

"You get it," I said. "That kind of love will become second nature to them."

"It's exciting to think our kids will have a chance to see God more clearly than we did, and that motivates me to keep working on my marriage," said Jenny.

Do you want to give your kids the gift of seeing God clearly? What could be a more wonderful gift? Those with a clear picture of what God's love is like will have far fewer struggles in life. When they can rely on His love to reassure and comfort them in life, they'll have a much easier time managing stress and anxiety later.

When you grow in your ability to love, your child's picture of God becomes understandable, relatable. This knowledge is the foundation, the framework of our parenting, and though we didn't give our kids a perfect picture of God and made plenty of mistakes, we loved each of them dearly and strived to make our faith tangible and real. Despite our shortcomings and failures early on, we committed to grow in our ability to love God and each of our kids, and today, we extend that commitment to the new families our kids have created.

Why did we choose Christianity as our foundation? Because the message of the gospel in the Bible is the most amazing model of relationship we know, and we can learn it by imitating it in our lives.

WHAT LOVE DOES

The Bible says God *is* love and that He relates to us in three primary ways: He *sees*, He *initiates*, and He *sacrifices* for us. And the result is *repair*, *reconnection*, and *restoration*.

What does God *see* when He looks at us through love? He sees the deepest problems and our greatest needs. He sees what's broken and what separates us from Him, from love. We've all made mistakes and will continue to make them, some small, some big. Just like our kids, we misbehave openly and secretly. But there is right and wrong, and wrong behavior results in consequences. That's called *justice*, and it is a vital part of real love. As parents, if our love contains justice that is fair, reasonable, and morally right, our kids will learn that a part of love is setting limits and saying no to what is morally wrong, hurtful, or evil. And they'll know that consequences result from what is wrong or false.

God's justice is always fair and loving. We deserve a consequence for our wrongdoing, and the Bible tells us what the consequence is: separation from love, which is separation from God, which ultimately leads to death. You've undoubtedly noticed how sin always separates and pulls people apart, putting them at odds. Secrets, gossip, backbiting, selfishness, lying, jealousy, betrayal, and adultery all cause division and discord. But love moves beyond punishment and initiates a plan to deal with the root of the problem. God's plan involves justice born of His love.

As you may have experienced, God's love causes Him to *initiate* reconnection with us, despite our sin. He walks *toward* our mess, not away from it. He's perfect and untouched by sin, so He cannot overlook our problems that arise from sin and evil (see Exodus 20:3–17), but He doesn't wait for us to make the first move. Instead, He does the unthinkable. He initiates and extends His love by sending His Son Jesus to bridge the gap and restore relationship with Him.

And like a parent, Jesus shows us who God is in a human way that we can understand. He shows us what God is really like and how His love takes on injustice. And as a perfect parent, He died in our place to take away the consequence we deserved.

Imagine what it required: the loss of freedom and tremendous *sacrifice*, the torment He endured, and choosing to hang on a cross, completely poured out. *That* is what love does; it goes all the way, whatever it takes to solve the problem, break down the barriers, and *restore relationship*. That's what the Cross is about—solving the problem of our sin so we wouldn't be separated from God.

Love sees your deepest need, initiates a plan of restoration, and is willing to endure loss and make enormous sacrifices to restore broken relationship. That's the heart of the gospel message. And our response is to imitate it. First, to respond to His love and accept the gift. And then to live the gift out in our relationships, in continual gratitude for it.

THE GREATEST GIFT A PARENT CAN GIVE

God is our perfect model for parenting. If we imitate God's love as detailed in 1 Corinthians 13, we will *see* our kids, seeking to know them for who they are, always trying to understand and meet their deepest needs. We'll *initiate* relationship by entering their world and walking toward the miracle and the mess, even when our kids don't appreciate it. We'll teach them to manage the consequences of their actions, but always with the loving goal of repair and restoration of relationship. And we'll seek to find the balance of offering justice in love.

At times parenting will require great sacrifice. We'll have to give up some of our freedom, endure losses, and sometimes grieve, but we must never give up trying to break down barriers that separate our kids from love. This is what God does. This is what we, as parents, do. And when it's all said and done, and we launch our kids into adulthood, they will have the power to accept or reject the gift, the same freedom Christ gives us.

What God does for us is what love looks like in action. This is our perfect model for our job as parents. As we grow out of our love styles, out of our injuries, and toward the ideal secure love style,[1] our love will become a clearer picture of God's. And by the time our kids leave home, relating to God will feel a lot like relating to Mom and Dad.

In our humble opinion, that's the greatest gift parents could give their kids.

Parenting is a tremendous responsibility, a wonderful privilege, an exciting adventure, and one of the most challenging undertakings you'll ever experience. It's a journey of laughter and tears. From the start, kids expose our flaws, so having God as an example, as a guide, and as a constant comfort and help is essential. Many times we ourselves gained wisdom and deep comfort during difficult seasons as we reached out for that primary relationship we had with Him. We hope you will find that too.

Here are words each of you can pray that incorporate many of the concepts within our book and that reflect the heart of God:

God, we want eyes to see the unique wonder of every child You entrust to us. Show us the right ways to help our children feel deeply known and loved, so they will know how to show that to others. Cover us with Your sacrificial, unconditional love, that we may provide the same covering to sustain our kids and help them accept their weaknesses and learn to overcome them. Let us show tenderness and be a shelter of comfort as our children face the harsh realities of life.

Prepare us now to release our children into adulthood and into Your capable hands. Mend the wounds we've caused them, and give us courage to express our regrets and acknowledge our shortcomings as parents. Give our kids grace to forgive us for the ways we failed them, and remind us often of the hope we have of heaven, where all things are as You intend and where we will know ultimate healing forever.

In closing, we'd like to share our prayer for you, the one we prayed together at the end of our writing here.

Lord, we come to You together right here to pray for the wonderful parents reading this book. May they seek hard after the Giver of life and love and learn to accept and emulate Jesus's love. May they find a constant refuge in Your grace as their kids expose inadequacies and weaknesses they have yet to address. Help them model humility and willingness to grow and change until they know how to love more like You do. Give them a clearer portrait of Your love today.

With our gratitude and sincere blessings,
Kay and Milan

Parent
Toolbox

COMFORT CIRCLE FOR PARENTING

1. Seek Awareness (Reflect)

Reflect on the meaning of your child's behavior, including possible stressors and underlying (unexpressed) feelings.

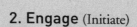

4. Resolve (Respond)

Resolution brings relief and comfort. Meet the needs of your child whenever possible, while at the same time being clear and direct as to what you can and cannot do. Do not make empty promises. If necessary, defer meeting your child's needs until an agreed-upon time.

2. Engage (Initiate)

Initiate a conversation with your child, exploring feelings and making guesses about stressors. Examples: "I wonder if you are grumpy because…," and, "I wonder what else you feel besides grumpy." (Use the Soul Words list or four basic feelings—mad, sad, afraid, happy.)

3. Find Out More (Curiosity and Openness)

Continue to listen and ask thoughtful questions to further clarify your child's inner emotions and perspective. Validate your child's feelings. Examples: "It makes sense that you feel…," or, "It's okay to feel…" Stay curious and find out more, even if you disagree with your child's perceptions; this process is about listening, not correcting. Conclude with the question, "What do you need?"

Note: The wonderful result of completing the Comfort Circle for Parenting will be increased trust, love, and bonding.

SOUL WORDS

HAPPY, cheerful, delighted, elated, encouraged, glad, gratified, joyful, lighthearted, overjoyed, pleased, relieved, satisfied, thrilled, secure

LOVING, affectionate, cozy, passionate, romantic, warm, tender, responsive, thankful, appreciative, refreshed, pleased

HIGH ENERGY, energetic, enthusiastic, excited, playful, rejuvenated, talkative, motivated, driven, determined, obsessed

AMAZED, stunned, surprised, shocked, jolted

ANXIOUS, uneasy, embarrassed, frustrated, nauseated, ashamed, nervous, restless, worried, stressed

CONFIDENT, positive, secure, self-assured, assertive

PEACEFUL, at ease, calm, comforted, cool, relaxed, serene

AFRAID, scared, anxious, apprehensive, boxed in, burdened, distressed, fearful, frightened, guarded, hard pressed, overwhelmed, panicky, paralyzed, tense, terrified, worried, insecure

TRAUMATIZED, shocked, disturbed, injured, damaged

ANGRY, annoyed, controlled, manipulated, furious, grouchy, grumpy, irritated, provoked, frustrated

LOW ENERGY, beaten down, exhausted, tired, weak, listless, depressed, detached, withdrawn, indifferent, apathetic

ALONE, avoidant, lonely, abandoned, deserted, forlorn, isolated, cut off, detached

SAD, unhappy, crushed, dejected, depressed, desperate, despondent, grieved, heartbroken, heavy, weepy

BETRAYED, deceived, fooled, duped, tricked

CONFUSED, baffled, perplexed, mystified, bewildered

ASHAMED, guilty, mortified, humiliated, embarrassed, exposed

CONVERSATION STARTERS

A good listener is able to ask good questions inviting conversation and inquiring about feelings and thoughts beneath the surface. Here are some ideas to get you started with your kids. Sadly, many people in our counseling offices reflect on their childhoods and remember questions as an indicator that they were in trouble or about to be interrogated. We want questions to have a positive connotation. Questions are how you discover all that goes on inside your child. At dinner or in the car ask, "What was your favorite part of your day and the worst (or most challenging) part of your day?"

For Young Kids

To develop self-awareness, imagination, sequential thinking, cause and effect, and reciprocity, here are some good ideas:

- Make up stories about imaginary characters that represent something current in the child's life. Take turns adding to the story. For example, "Once upon a time there was a little bear that was off to his first day of preschool, and he was very, very…" (Your child fills in some of the story and then gives you a turn.)

- At bedtime take a few minutes to reflect on the day, linking feelings to events, allowing your child to complete each thought with a soul word and whatever else is applicable. For example, "Today Tommy got to go play with Shawn, and Tommy felt very… Shawn was a little grumpy and hard to get along with. That made Tommy feel… Later in the day Tommy got to go to the pet store. His favorite animal was… Holding the puppies made Tommy feel…"

- Who is your favorite playmate at school? What makes him different from the other kids? What do you like best about your best friend? What kind of games do you play together?
- What do you think your friend likes best about you?

For Older Kids

It's important to let older kids voice opinions and thoughts that may be different from yours. You don't have to agree to be interested and find out more. Here are some ideas:

- "If you could change one thing about me as a person (and parent) what would you change?"
- "If you could design the optimal school that you would love, what would it be like?"
- "If you could travel anywhere in the world, where would you like to go?"
- "If you planned our next family vacation, what would it look like?"
- "How could church be more relevant to kids of your age?"
- "What charity or societal need are you most drawn too?"
- "What is the hardest thing about being your age?"

POSITIVE DESCRIPTIVE WORDS

accommodating
adaptable
adventurous
affectionate
agreeable
alert
ambitious
aware
bubbly
brave
capable
charming
cheerful
clever
compassionate
considerate
contemplative
cooperative
courteous
creative
decisive
dedicated
dependable
determined
devoted
diligent
discerning
disciplined

dynamic
eager
efficient
enchanting
encouraging
energetic
engaging
enjoyable
entertaining
enthusiastic
exuberant
fair
faithful
fearless
forgiving
frank
friendly
funny
generous
gentle
giving
gracious
happy
harmonious
helpful
hilarious
honest
hopeful

industrious
insightful
inspiring
intelligent
kind
likeable
lively
logical
lovely
loyal
nice
observant
optimistic
organized
patient
peaceful
perceptive
pleasant
polite
positive
productive
protective
quiet
receptive
reflective
resilient
responsive
self-assured

sensitive
silly
secure
sentimental
sincere
smart
smiling
steadfast
supportive
sympathetic
talkative
thoughtful
trustworthy
upbeat
vivacious
warm
willing
wise
witty

LISTENER GUIDE

Listener Goals

"Be quick to hear, slow to speak and slow to anger" (James 1:19). The goal is to enter the perspective and mind-set of the other person until you can see the situation through the other's eyes. We need to ask questions and probe for deeper understanding and expand our knowledge of the other's feelings, thoughts, and experiences. Do this for your children and help them learn to listen to others in the same way. Remember that conflicts between siblings or friends are a good time to teach listener-speaker roles, as each child takes a turn being the listener, then the speaker.

Listen Calmly

- Don't defend yourself, argue, explain, or problem solve. You don't have to agree with what you are hearing in order to listen and explore.
- Focus on the speaker's (your child's) experience, not yours.

Control Your Reactivity

When defenses go up, listening goes down. Remind yourself, *I can listen with an open mind even if I disagree.* The speaker is a separate person with her own feelings, thoughts, personality, and family history.

Be Aware of Your Nonverbal Responses

- Don't roll eyes, sigh, groan, or give responses that stop communication.
- Maintain eye contact and encourage the speaker to continue.

(continued on the next page)

Four Steps of Listening

1. Listen, asking the speaker to stop and let you summarize if it gets too long.
2. Repeat back in your own words what you heard and check for accuracy.
3. Ask questions that will broaden your understanding.
4. Validate feelings and respond with empathy: "I see what you are saying," or, "I can see how you might feel that way."

Good Questions to Ask

- "Tell me more; I want to understand."
- "How does that make you feel?"
- "Are there other times you have felt this? Are you hurt? afraid? scared? angry?"
- "What are your hopes? expectations? desires?"
- Don't ask "Why?" because it is often accusatory. Instead, ask "Where? How? Who? What?" questions.
- If you are wrong, don't apologize until you have fully listened as to how your actions affected your child.

Resolution

- Key guiding question: "What do *you* need right now?"
- Ownership: "I need you to admit and own the problem, infraction, or mistake."
- Forgiveness: "I need a well-thought-through forgiveness statement and an apology."
- Little or nothing: "You know, I don't think I need anything right now. I just feel better having gotten that off my chest."

- Reassurance: "I need to hear from you that things will be okay…or that you will work on this…or that you still really love me!"
- Agree to disagree: "While we still do not agree on this, I do feel like we understand and accept each other."
- Negotiation: "I need for us to find some middle ground or a compromise on this."
- Analysis / problem solving: "Please help me figure out how to solve the problem I'm facing."
- Comfort and nurture: "Would you please hold me and comfort me while I cry?"

SPEAKER GUIDE

Speaker Goals

"Speak truth each one of you…for we are members of one another" (Ephesians 4:25). The goal is to choose a topic of concern that you would like to explore and to share your concerns in a way that minimizes defensiveness in the listener. In order to know your child deeply, you as a parent will most often be the listener and your child will be the speaker. The older your child gets, the more he should be able to follow the guidelines below. When you need to confront your child about something, use the guidelines below.

Get Started

- At first, parents initiate conversations and trips around the comfort circle. Over time, teach your child to initiate conversations with clear, direct "I feel…I need…" statements. (For example, "I feel angry about the comment you made in front of my friends, and I need to talk to you about it.")
- Check the listener's readiness to listen and agree upon a time. "When would be a good time for you to discuss this?"

Tips to Try

- Introduce the issue you'd like to discuss by talking about yourself, your experiences, and your feelings.
- Use "I" statements rather than "you" statements. For example, "I am feeling sad that I didn't get to spend any time with you," instead of, "You are always busy and never have time for me." If you need to share something negative about the listener, start and end with a positive affirmation about that person.

- If the listener is causing you to feel unsafe, share what is happening (or could happen) that is making you feel unsafe. For example, "I am feeling unsafe because your tone of voice sounds disinterested and defensive."
- If you have a concern about how the talk might go, start with that. For example, "I need to have you listen without the television on."

Express Your Thoughts and Feelings
- Use feeling words to help explain your experience.
- Be honest. Pretending or minimizing is dishonest. Speak the truth in the most loving way you can.
- Be vulnerable. Try not to avoid pain or embarrassment that may be a part of sharing deep feelings.

If You Are Angry
- Try to discover the feeling under the anger. Hurt and sad feelings are usually underneath the anger.
- Take a time-out if necessary, but don't use a time-out as a way to escape and avoid. The following statement works well: "I'm getting so angry that I need to call a time-out so I can cool down. We will continue this talk in [ten minutes, one hour, or so on]." *Do not* blame, accuse, or name call. Doing so is always destructive.

AWARENESS AND REFLECTION SKILLS

	Avoider	Pleaser
Self-Awareness Has the ability to internally reflect, understand, and evaluate inner responses and outward behaviors. Can communicate this awareness to others.	No practice as a child. Never asked to talk about feelings. No opportunity for self-reflection, so feelings are minimized, restricted, and devalued.	Other focused since childhood, so unaware of their feelings and needs. Poor receivers. Often unaware of the anxiety that drives their "fixing" behaviors.
Other-Awareness Has the ability to reflect on, ask about, and describe internal feelings, thoughts, and reactions of others. Is able to put self in others' shoes and see from their perspective.	Does not occur to them to ask about internal feelings and thoughts of others. Assumes they are "fine" or will solve problems on their own.	Indirectly attempts to read the thoughts, feelings, and nonverbal communication of others to determine if they are happy or unhappy. Asks indirect questions to "take emotional temperature."
Comfort in Dealing with Negative Emotions Has the ability to recognize and respond to negative emotions.	Unaware of, minimizes, or avoids negative emotions of self and others. Self-reliant and expects others to be the same.	Gives and appeases to avoid dealing with negative emotions. Acts "nice" to appease negative emotions in others and distract from negative emotions in self.

Vacillator	Controller	Victim
Other focused since childhood. Only aware of how others hurt or anger them. Little awareness or ability to reflect on how their behavior contributes to relational dynamics.	Faced humiliation as a child. Anger covers awareness of all vulnerable emotions. Self-reflection would mean facing pain, so it is avoided.	Too much pain to self-reflect. Depression or dissociation keeps feelings from surfacing. Nothing helps: they see little value in telling others what they think and feel.
Little ability to put themselves in others' shoes or put aside their own feelings to listen to and understand the perspective of others. Preoccupied with how others hurt or anger them.	Never listened to as a kid. It's all about having control, so insecurities do not arise. Little to no ability to explore or understanding the feelings of others.	No skills. Has experienced the feelings, opinions, and thoughts of others as critical and negative. Little motivation to listen to more of the same.
Angry, but unaware of underlying emotions in self. Little awareness of the impact of their anger on others. Sees own emotions as valid and others' negative emotions as invalid.	Responds to own negative emotions with a heightened need to control. Others' negative emotions cause anger, as the controller attempts to discount and stop others from expressing those emotions.	Others' negative emotions signal danger or are reminders of unresolved pain. Tries to stop the expression or withdraws. Has never learned to constructively manage negative emotions.

For Further Study: Attachment Theory

The central concepts of attachment theory come from a multitude of researchers. Some of the most important figures giving rise to the concepts in this book are, among many others, John Bowlby, Mary Ainsworth, Mary Main, Selma Fraiberg, Allan Schore, Daniel Siegel, Robert Karen, Jude Cassidy, and Phillip R. Shaver (see "Notes" and "Bibliography" for further credits). Ainsworth discovered and described patterns of attachment by watching toddlers interact with their mothers. She observed the differences and categorized the children's responses to their mothers as secure or insecure. Insecure responses were further divided into two groups: children with avoidant responses and children with ambivalent responses.

Ainsworth observed that secure toddlers were distressed when their moms would leave but readily approached them for comfort when they returned. When they were upset, avoidant toddlers ignored their mothers, but ambivalent children wanted soothing. These children approached Mom when they were distressed, but they became angry and resistant to comfort when Mom picked them up and held them.[1] Ainsworth's student Mary Main discovered a fourth category that she labeled as "disorganized" and used the term to describe the effects of abuse, loss, or trauma on attachment. These children displayed both avoidant and ambivalent responses, but in extremely disorganized and unpredictable ways.[2]

As a result of the Adult Berkeley Attachment Interview, Main and her colleagues demonstrated that the groupings of love styles can be observed in an adult's overall "state of mind with respect to attachment."[3] Hazan, Shaver, and Bradshaw agreed. Feeney summarizes their findings:

"In these papers, Hazan and Shaver argued that romantic love can be conceptualized as an attachment process. That is, relationships between spouses and between unmarried but committed lovers are affectional bonds that involve complex socioemotional processes. They further argued that variations in early social experience produce relatively lasting differences in relationship styles, and that the three major love styles described in the infant literature ('secure,' 'avoidant,' and 'ambivalent') are manifested in romantic love."[4]

Research shows that relationship styles learned early on establish belief systems about relationships that shape our expectations, beliefs, and behaviors in all future relationships. While most of the research utilizes the four-group approach—secure (sometimes called "autonomous"), avoidant (sometimes called "dismissing"), ambivalent (sometimes called "preoccupied"), and disorganized (sometimes called "unresolved" or "chaotic")—some researchers add one more category. Judith Feeney summarizes research supporting the four-group model (five groups including secure) and concludes, "Given these findings, researchers have increasingly adopted the four-group model of adult attachment. This model is consistent with infant research suggesting the importance of a fourth attachment group showing characteristics of both avoidance and ambivalence (Crittenden, 1985); in particular, fearful adults tend to endorse both avoidant and ambivalent attachment prototypes (Brennan et al., 1991)."[5] Fearful people (pleasers) desire connection to reduce their anxiety (like ambivalents), but avoid their own feelings and needs in relationships (like avoidants).

Bartholomew and Horowitz also add a fourth category by dividing avoidant attachment into "fearful" and "dismissing" types. John Byng-Hall summarizes their views: "Avoidants with high self-esteem are categorized as dismissing; they emphasize achievement and self-reliance, maintaining a sense of self-worth at the expense of intimacy. In contrast, avoidants with low self-esteem are categorized as fearful; they desire intimacy but distrust others, avoiding close involvements that may lead to loss or rejection."[6] Although we do see fearful people's attempts to avoid rejection, we have difficulty seeing them as a type of avoidant because of their tendencies to pursue and seek closeness when fearful.

In his book *Loss: Sadness and Depression,* Bowlby identifies a fearful group as well. He describes three relational styles as follows: "In one such group affectional relationships tend to be marked by a high degree of anxious attachment, suffused with overt or covert ambivalence. In a second and related group there is a strong disposition to engage in compulsive caregiving.... In a third and contrasting group there are strenuous attempts to claim emotional self-sufficiency and independence of all affectional ties."[7] Bowlby goes on to say that people with these three types of affectional ties (relational styles) will have greater adverse reactions to loss. Bowlby believes the fearful group is related to the ambivalent group due to the anxiety that drives each style. He sees the self-sufficient (avoidant) as a contrasting style because these people reduce anxiety by disavowing their needs and do not pursue others.

In *How We Love,* we included the "fearful" or pleaser style because we find that many people relate to this pattern of attachment. In an attempt to simplify terms, we have adopted different labels, but they come from the original framework of this body of research. We find these same groups in our seminars as well as in our work with clients.

Our purpose has not been to reflect all the current data on attachment theory, though we've tried to include as much of the supporting materials we leaned on as was feasible. We offer our heartfelt thanks to the researchers, psychologists, and authors who have helped make this book possible. Their work has changed lives—including ours—by transforming relationships and revolutionizing our approach to life and love.

Notes

Chapter 1: *The Miracle and the Mess*

1. John Bowlby, *Attachment and Loss,* vol. 1, *Attachment* (New York: Basic, 1982).
2. Louis Cozolino, *The Neuroscience of Human Relationships: Attachment and the Developing Social Brain* (New York: Norton, 2006), 6.
3. Margaret Mahler, *On Human Symbiosis and the Vicissitudes of Individuation* (New York: International Universities Press, 1968), 11, quoted in Alice Miller, *The Drama of the Gifted Child* (New York: Basic, 1981), 7.

Chapter 2: *What Determines How We Parent*

1. Robert Karen, *Becoming Attached: Unfolding the Mystery of the Infant-Mother Bond and Its Impact on Later Life* (New York: Warner, 1994), 375.
2. Alice Miller, *The Drama of the Gifted Child* (New York: Basic, 1981), 7. Miller's actual quotes: "In an atmosphere of respect and tolerance for his feelings, the child, in the phase of separation, will be able to give up symbiosis [mutual dependency] with the mother and accomplish the steps toward individuation [becoming their own individual] and autonomy," and, "If they [the parents] are to furnish these prerequisites for a healthy narcissism [view of oneself], the parents themselves ought to have grown up in such an atmosphere."
3. Karen, *Becoming Attached,* 379.
4. Karen, *Becoming Attached,* 375.
5. *Attachment Theory and Close Relationships*, ed. Jeffry A. Simpson and W. Steven Rholes (New York: Guilford, 1998), 411. Actual quote: "The tendency to pay attention to feelings was most associated with the use of touch to convey affection.... Individuals open to feelings are more apt to

use touch as a means to establish proximity and emotional closeness.... Individuals unsure of what emotion they are experiencing are more likely to report a host of negative reactions to touching."

6. Miller, *Drama*, 22.
7. Miller, *Drama*, 30.
8. Louis Cozolino, *The Neuroscience of Human Relationships: Attachment and the Developing Social Brain* (New York: Norton, 2006), 8. Actual quote: "Those of us who study interpersonal neurobiology believe that friendships, marriage, psychotherapy—in fact, any meaningful relationship—can reactivate neuroplastic processes and actually change the structure of the brain."

Chapter 3: The Avoider Parent

1. The term *avoider* comes from the original attachment term *avoidant,* coined by John Bowlby and Mary Ainsworth. For further characteristics and descriptions, see Robert Karen, *Becoming Attached: Unfolding the Mystery of the Infant-Mother Bond and Its Impact on Later Life* (New York: Warner, 1994), 367–8, 388, 443; Judith A. Feeney, "Adult Romantic Attachment and Couple Relationships," in *Handbook of Attachment: Theory, Research, and Clinical Applications,* ed. Jude Cassidy and Phillip R. Shaver (New York: Guilford, 1999), 364; John Byng-Hall, "Family and Couple Therapy: Toward Greater Security," in *Handbook of Attachment,* 628–9.
2. Judith A. Crowell, R. Chris Fraley, and Phillip R. Shaver, "Measurement of Individual Differences in Adolescent and Adult Attachment," in *Handbook of Attachment,* 443.

Chapter 4: The Pleaser Parent

1. William Hillcourt, *Boy Scout Handbook* (New Brunswick, NJ: National Council Boy Scouts of America, 1959), 84.
2. The term *pleaser* comes from an insecure attachment type that clearly shows tendencies toward pleasing and pursuing—tendencies that are born of fear-based insecurities. This fear-based type is noted in John

Bowlby, *Attachment and Loss,* vol. 3, *Loss: Sadness and Depression* (New York: Basic, 1980), 202, 206. See also Judith A. Feeney, "Adult Romantic Attachment and Couple Relationships" in *Handbook of Attachment: Theory, Research, and Clinical Applications,* ed. Jude Cassidy and Phillip R. Shaver (New York: Guilford, 1999), 361–2, and John Byng-Hall, "Family and Couple Therapy," in *Handbook of Attachment,* 629.

3. Loose paraphrase from Dr. Bruce Perry, *Trauma, Brain and Relationship: Helping Children Heal,* DVD (Santa Barbara: Santa Barbara Graduate Institute, 2004), www.healingresources.info/emotional_trauma_online_video.htm.

4. Mary Dozier, K. Chase Stovall-McClough, and Kathleen E. Albus, "Attachment and Psychopathology in Adulthood," in *Handbook of Attachment: Theory, Research, and Clinical Applications, Second Edition,* ed. Jude Cassidy and Phillip R. Shaver (New York: Guilford, 2008), 730.

Chapter 5: The Vacillator Parent

1. The term *vacillator* is a term we coined referring to the classic ambivalent style and was so named by Bowlby and Ainsworth. For further information, see Robert Karen, *Becoming Attached: Unfolding the Mystery of the Infant-Mother Bond and Its Impact on Later Life* (New York: Warner, 1994), 368–9, 388, 443; Judith A. Feeney, "Adult Romantic Attachment and Couple Relationships," in *Handbook of Attachment: Theory, Research, and Clinical Applications,* ed. Jude Cassidy and Phillip R. Shaver (New York: Guilford, 1999), 364; and John Byng-Hall, "Family and Couple Therapy," in *Handbook of Attachment,* 628.

Chapter 6: The Controller Parent

1. The term *controller* refers to the chaotic-disorganized-disoriented attachment style. M. Main and E. Hesse, "Parents' Unresolved Traumatic Experiences Are Related to Infant Disorganized Attachment Status: Is Frightened and/or Frightening Parental Behavior the Linking

Mechanism?" in *Attachment in the Preschool Years: Theory, Research, and Intervention,* ed. M. T. Greenberg, D. Cicchetti, and E. M. Cummings (Chicago: University of Chicago Press, 1990), 161–182; Roger Kobak, "The Emotional Dynamics of Disruptions in Attachment Relationships: Implications for Theory, Research, and Clinical Intervention," in *Handbook of Attachment: Theory, Research, and Clinical Applications,* ed. Jude Cassidy and Phillip R. Shaver (New York: Guilford, 1999), 34-35; Karlen Lyons-Ruth and Deborah Jacobvitz, "Attachment Disorganization: Unresolved Loss, Relational Violence, and Lapses in Behavioral and Attentional Strategies," in *Handbook of Attachment,* 532–3.

2. Mary Dozier, K. Chase Stovall, and Kathleen E. Albus, "Attachment and Psychopathology in Adulthood," in *Handbook of Attachment,* 506.

Chapter 7: The Victim Parent

1. The term *victim* also arises from the chaotic-disorganized attachment style. Karlen Lyons-Ruth and Deborah Jacobvitz, "Attachment Disorganization: Unresolved Loss, Relational Violence, and Lapses in Behavioral and Attentional Strategies," in *Handbook of Attachment: Theory, Research, and Clinical Applications,* ed. Jude Cassidy and Phillip R. Shaver (New York: Guilford, 1999), 543–6, 550; Carol George and Judith Solomon, "Attachment and Caregiving: The Caregiving Behavioral System," in *Handbook of Attachment,* 662–3.

2. "Battered Men Statistics," National Coalition of Free Men, Los Angeles Chapter, www.ncfm.org/chapters/la/dv_data.html.

Chapter 9: The Avoider Child

1. Many of the traits listed in this section, and the ones in following chapters, are compiled from the excellent research papers documented within *The Handbook of Attachment: Theory, Research, and Clinical Applications,* ed. Jude Cassidy and Phillip R. Shaver (New York: Guilford, 1999) and Robert Karen's book *Becoming Attached: Unfolding the Mystery of the Infant-Mother Bond and Its Impact on Later Life* (New York: Warner, 1994).

Chapter 10: The Pleaser Child

1. Jay Belsky, "Modern Evolutionary Theory and Patterns of Attachment," in *Handbook of Attachment: Theory, Research, and Clinical Applications,* ed. Jude Cassidy and Phillip R. Shaver (New York: Guilford, 1999), 157. Actual quote: "Preoccupied mothers appear especially oriented and responsive toward expressions of fear in their babies."

Chapter 12: Controller and Victim Children

1. Bruce D. Perry et al., "Childhood Trauma, the Neurobiology of Adaptation, and 'Use-Dependent' Development of the Brain: How 'States' become 'Traits,'" *Infant Mental Health Journal* 16, no. 4 (1995): 278.
2. Teen suicide is often linked to bullying. See Jill Smolowe and others, "Bullied to Death?" *People,* April 26, 2010.

Chapter 13: The Introverted Child

1. For more on introversion, see David Keirsey and Marilyn Bates, *Please Understand Me: Character and Temperament Types* (Del Mar, CA: Prometheus Nemesis, 1984), 14.
2. Marti Olsen Laney, *The Introvert Advantage: How to Thrive in an Extrovert World* (New York: Workman, 2002), 43, 156.
3. Several of these traits come from Keirsey and Bates, *Please Understand Me.*

Chapter 17: The Premature Child

1. K. J. S. Anand and Frank M. Scalzo, "Can Adverse Neonatal Experiences Alter Brain Development and Subsequent Behavior?" *Biology of the Neonate* 77, no. 2 (February 2000): 69–82.
2. Robin Grille, "What Your Child Remembers: New Discoveries About Early Memory and How It Affects Us," *Sydney's Child* 14, no. 4 (May 2003): 2.
3. Jonna Jepsen, *Born Too Early: Hidden Handicaps of Premature Children* (London: Karnac, 2006), 169.
4. Jepsen, *Born Too Early,* 170–71.

Chapter 19: The Gift of Comfort

1. Norman Doidge, *The Brain That Changes Itself: Stories of Personal Triumph from the Frontiers of Brain Science* (New York: Penguin, 2007), 191.
2. Louis Cozolino, *The Neuroscience of Human Relationships: Attachment and the Developing Social Brain* (New York: Norton, 2006), 14.
3. Steven E. Gutstein, *The RDI Book: Forging New Pathways for Autism, Asperger's and PDD with the Relationship Development Intervention Program* (Houston: Connections Center, 2009), 111.
4. T. Berry Brazelton and Bertrand G. Cramer, *The Earliest Relationship: Parents, Infants, and the Drama of Early Attachment* (New York: Addison-Wesley, 1990), 126.
5. Cozolino, *Human Relationships*, 128.
6. Cozolino, *Human Relationships*, 129.

Chapter 20: The Gift of Power

1. Po Bronson and Ashley Merryman, *NurtureShock: New Thinking about Children* (New York: Twelve, 2009), 161, 165.

Chapter 24: The Gift of God: The Perfect Parent

1. Regarding the parenting style that creates a secure child, "A secure family base allows family members to engage in conflicts, safe in the knowledge that care will not be threatened. As resolving conflict is a necessary aspect of authority, a secure family base supports functional authority systems. In turn, functional authority facilitates caregiving, especially when parents are setting limits (e.g., sending children to bed). Conversely, insecure family bases help to disrupt authority, and dysfunctional authority disrupts security." John Byng-Hall, "Family and Couple Therapy: Toward Greater Security," in *Handbook of Attachment: Theory, Research, and Clinical Applications,* ed. Jude Cassidy and Phillip R. Shaver (New York: Guilford, 1999), 637.

For Further Study: Attachment Theory

1. Robert Karen, *Becoming Attached: Unfolding the Mystery of the Infant-Mother Bond and Its Impact on Later Life* (New York: Warner, 1994), 146–64.

2. Karen, *Becoming Attached,* 216.

3. Quoted in Erik Hesse, "The Adult Attachment Interview: Historical and Current Perspectives," in *Handbook of Attachment: Theory, Research, and Clinical Applications,* ed. Jude Cassidy and Phillip R. Shaver (New York: Guilford, 1999), 421.

4. P. R. Shaver, C. Hazan, and D. Bradshaw, "Love as Attachment: The Integration of Three Behavioral Systems," in *The Psychology of Love,* ed. Robert J. Sternberg and Michael L. Barnes (New Haven, CT: Yale University Press, 1988), 68–99, summarized in Judith A. Feeney, "Adult Romantic Attachment and Couple Relationships," in *Handbook of Attachment,* 356.

5. Feeney, "Adult Romantic Attachment," 362.

6. K. Bartholomew and L. M. Horowitz, "Attachment Styles Among Young Adults: A Test of a Four-Category Model," *Journal of Personality and Social Psychology* 61, no. 2 (American Psychological Association, 1991), 226–44, summarized in John Byng-Hall, "Family and Couple Therapy: Toward Greater Security," in *Handbook of Attachment,* 629.

7. John Bowlby, *Attachment and Loss,* vol. 3, *Loss: Sadness and Depression* (New York: Basic, 1980), 202.

Bibliography

American Psychiatric Association. *Diagnostic and Statistical Manual of Mental Disorders,* Fourth Edition, Text Revision. Washington, DC: American Psychiatric Association, 2000.

Aron, Elaine N. *The Highly Sensitive Child: Helping Our Children Thrive When the World Overwhelms Them.* New York: Broadway, 2002.

————. *The Highly Sensitive Person: How to Thrive When the World Overwhelms You.* New York: Broadway, 1996.

Bauer, Walter, and Frederick William Danker. *A Greek-English Lexicon of the New Testament and Other Early Christian Literature.* Chicago: University of Chicago Press, 1974.

Belsky, Jay. "Modern Evolutionary Theory and Patterns of Attachment." In *Handbook of Attachment: Theory, Research, and Clinical Applications,* ed. Jude Cassidy and Phillip R. Shaver. New York: Guilford, 1999.

Bowlby, John. *Attachment and Loss.* Vol. 1, *Attachment.* New York: Basic, 1982.

————. *Attachment and Loss.* Vol. 2, *Separation: Anxiety and Anger.* New York: Basic, 1976.

————. *Attachment and Loss.* Vol. 3, *Loss: Sadness and Depression.* New York: Basic, 1980.

Brazelton, T. Berry, and Bertrand G. Cramer. *The Earliest Relationship: Parents, Infants, and the Drama of Early Attachment.* New York: Addison-Wesley, 1990.

Brennan, Kelly, Shey Wu, and Jennifer Loev. "Adult Romantic Attachment and Individual Differences in Attitudes toward Physical Contact in the Context of Adult Romantic Relationships." In *Attachment Theory and Close Relationships,* ed. Jeffry A. Simpson and W. Steven Rholes. New York: Guilford, 1998.

Bretherton, Inge, and Kristine A. Munholland. "Internal Working Models in Attachment Relationships: A Construct Revisited." In *Handbook of Attachment: Theory, Research, and Clinical Applications,* ed. Jude Cassidy and Phillip R. Shaver. New York: Guilford, 1999.

Bronson, Po, and Ashley Merryman. *NurtureShock: New Thinking about Children.* New York: Twelve, 2009.

Byng-Hall, John. "Family and Couple Therapy: Toward Greater Security." In *Handbook of Attachment: Theory, Research, and Clinical Applications,* ed. Jude Cassidy and Phillip R. Shaver. New York: Guilford, 1999.

Carnes, Patrick J. *The Betrayal Bond: Breaking Free of Exploitive Relationships.* Deerfield Beach, FL: Health Communications, 1997.

Cassidy, Jude. "The Nature of the Child's Ties." In *Handbook of Attachment: Theory, Research, and Clinical Applications,* ed. Jude Cassidy and Phillip R. Shaver. New York: Guilford, 1999.

Cassidy, Jude, and Phillip R. Shaver, eds. *Handbook of Attachment: Theory, Research, and Clinical Applications.* New York: Guilford, 1999.

————. *Handbook of Attachment: Theory, Research, and Clinical Applications, Second Edition.* New York: Guilford, 2008.

Cline, Foster, and Jim Fay. *Parenting Teens with Love and Logic: Preparing Adolescents for Responsible Adulthood.* Colorado Springs: Piñon Press, 1992.

————. *Parenting with Love and Logic: Teaching Children Responsibility.* Colorado Springs: Piñon Press, 1990.

Cloud, Henry. *Changes That Heal.* Grand Rapids, MI: Zondervan, 1990.

Cozolino, Louis. *The Neuroscience of Human Relationships: Attachment and the Developing Social Brain.* New York: Norton, 2006.

Doidge, Norman. *The Brain That Changes Itself: Stories of Personal Triumph from the Frontiers of Brain Science.* New York: Penguin, 2007.

Feeney, Judith A. "Adult Romantic Attachment and Couple Relationships." In *Handbook of Attachment: Theory, Research, and Clinical Applications,* ed. Jude Cassidy and Phillip R. Shaver. New York: Guilford, 1999.

George, Carol, and Judith Solomon. "Attachment and Caregiving: The Caregiving Behavioral System." In *Handbook of Attachment: Theory, Research, and Clinical Applications,* ed. Jude Cassidy and Phillip R. Shaver. New York: Guilford, 1999.

Gladwell, Malcolm. *The Tipping Point: How Little Things Can Make a Big Difference.* New York: Back Bay, 2002.

Glasser, Howard, and Jennifer Easley. *Transforming the Difficult Child: The Nurtured Heart Approach.* Nashville, TN: Vaughan, 2008.

Gutstein, Steven E. *The RDI Book: Forging New Pathways for Autism, Asperger's and PDD with the Relationship Development Intervention Program.* Houston: Connections Center, 2009.

Hesse, Erik. "The Adult Attachment Interview: Historical and Current Perspectives." In *Handbook of Attachment: Theory, Research, and Clinical Applications,* ed. Jude Cassidy and Phillip R. Shaver. New York: Guilford, 1999.

Hillcourt, William. *Boy Scout Handbook.* New Brunswick, NJ: National Council Boy Scouts of America, 1959.

Jepsen, Jonna. *Born Too Early: Hidden Handicaps of Premature Children.* London: Karnac Books, 2006.

Karen, Robert. *Becoming Attached: Unfolding the Mystery of the Infant-Mother Bond and Its Impact on Later Life.* New York: Warner, 1994.

Keirsey, David, and Marilyn Bates. *Please Understand Me: Character and Temperament Types.* Del Mar, CA: Prometheus Nemesis, 1984.

Kobak, Roger. "The Emotional Dynamics of Disruptions in Attachment Relationships: Implications for Theory, Research, and Clinical Intervention." In *Handbook of Attachment: Theory, Research, and Clinical Applications,* ed. Jude Cassidy and Phillip R. Shaver. New York: Guilford, 1999.

Laney, Marti Olsen. *The Introvert Advantage: How to Thrive in an Extrovert World.* New York: Workman, 2002.

Lieberman, Alicia F. *The Emotional Life of the Toddler.* New York: Free Press, 1993.

Lyons-Ruth, Karlen, and Deborah Jacobvitz. "Attachment Disorganization: Unresolved Loss, Relational Violence, and Lapses in Behavioral and Attentional Strategies." In *Handbook of Attachment: Theory, Research, and Clinical Applications,* ed. Jude Cassidy and Phillip R. Shaver. New York: Guilford, 1999.

Magai, Carol. "Affect, Imagery, and Attachment: Working Models of Inter-personal Affect and the Socialization of Emotion." In *Handbook of Attachment: Theory, Research, and Clinical Applications,* ed. Jude Cassidy and Phillip R. Shaver. New York: Guilford, 1999.

Maggio, Rosalie. *The Art of Talking to Anyone: Essential People Skills for Success in Any Situation.* New York: McGraw-Hill, 2005.

Marvin, Robert S., and Preston A. Britner. "Normative Development: The Ontogeny of Attachment." In *Handbook of Attachment: Theory, Research, and Clinical Applications,* ed. Jude Cassidy and Phillip R. Shaver. New York: Guilford, 1999.

Mason, Mike. *The Mystery of Marriage: Meditations on the Miracle.* Sisters, OR: Multnomah, 1985.

Miller, Alice. *The Drama of the Gifted Child.* New York: Basic, 1981.

Myers, Isabel Briggs. *Gifts Differing: Understanding Personality Type.* Palo Alto, CA: Consulting Psychologists, 1980.

Newton, Ruth P. *The Attachment Connection: Parenting a Secure and Confident Child Using the Science of Attachment Theory.* Oakland, CA: New Harbinger, 2008.

Purvis, Karyn B., David R. Cross, and Wendy Lyons Sunshine. *The Connected Child: Bringing Hope and Healing to Your Adoptive Family.* New York: McGraw-Hill, 2007.

Sears, William, and Martha Sears. *Parenting the Fussy Baby and High-Need Child.* New York: Little, Brown and Company, 1996.

Siegel, Daniel J. *The Developing Mind: How Relationships and the Brain Interact to Shape Who We Are.* New York: Guilford, 1999.

———. *The Mindful Brain: Reflection and Attunement in the Cultivation of Well-Being.* New York: Norton, 2007.

Simpson, Jeffry A., and W. Steven Rholes, eds. *Attachment Theory and Close Relationships.* New York, Guilford, 1998.

Suomi, Stephen J. "Attachment in Rhesus Monkeys." In *Handbook of Attachment: Theory, Research, and Clinical Applications,* ed. Jude Cassidy and Phillip R. Shaver. New York: Guilford, 1999.

Vaughn, Brian E., and Kelly K. Bost. "Attachment and Temperament: Redundant, Independent, or Interacting Influences on Interpersonal Adaptation and Personality Development?" In *Handbook of Attachment: Theory, Research, and Clinical Applications,* ed. Jude Cassidy and Phillip R. Shaver. New York: Guilford, 1999.

Weinfield, Nancy S., L. Alan Sroufe, Byron Egeland, and Elizabeth A. Carlson. "The Nature of Individual Differences in Infant-Caregiver Attachment." In *Handbook of Attachment: Theory, Research, and Clinical Applications,* ed. Jude Cassidy and Phillip R. Shaver. New York: Guilford, 1999.